KT-222-906

HAMLYN

COMPLETE CHRISTMAS BOOK

HAMLYN

COMPLETE CHRISTMAS BOOK

Carol Hupping

HAMLYN

This edition published in 1991
by Paul Hamlyn Publishing, part of
Reed International Books Limited,
Michelin House, 81 Fulham Road,
London SW3 6RB.

ISBN 0 600 57394 X

Produced by Mandarin Offset –
printed in China

CONTENTS

THE SPIRIT OF CHRISTMAS

OF CHRISTMASSES PAST

CHRISTMAS is a time of merriment and feasting, a time for indulging in all the traditional pleasures: the Christmas tree, presents from Santa Claus, turkey and all the trimmings, cards and carols. Yet it has not always been so.

Indeed, there have been midwinter festivals for hundreds of years, long before Christian times. The gods had to be propitiated during the bleak days of winter in order to ensure the return of the life-giving sun. For the Romans it was Saturnalia, celebrated with ever-green decorations, the exchange of presents and a great deal of drinking. In Northern Europe they called it Yuletide, and it featured feasting and wassailing around the Yule log fire.

When the Christian Church took over the midwinter festival to celebrate the birth of Christ and declared that the whole of the 12 days between the Nativity and Epiphany should be a sacred and festive season, many of the pagan customs were adopted. At courts and manor houses in England a "Lord of Misrule" was appointed, and by Tudor times, in spite of the Church's admonitions, Christmas was being celebrated in a positive orgy of feasting, dancing and gambling.

Such conspicuous jollity was, of course, anathema to the Puritans, under the leadership of Oliver Cromwell. The Puritans attempted to abolish Christmas, one of those misguided attempts to legislate against people having fun. It was proclaimed that Christmas Day should be kept as a fast and a penance, and for 12 years any sort of festivity was banned. Parliament sat on Christmas Day, its soldiers made sure that the shops stayed open, and the churches closed. Decking the halls with boughs of holly was taboo, and it was definitely not the season to be jolly.

The Restoration of the monarchy in 1660 ensured that the laws against Christmas were repealed, but the old ways of celebrating Christmas had taken a knock from which they never really recovered. Also society was beginning to change quite dramatically. People whose families had for generations worked on the land began to move to the great industrial cities in search of work. They left behind the country house, the farm, and the village and the seasonal customs associated with them. Many of the country estates were bought up by "new money", and the mediaeval style of Christmas revelry became for most people just a fond memory.

It was Charles Dickens who identified the general mood of nostalgia for Christmas past, and set about recreating it in his writing. Christmas as decribed in *The Pickwick Papers* was a thoroughly romanticized version of the country festivities in days gone by. Images of this mythical "Merrie England" still adorn our Christmas cards today; jovial squires dispensing good cheer by roaring fires, and coaches bowling along snow-covered lanes towards picturesque inns, full of cheery revellers.

But Victorian Britain was a stark contrast to this cosy imagined past. The country's new-found industrial prosperity had also brought terrible hardship to the urban poor, and so charitable work and benevolence to the poor became the duty of the pious Victorian. In 1843 Dickens published *A Christmas Carol*. Gone is the unallayed jollity, and it its place are the worthy philanthropic sentiments so graphically illustrated in the tale of Scrooge

The Lord of Misrule, master of the revels in the seventeenth century.

and Bob Crachit. Poor crippled Tiny Tim moved the sentimental hearts of the nation, and *A Christmad Carol* was an instant and popular success. Most people today, if asked what they thought about Christmas, would say, "Well, it's really for the children, isn't it?" And this is perhaps the most significant change that the Victorians made in the seasonal celebrations. From being a social occasion when whole communities would get together in general revelry, Christmas became centred on hearth and home.

So the Victorians breathed new life into Christmas. They transformed a half-forgotten festival into a great family jamboree, a time for surrounding oneself with nearest and dearest, a time for goodwill and generosity, particularly towards children, and of course, a time for Christmas charity and benevolence towards the poor.

It was in Victorian times too that the Father Christmas, alias St. Nicholas, or Santa Claus, was first introduced to Britain, and thus America. In 1822 Clement Clark Moore painted a vivid picture of Saint Nick, or Santa Claus, a jolly old man who filled children's stockings with presents on Christmas Eve, in his famous poem, *A Visit from St. Nicholas,* better known as *The Night Before Christmas.*

"T'was the night before Christmas," begins Clement Clark Moore's poem *A Visit from St. Nicholas,* and it goes on to describe the arrival of St. Nick at the sleeping house:

He was dressed all in fur from his head to his foot,
And his clothes were all tarnished with ashes and soot;
A bundle of toys he had flung on his back,
And he looked like a peddler just opening his pack.
His eyes how they twinkled! his dimples how merry!
His cheeks were like roses, his nose like a cherry;
His droll little mouth was drawn up in a bow,
And the beard on his chin was as white as the snow.
The stump of a pipe he held tight in his teeth,
And the smoke it encircled his head like a wreath.
He had a broad face, and a little round belly
That shook, when he laughed, like a bowl full of jelly.
He was chubby and plump, – a right jolly old elf –
And I laughed when I saw him, in spite of myself.

Immigrants to America from Europe helped to keep the celebration of Christmas very much alive by bringing with them their own Christmas customs. The Germans introduced the Christmas tree, and they made the lavishly decorated ginger-bread house, cookies, mince pie and Putz (or nativity scene) very much a part of American Christmasses. Settlers from Scandinavia had holiday cakes, breads, rice puddings and cookies. They also had their Yule Log, a special water-soaked log that burned slowly all Christmas Day and was used to light the Yule candles.

The French, who have their Yule Log often in the shape of a cake, gave that delicious sweet idea, Hungarians brought their poppy seed cake with them and Serbian Russians bake a cake with a coin hidden inside assuring a good year to whoever gets it.

Queen Victoria and her beloved Prince Albert made Christmas a big event in their lives, and they had a tremendous influence on the population, which until then was still feeling the effects of the religious opposition to Christmas festivities instilled by the Puritans almost 200 years earlier. The Queen and her husband transformed a half-forgotten festival into a great family affair, a time for surrounding oneself with family and special friends, a time for goodwill and generosity, particularly toward children.

The custom of decking the halls with holly and evergreens began in Victorian England, and the tree became the centrepiece of their holiday; it was covered with glass balls, candies and little gifts and sweets wrapped up in bright paper. Many of the games played by the Victorians at Christmastime are still with us, like "Simon Says", "Blindman's Bluff", "'Charades" and "Hide and Seek". We can thank them for reviving Christmas carol singing; they collected many songs that were in danger of being forgotten and wrote many new ones. They also established the custom of sending cards at Christmas.

Mistletoe began with the Druids, who considered it a sign of fertility and a plant with healing powers. It played a big role in their religious rites, and they hung it in their places of worship to provide protection for the fairies during the long winter. While the English did not consider it a sacred plant, they adopted the practice of hanging it during the holidays. (See pp 88-89 for more information on the significance of mistletoe.)

CHRISTMAS, A TIME FOR TRADITIONS

So many of these holiday traditions, whether they can be considered truly British in origin, or contributions from other cultures, come alive again each Christmas. And, as many of us feel the commercialization of Christmas taking some of the joy out of the holiday for us, such deep-felt traditions become even more important. They remind us of our roots, they help to preserve our cultural heritage, they remind us of what Christmas is really all about.

Filling the house with evergreens and pretty ribbons and putting up a tree is more than just decorating for the holidays; it is a way to express the importance of home and hearth in our lives. Making special foods to share with others brings family and friends together – to celebrate the love we have for one another and to rejoice in our good fortune.

Gift-making and gift-giving is one way to make others happy and to show how much they mean to us, and to share our bounty with those who have less than we do. Cards let us exchange greetings for Christmas and the New Year with people we are not able to be with. Even the songs we sing reaffirm our heritage and put us closer in touch with our beliefs and our feelings about our place in the world, be it feelings of worship, thankfulness, happiness, goodwill, peace – or them all.

This Norman Rockwell illustration for the cover of The Saturday Evening Post *captures the bustle of Christmas.*

SWAGS, BOWS AND BELLS

🎄 ALL DRESSED UP FOR CHRISTMAS 🎄

Christmas, what a delightful reason for giving your house a festive facelift, and for bringing much-needed relief from the doldrums of winter. Holiday greenery and flowers, candles and handmade decorations can quickly conjure up an atmosphere of warm welcome and sincere good cheer.

Much of the pleasure of dressing up the house for Christmas is knowing that your special touches are everywhere – treasured objects from past holidays and bright new things you will be making and buying. But before you start to think about what decorations will go where, take a little time to do some cool, calm planning.

Think about your house room by room, making a cool appraisal of those areas that are in most need of something festive; where there is a usable flat surface for a floor arrangement or a blank wall for an evergreen wreath; a dark corner that would benefit from a vase of white everlastings, a high ceiling that would show off a hanging decoration to advantage.

The next thing to decide is an overall colour theme. Shop windows show us just how effective a planned colour scheme can be when it is carried through from the Christmas tree to gift wrappings and the smallest

decorations. Your scheme will naturally depend to a large extent on the colours of your room furnishings, on your personal preferences—whether you like your festive themes to be dazzling or understated – and on the collection of decorations you already have.

Choosing a colour theme

Are you going to be traditional and go for holly green, berry red, or snowy white – or a combination of all three? Or perhaps you will make this Christmas a real sparkler, and add more touches of silver or gold to your scheme – easy to do with shiny Christmas balls, paint-sprayed twigs, nuts and seedheads.

Consider which approach would do most to flatter your home and – to be totally practical – which would be the easiest to achieve by adding to and adapting the materials you already have.

Once you have made some of those basic decisions you can start planning specific decorations for particular places. On the pages that follow you will find many ideas for dressing up fireplaces and walls, tables, shelves and odd corners of the house. Some

A glistening turkey with all the trimmings and fine wine provide the ingredients of a traditional Christmas dinner.

should surely fit nicely into your overall approach for this Christmas.

WREATHS AND GARLANDS

Christmas wreaths and garlands are on sale from the end of November onwards, but it is just as easy to make your own. It's also cheaper – for the cost of a plain ready-made wreath, you can buy what you need to make your own, including the festive decorations such as brightly coloured wooden cherries and holly berries used here. And, if you have plenty of evergreens in your garden, you could even make one or two extra wreaths as presents for your friends.

Choosing the material

Foliage is the mainstay of most Christmas wreaths and garlands and there is a long tradition of using holly, ivy and conifers at Christmastime. Of the broad-leaved evergreens, plain-leaved ivy and variegated holly are best. There are dozens of variegated hollies, with silver or gold splashes, stripes or edges, any of which are fine. Or you might choose variegated ivy – again, there are dozens available – partnered with plain-leaved holly. Keep away from too many different variegations, though, or you'll end up with a confused effect. If you can't get variegated ivy or holly, variegated elaeagnus would be a good substitute.

Cupresses, or true cypress, and its close relatives, chamaecyparis, or false cypress, and Leyland's cypress also make good foliage, and branches of these quick-growing screen and hedging plants are often included by florists in mixed bunches, so they're fairly easy to buy. Blue cedar also features in this wreath, but is less common in the shops.

WIRING CANDLES

Table top garlands make wonderfully festive dining table centrepieces. Add short red candles to provide bright highlights to a predominantly green base. Cut a piece of thick stub wire, approximately 15-20cm (6-8 inches) long, in half. Insert the 2 pieces, spaced evenly apart, into the base of the candle. Don't insert them too near the rim, or the wax may chip off.

Fortunately, florists are now starting to stock more unusual conifer foliage, and you could use blue spruce instead. (See Chapter 5 for more about types of Christmas greenery.)

Whatever foliage you choose, it helps to lay it all out in separate piles in front of you when you work. Buy generous sized bunches – you can always use what's left in other floral displays, and it's better than running out halfway through. However, if you're using holly from your garden, remember that it is quite slow growing, so don't go overboard. You can always run outside for a few extra sprigs.

Holly berries are a traditional Christmas decoration, but birds tend to strip holly berries long before December 25. You can pick some berried sprigs in advance and keep them fresh in a plastic bag in a cool place. If the berries start to shrivel, spray them lightly.

This aromatic nut and herb kitchen wreath is pretty all year round. Straw moulded into a sausage shape, bound with natural string forms the circular base. Ivy and other ornaments are glued on, then golden bows added to finish.

Adding festive ingredients

Once you have formed the basis of your wreath you can let your imagination and creativity run wild when deciding on additional materials to make it both sumptuous and eye-catching for Christmas. Use traditional red and gold coloured ingredients; red and gold ribbons to make large bows, and short candles for a tabletop arrangement, or tall ones for a sideboard, to add light and lustre to your design. Wire nuts and cones and spray them gold and silver, or sprinkle them with a covering of glitter so that they shimmer in the candlelight, or simply varnish them if they are to be mixed with brightly-coloured flowers.

Kitchen wreath materials

Spices and herbs are ideal ingredients for a more unusual, sweet-smelling Christmas wreath to hang on your kitchen door or at

A flat wreath studded with ribbons, pine cones and candles makes a perfect dining table centrepiece.

your window. They are an attractive natural way to display nutmeg, cinnamon sticks, lemon sticks, and star anise. Choose complementary herbs so that the wreath fills the kitchen with a delicious aroma. Don't include anything too overpowering that will cancel out the more subtle smells of other herbs. If you look after the wreath carefully and do not use too many of its ingredients in your cooking, your wreath should last well into the new year. Our kitchen arrangement is built upon an ivy base, but as an alternative you could use laurel leaves. Long spikes of rosemary also look lovely in winter arrangements and would mix well with holly and ivy featured here. Lastly, the seedheads of fennel, caraway and dill could also have an aromatic part to play in Christmas wreaths.

Choosing the frame

There are many types of frames for Christmas wreaths and garlands, but we have used the simplest here – copper wire formed into a rough circle. Don't worry about a perfect shape – once you get a thick cover of foliage over the wire, any unevenness is less obvious, and the slight variation on a perfect circle gives it character. If you're really keen on a perfect circle, you could use a wire-frame lampshade base instead.

You can buy plastic-backed foam rings in a range of diameters and in oval or round shapes: the dining table wreath here is built on a foam ring. A more traditional foundation is wire-mesh netting formed into a circular tube and stuffed with moss. Unfortunately, moss tends to stain white paint or wallpaper so is often unsuitable for indoors. For a rustic, informal dried wreath, teased-out straw (available from pet shops) can be bound into a long sausage shape with natural twine, then tied together at the ends to form a circular base.

Displaying your wreath

The front door is the traditional location for Christmas wreaths but they look equally as nice on inside doors. Wreaths made with dried flowers or herbs must be kept under cover, as rain or even a damp atmosphere will ruin them. Indoors, you can hang a wreath over a mantelpiece mirror, from a picture hook on a wall, or on an ornate and decorative piece of furniture, ideally one that will not be in use.

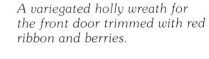

A variegated holly wreath for the front door trimmed with red ribbon and berries.

A gloriously traditional Christmas wreath made of holly, ivy and conifer foliage, displayed on an antique wooden chair. Dark green leaves on their own can be rather sombre but here, blue cedar, variegated holly, ribbons and artificial fruit provide festive colour.

A TRADITIONAL CHRISTMAS GARLAND

MATERIALS

1   variegated holly
2   blue cedar
3   ivy
4   cupressus
5   fake holly berries
6   large and small cones
7   wooden cherries
8   copper wire
9   scissors
10 green twine
11 red ribbon
12 transparent glue
13 plate moss (optional)

HANGING YOUR CHRISTMAS WREATH

To make a hook for your Christmas wreath, cover a piece of stub wire in green tape.

1 Twist a circle in the middle of the wire and push the ends into the back of the wreath at the top.

2 Pull the wire ends back under the wreath, then push each end into each side of the wreath to secure.

3 The loop should be fixed in the middle of the wreath on the top back, with the ends tucked in.

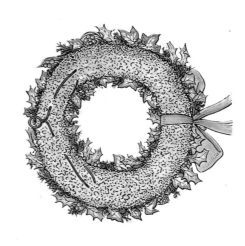

1 Bend copper wire (length depends on how big you want your wreath to be) into a circle, then firmly bind with uncut green twine. Take 5 or 6 sprays of foliage from the cupressus and strip some of the lower fronds to leave bare stems. Bunch 2 or 3 stems together, then hold them against the bound wire, and start binding onto the wire with the twine still attached to the reel.

2 Using the same uncut twine, keep binding overlapping bunches of foliage and moss, if used, to the frame. Select 3 or 4 long-stalked ivy leaves, then add them, as a tight group, wrapping the twine around the stalks 5 or 6 times. Break off small lengths of blue cedar, strip the lower stems, then bind a small bunch overlapping the ivy. Keep following the curve of the ring as you work.

3 Divide the holly into small sprigs, then secure a bunch of 5 or 6 sprigs to the wire ring, in the same way. Use small bunches of holly to give a more interesting shape. You should now be roughly halfway around the ring, but if not, don't worry – you simply repeat the ingredients in the same order, and carry on adding more material until the entire ring is completely covered with overlapping foliage.

4 Once the ring is completely covered, cut and knot the twine. Inspect the wreath from all sides and trim off any stray pieces that don't follow the general line and flow. Don't tidy up too much, though, or the wreath will look artificial and the final effect spoiled. If there are bare patches, you can usually gently manipulate the foliage to cover them, or at least make them smaller.

5 To add colour, glue on the red-painted wooden cherries in clusters or pairs, using quick-drying transparent glue. Fake holly berries do not always look authentic but real berries tend to shrivel after a couple of weeks. Glue on fake berry clusters instead of, or as well as, real berries evenly spaced apart. Glue pine, fir or larch cones onto the cedar branches.

6 Hold the wreath up or prop it on the mantelpiece, so that you can decide which way it looks best. Then, when you have decided where the top of the wreath is, glue on a large bow, both for decoration and to disguise the hook. Glue another ribbon, with long trailing ends, onto the bottom, and glue small bows all around the greenery for added Christmas sparkle.

FIREPLACE DECORATIONS

At Christmastime the fireplace is rightly the focal point of a room. After all, this is Santa Claus's doorway to your home, and as such has a very special place in the family's affections. Make sure the hearth and mantelpiece live up to traditional expectations by giving it a high-priority decoration scheme.

Swags and ribbons of evergreens, cones, Christmas balls or false fruits looped over the mantelpiece – though not in reach of stray sparks – are a decorative way to frame this important architectural feature. All you need is a length of strong rope or thick string, a roll of fine wire, and a handful of ingredients. Dried flowers, artificial berries, loops of tinsel, ribbon bows, they can all enhance a "trail of leaves".

If your fireplace has a mirror above it, work that into your scheme of things, too, with a slender version of the fireplace decoration outlining its frame.

Some fireplaces just weren't built for loops and drapes – there may not be space to spare above the opening. Such features look especially attractive with a simple hanging decoration on each side, a ribbon of evergreens, a posy of dried flowers on a pretend woodcarving made up of cones, nuts and seedheads wired to a base. The braided frame used for garlic strings makes a perfect base for this type of hanging.

The wall area above a fireplace is too precious to ignore. Make it the focus of attention by adorning it with a hanging wreath of Christmas tree trimmings, other evergreens and dried flowers, or a glittering version composed of tinsel and Christmas balls. Make a Christmas card collage on a piece of softboard outlined with sprigs of holly, or string a spare set of Christmas lights in loops and fix small balls along the wire to maximize the effect.

If you don't have a fireplace, you may be able to treat another architectural feature – an alcove, arch or even a doorway – in a similar way.

A charmingly decorated mantelpiece using greenery combined with beautiful fruits to create an unusual effect.

If the shape of your tree leaves something to be desired, cut off the offending branches, and use the trimmings to make a cheerful wall decoration.

Just because a fireplace is not in use, there's no need to leave it out in the cold! These bright and colourful swags make sure that it retains its rightful place as the focal point of the room. Cones, silk leaves and brilliant red fruit look-alikes are tied to scarlet ribbons to make an original and festive design.

CLEVER CANDLECUPS

Candles, so much a part of Christmas tradition, can be incorporated in your festive flower arrangements.

A candelabrum is easily converted into a holder for flowers and foliage by the simple addition of a candlecup obtainable from flower shops. Candlecup knobs do vary in size, so before buying one, first measure the diameter of the candelabrum cavity. A small to medium cup is better than a large one that can look too obvious and ungainly. A cakeboard covered in a plain fabric to tone with the candle will provide a suitable base.

1 To secure the candlecup use a pencil-thin length of florist's foam. Fix to follow the circular shape of the cup base and press firmly onto the candlestick opening.

2 Place presoaked florist's foam in the cup and tape securely. (To remove cup, gently twist off. Pull off the florist's foam fix and clean the candelabrum with polish.)

Flowers and foliage should be well conditioned before arranging, and attention to scale should be considered. A carnation is large enough, a chrysanthemum bloom overlarge. Spray chrysanthemums, spray carnations and alstroemeria have several flowerheads on the main stem, so can be cut up into smaller pieces. Ivy trails look pretty and the individual leaves around the centre hide the florist's foam. Add holly and shiny red shiny red berries to complete the seasonal touch.

If the candelabrum design is for the dinner table, match the flower colours and candles to the napkins and dinner service. Make sure that plant material does not overhang food, it

The elegance of a candelabra is ideally suited to displaying flowers. Here, red spray carnations, spray chrysanthemums and alstroemeria combine with greenery to make a charming arrangement for any Christmas occasion.

could be embarrassing if unpalatable petals found their way into the main dish!

To prevent the candle making a big hole in the florist's foam, tape toothpicks to the bottom of the candle so they extend beyond the end. Push these into the florist's foam and check that the candle sits straight.

Remember, lighted candles are a fire hazard so never leave them unattended and keep them well above plant material replacing candles as they burn down. Dried material carries a greater fire risk than fresh.

Candles make a delightful focal point on the table as well as providing a beautifully flattering soft light which is guaranteed to cheer your guests. The combined flames of these slender, taper candles create a good deal of light of a very diffuse nature.

If you don't own a candelabrum, the candlecup can be inserted in the neck of a bottle. When the florist's foam is in place, a candle can be added before the flowers are arranged.

LIGHTING DARK CORNERS

Banish dark and gloomy corners from your house for the holiday season and beyond.

Brighten up by installing spotlights to bathe special flower arrangements, pieces of furniture and ornaments in a flattering light.

Careful selection of light-reflecting table surfaces, containers and even the flowers and foliage themselves is important. White, followed by pastel shades of all kinds, is beautiful when it comes to choosing flowers to lighten the darkness.

For "here and now" pools of light, do not overlook the possibility of extending the use of Christmas lights. String them over a party table, fix them around the edge of a buffet table, or use them to outline the door frame leading to a party dining room to create a festive feel.

You don't need to give a party, or have any excuse at all, though, to make use of candlepower. Nightlights have the twin advantages of being inexpensive and long-lasting, and they don't need any special holders. Not only that, they float! Try some of these ideas this Christmas.

Group a dozen or so nightlights on a plate or dish to draw the eye to a room-corner flower arrangement; place a handful of them haphazardly around a large flat plate or dish with the tiniest of flower groupings, and they will make even a single flower look like a million dollar bunch.

Float nightlights and flowerheads in a glass bowl for an exotic look. A design like this, assembled in moments, would be especially suitable for a hall table or, scaled down a little, a guest bedroom or bathroom. More practically, put a nightlight and a couple of tiny floating flowers into a grapefruit glass or jam jar for a pretty way to light a staircase or landing.

LEFT Half-a-dozen nightlights and a handful of flowerheads show the decorative potential of candlepower. The cut chrysanthemums float in a glass bowl of water.

OPPOSITE Children and candles go together – the magic and joy of Christmas seems to be held in the flickering flames. Nightlights – which come in all the colours of the rainbow, and perfumed, too – are safest where there are young children about. They are especially pretty if you group several of the same colour on a large, flat plate.

A DRIED CENTREPIECE FOR THE TABLE

This centrepiece obeys one of the most important rules of dining table flower arrangement: the display must be low enough for everyone to see each other across the table, otherwise, conversation can't flow, see page 26 for step-by-step instructions on making this beautiful project.

Choosing the materials

Only two types of flowers are used; helichrysum, or strawflowers, and safari grass. The larger ones are yellow and orange helichrysums. Red helichrysums would be a more traditional choice of colour for Christmas, but the yellow and orange echo the gold of the accessories and gilded conifer cones. Alternatively, you could match the colour of the helichrysums to the colour scheme of your dining room or china and table linen. The smaller flowers are bleached safari glass, also called broom bloom. These add a delicate touch and, because they are neutral, will blend in with any decor. Use dried gypsophila, if you can't find safari grass.

Preserved foliage

Cones, seedpods and preserved foliage make up the bulk of the display. Beech mast (the empty seedheads of the beech tree) look like open flowers with petals of pale wood. They have no stems, so are wired into natural-looking groups, as well as singly. The wire

FINDING MATERIALS

Many florist shops do not sell safari grass stems individually, although a friendly local florist may order them specially for you if given plenty of advance warning.

Safari grass, or broom bloom, is usually sold in a made-up, mixed "Safari Pack" that includes other dried materials as well. If you need to buy 2 safari packs so that you have the right amount of grass for this arrangement, check the packs before buying to make sure that they contain plenty of safari grass.

Larch cones are sometimes difficult to find, but ordinary fir cones will do just as well. Use them singly or wired onto a sturdy twig.

SAFETY TIPS

Dried flowers are highly flammable, so before lighting the candles for this or any other dried arrangement make sure that dried material is positioned well away from the candle flames. Nor should you light candles anywhere near curtains or furnishing fabrics in case they catch. Don't leave your display unattended, particularly if children or pets are around, and lastly, make sure that lighted candles are fully extinguished before leaving the room.

would be visible in the finished display, so it is camouflaged here with brown florist's tape. The large larch cones are also wired, while the smaller ones are used still attached to their own leafless branches (larch is one of the few conifers to shed its foliage in winter).

Glycerining beech

The rich brown leaves are those of glycerined beech. Beech leaves are among the easiest and most popular to glycerine – the secret is to pick and preserve them in the summer, before they go brown naturally. (Green beech leaves become brown during the glycerining process – those that have already started to turn brown on the trees cannot take up glycerine, and shrivel up instead.) The delicacy of woodland fern is captured with the pressed fronds of the male fern, *Dryopteris filix-mas*, but any fern, or even bracken, would do equally well.

The nonfloral material – candles, gold ribbon, gold spray and prewired balls – are available from florists, gift shops, craft shops and notions sections of department stores. For the gold spray paint, you could also try hardware stores and car accessory stores.

Choosing the container

The base for this display is a commercially-prepared teak board, cut with a band saw and carved to give the gently sculpted effect. Your florist may be able to order one for you if you give enough notice (Christmas is the busiest time of the year for florists, so don't leave it too late). Though beautiful, teak is one of the hardest woods to work. If you want to make the base yourself, a softwood,

such as fir or pine, would be a better choice. You could also stain or oil the wood, to enrich its colour. (Wood staining products are available from hardware stores.)

Alternatively, make do with an old, oval breadboard or a thick, woven straw placemat. Both are often cheaply available at jumble sales.

This glorious table centerpiece comprises holly, peachy orange roses and a striking orange gourd at the centre.

6 STEPS TO A FESTIVE DINING TABLE DISPLAY

MATERIALS

1 8 helichrysum flowerheads in gold and orange (or in colours of your choice)
2 10-12 safari grass stems
3 6 large larch cones and 2 branches with cones on
4 2 sprays of beech mast
5 12 beech leaves
6 7-8 single stems of fern
7 2 slim cream candles
8 2 ribbons
9 5 Christmas balls
10 wooden base
11 block of dry florist's foam
12 plastic flowerpot saucer
13 tape
14 wire
15 florist's scissors
16 gold spray paint

MAKING RIBBON BOWS

1 Take a length of ribbon about 60cm (24 inches) long and beginning at 1 end, leaving a small tail, loop the ribbon into a figure-of-eight. Hold the point where you are forming the loops firmly between thumb and forefinger.

2 Holding the centre of the figure-of-eight, make a second figure-of-eight on top of the first. Keep holding the ribbon securely as you work, or it will slip out of shape.

3 Pinch together the point you are holding between thumb and forefinger and bind a length of stub wire around this point to secure the bow. Cut the wire, leaving 10cm (4 inches) over to push into the foam.

1 Measure and cut the dried-flower foam block to fit in a plastic flowerpot saucer. Tape the block in place, then spray everything gold. When dry, position it slightly off-centre on the base, then fix it firmly with adhesive clay. Slightly shorten 1 candle, then tape toothpicks to the ends of both candles to make insertion easier. Firmly fix them together (but not touching) in the centre of the foam block.

2 Cut the beech diagonally into sprigs, with easy-to-insert, pointed ends. Use 7 sprigs, evenly spaced, to set the basic width of the display. Place long sprigs of safari grass over the longest length of base – on the righthand side – and shorter pieces all the way around, roughly parallel to the beech. To set the height and conceal the tape, place sprigs of safari grass between the candles.

3 Trim the lower segments off the fern fronds. Insert the bare stalks horizontally into the foam block, above the beech leaves and evenly spaced out. Wire the stalks if they are too soft to insert. Spray the larch branches and cones gold. When dry, insert branches low down, with the longest on the righthand side to emphasize the asymmetric design. It doesn't matter if they rest on the base.

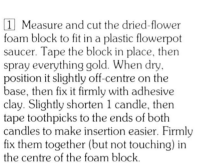

4 Wire up the larger sprayed gold larch cones on short stems and insert them, evenly spaced out, to help conceal the foam block. Place some in the centre, others at the base of the candles, and the remainder on the lefthand side to balance the branches on the right. At this stage, inspect the display from all sides to ensure that it is evenly dense and attractive from every angle. Adjust as necessary.

5 Wire and tape the beech mast, singly and in sprigs of two or more. Place longer sprigs on the righthand side, reinforcing the asymmetry. Insert a cluster of three on the lefthand side, for balance and to hide the foam block. Make 2 ribbon loop "flowers", twisting and tying the centre with stub wire to form the "petals". Insert 1 ribbon flower at the front of the display, the other at the back.

6 Place 2 balls on the lefthand side of the display, and three on the right, to create areas of highlight. Wire the helichrysum, fixing the smaller flowers on the long wires, and the larger flowers on shorter wires, to keep the mass of colour close to the centre. Form a staggered line of flowers diagonally across the display, varying the height of the flowers to break up the outline.

FLORAL CONE

This pretty little spiral cone is ideal for festive occasions. It's cheerful, glittery, and versatile, too. It can be moved from coffee table to dinner table and from buffet table to sideboard – or wherever a festive feature is required. You could even use it as a welcoming hallway display if you run out of fresh or dried flowers over the Christmas period. Florist's foam cones are available in a variety of sizes, so you can make one the same size as here, or in a different size. Use ingredients in colours of your own choice, but if you prefer to follow our steps for this purple and silver cone you will need the items below.

MATERIALS

florist's foam cone
    (sprayed silver)
cake board (slightly wider
    than the cone)
purple felt
glue or pins
purple dried
    xeranthemums

white dried helichrysums
alder cones (or any small
    cones sprayed silver)
dried hydrangea head
    florets (sprayed silver)
silver ribbon
thin stub wire

1 Using a piece of strong wire etch a spiral guideline for the flowers from the top of the cone to the bottom. Make sure you keep the spacing even. Cover the cake board with purple felt; glue it to the underside of the board or secure it with pins, then glue the cone to this base. Start by inserting the xeranthemums, following the etched line, to create the basic outline of your design.

2 Next insert the silver cones, following the first line of purple flowers and then make a third line with the helichrysums (the line of cones will stand out between the flowers and give the arrangement textural contrast). Try to insert all the flowers so that their heads are pointing slightly downward. By this stage the arrangement will really be taking shape and the cone should look fairly dense and evenly covered.

3 Break off florets from a sprayed-silver hydrangea head, wire the floret stems and insert them randomly in the cone to fill out any gaps. Make silver ribbon loops and twist stub wire around a section of each loop leaving a long enough length of wire to insert in the cone. Place the ribbon loops at intervals all over the arrangement. Lastly, insert 1 or 2 helichrysum flowers in the top of the cone.

ADDING SPARKLE THROUGHOUT THE HOUSE

All that glitters may not be gold, but in the short, dark days of winter any additional shine or sparkle, glint or glitter you can add to your home will bring a welcome glow.

Gather together a group of shiny containers and ornaments; arrange them on a surface you can almost see your face in; invest in a handful of dried or long-lasting fresh flowers for an arrangement with a difference and you can create an eye-catching still-life.

Shiny surfaces

This is not the time for best linen tablecloths. Concentrate attention instead on a highly polished wooden surface, whether an occasional table, a sideboard, a glass shelf or coffee table.

Look out for bargain lengths of shiny-coated plasticized cotton, the up-dated version of the old-fashioned oilcloth, which is sold to match conventional cotton furnishing fabrics in a wide range of modern and classic patterns.

Give new, if temporary, prominence to a brass or copper tray or large plate or improvise by using sheets of gold, silver or brightly coloured foil paper.

Sparkling containers

Once you have decided on the base for your attention-grabbing display, look around your home for imaginative containers with a high gloss factor. If you happen to have a glass vase, particularly one of the pearlized type, or an old lustre jug or teapot, that's fine. If not, use a shiny stainless steel pot or an enamel saucepan from the kitchen.

Glossy flowers and foliage

Seek out the shiniest specimens among everlasting and dried flowers, preserved and evergreen foliage, and fresh flowers. Each category has some that have a higher gloss factor than others; these are the ones you want.

Everlasting flowers, which dry naturally on the plant or hung up in a warm, airy room, have more built-in sparkle than other dried flowers. The pick of the bunch must be strawflowers, which grow in many lovely colors, and rhodanthe (also known as helipterum), which grow in shiny sugar-almond pink and snowy white. Both of these are pretty daisy-shaped species and blend well with other dried materials.

When it comes to seedheads, there is no contest. Honesty, those translucent, silvery-papery "moon petals", stand out a mile. Stems and clippings of honesty are excellent mixers and provide pretty highlights in arrangements of both dried and fresh flowers. And a casual bunch of honesty (once you have rubbed off the drab beige outer covers of the seed carriers) will brighten a dark corner.

Evergreen leaves and most foliage preserved in glycerine are good for shine. Ivy, magnolia, laurel, elaeagnus, pittosporum, camellia, pyracanthus and many other evergreens will fit perfectly into your design, as will preserved beech, oak, maple and many other types.

It is well worth giving any slightly weary-looking foliage a bit of "spit and polish". Dust large leaves with pot plant leaf-shine wipes. Alternatively, use a soft dry cloth. Then for extra gloss, polish the leaves with a cloth sprinkled with a couple of drops of salad oil. It makes all the difference. One word of warning though; leaves treated with this special dressing do tend to attract and hold the dust, so it is not suitable for a dusty environment. Fortunately, some of the shiniest fresh flowers also have the longest vase life. Lilies of all kinds, including alstroemeria, orchids and, as the season merges into spring, tulips, all have glossy waxlike petals that act like reflectors to every shaft of sunlight or lamplight. It is not necessary to buy a lot of these – if you plan your arrangement carefully a few stems will go a long way. Condition them well before designing the display for longer life.

Not quite natural

You don't have to rely on nature – a can or two of spray paint and a few brushfuls of clear varnish can turn a collection of lack-lustre seedheads, twigs and foliage into a dazzlingly different display. Spray love-in-a mist seedheads silver, stately poppy "urns" red and tough little windfall apples golden.

Find some teasels and spray them very lightly with silver paint so they have a frosted appearance. Spray spare apples and pears and a few oranges with a touch or two of red paint. Leave to dry, then touch up with silver, gold or bronze. Bunches of plastic grapes also take well to this treatment, and add an interesting change of size and shape to a decorative bowl of sprayed fruits. Lemons, tangerines and clementines can also be sprayed and included in your display.

Sizing your table decorations

Christmas is the time to let your imagination run riot on table decorations. Put a little thought beforehand into the size of your table, the number of guests you are expecting, and the food you will be serving. You will not want to constantly be moving your decorations to find extra space for dishes, and nor will you want to run the risk of greenery getting into the food – so if space is limited, content yourself with making small, dainty, decorations. On the other hand, if you have plenty of table space you can add your decorations with a freer hand, making your table a feature of the festive living room.

Polished wood

With woody-looking subjects such as cones, nuts and seedheads, all you need is a coat of varnish. Choose a clear, colourless type – you can buy it in bottles, cans or spray cans – and apply a thin, even coat to your chosen materials. Cones look like intricate and highly polished wood carvings; walnuts, chestnuts and hazelnuts glisten like tiny Christmas balls, and stems or sideshoots of seedheads – hollyhock or delphinium, for example – sparkle as never before. Do keep treated fruit out of children's reach, as it look tempting but is poisonous to eat.

Accessories after the fact

Now you have chosen the 3 main ingredients – the surface, the container and the flowers – increase the effect with a few accessories.

Christmas balls and tinsels are obvious and cheerful candidates. Gift wrap ribbons, especially ones with a metallic thread, snaking in and out of the items in the group, visually link the components and add extra colour. For the finishing touch, a dish of the brightest boiled sweets or chocolate in gold foil wrappings make stunning accessories.

Nestling in coils of glossy ivy leaves, apples and pears, cones and tiny teazels show themselves in a new light. Spray the fruits with one gloss colour – perhaps red as here – and then overspray with a metallic one for an interesting finish.

SUGAR BASKETS

Glistening sugar baskets are very easy to make and they are a good way of using old cotton crocheted mats that might have been put away and forgotten. They make effective and pretty containers for Christmas goodies.

Fill the baskets with sweets, dried fruit, nuts or Christmas balls for table decoration. If the mat is not too valuable, crocheted cotton can also be gold-sprayed. Thread gold or silver ribbons through the holes, or make handles by sugaring strips of insertion lace or bending florist's wire. The baskets can subsequently be washed to remove the syrup after Christmas is over.

Sugar baskets can also be used to present gifts of food or arrangements of dried flowers and leaves.

MATERIALS

cotton crocheted mats or doilies
50g (2 oz) sugar for each mat
1 tablespoon water
a mould (bowls, glasses, dishes, etc.)
spray varnish (optional)
gold spray paint (optional)
florist's wire
satin ribbon

1 Stir the sugar into the water until it has dissolved, then bring gently to a boil. Remove the pan from the heat as soon as the syrup has formed.
2 Dip the crocheted mat or doily into the syrup and squeeze out the excess sugar with your fingers.
3 Put the mould on a pastry board and place the mat over it. Smooth it down the sides of the mould and spread out the decorative edges. Pin the edges to the board. The mats will take between 2 and 3 hours to dry out. After about 1 hour, the decorative edges can be bent to a particular pattern or shape if desired.
4 Remove the sugar basket from the mould and leave overnight in a warm place to dry out completely.
5 If desired, sugar baskets can be given a protective coating of spray varnish and the edges can be highlighted with a touch of gold or silver paint.

6 Make handles by bending florist's wire to shape and wrapping with ribbon. Loop the wire handle through the holes in the rim of the basket and glue to the basket edges.

SPRAYING FRUIT

To make the job of paint spraying fruit and seedheads easier, follow these simple steps for a cleaner finish.
● If you are going to spray paint, remember to use the aerosol in a well-ventilated room.
● Pierce the fruits with wooden skewers or cocktail sticks, and secure them in a firm base such as a metal pinholder or even a large potato.
● Stand the base on newspaper to prevent paint spray from falling on the floor or furniture – or put it into a cardboard box turned on 1 side and spray it there.
● Spray the paint as you turn the base in an even, all-around motion.
● Leave the fruits to dry thoroughly overnight before arranging them.

KIDS' CREATIONS FOR CHRISTMAS

Many children could teach their parents a thing or two when it comes to imaginative ideas for Christmas and party time. With their natural exuberance and flair for self-expression, school children often produce artistic triumphs that the older generation wouldn't dream up in a million years!

It's fun to allow children to play a large part in decorating the house for Christmas – after all, it is their own special festival and it will keep them occupied for some time over the Christmas holidays. Give them the tools – brightly coloured paper, felt and plastic; odds and ends of ribbon and tinsel; pens, paints and pencils; sprays of evergreens, and artificial berries, dried flower trimmings and un-breakable containers; and they will surely come up with some surprises.

Young people rarely appreciate decorative understatement – they are more attracted to brightly-coloured bold designs. Evergreen branches emblazoned with bright red paper flowers, cut woollen balls, or clusters of cellophane-wrapped sweets; or a handful of knobbly branches sprayed bright red, spattered with glitter and hung with painted play-dough flowers and lantern shapes, are more likely to appeal. Spray-paint twigs, cones, nuts, teasels, seedheads, small under-ripe apples to turn into shiny balls.

Discarded herb and spice jars, spray-painted or given a silver-foil covering serve as pretty containers for candles, evergreens or dried flower posies.

Imagination knows no bounds in these colourful tree decorations. Flower and leaf shapes cut from felt, felt, paper and plastic and placed one over the other, collage style, are fixed to the branches with huge paperclips, and there are tempting gingerbread shapes and sweetmeats. Provide a range of paper and other scraps, and let the children go to it!

A NATIVITY SCENE

This charming Nativity depicts the birth of Jesus in Bethlehem, a Middle Eastern town complete with a palm tree in the inn's courtyard and the pale blue winter moonlight outside the stable. Empty food cartons are used for the stable and for the figures, with pieces of felt, beads, buttons, etc. to dress them. Smaller children could make a whole flock of salt dough sheep (see the recipe, in Chapter 3: The Christmas Tree), while older children construct the stable and make the figures.

MATERIALS

For the stable:
2 × 225g (8 oz) cornflakes boxes
clear adhesive tape
instant adhesive
30cm (12 inch) piece of blue transparent cellophane
1 roll of white kitchen paper
white powder paint
30 × 45cm (12 × 18 inch) base card
1 sheet grey or brown gift wrap
matchsticks
brown wrapping paper
13 × 13cm (5 × 5 inch) piece of gold paper
1 sheet red patterned gift wrap
1 packet pink crêpe paper
thin white card
silver glitter
felt-tip pens

7.5 × 25cm (3 × 10 inch) piece of dark green felt
very small box (eg jewelry or complimentary soap box)
raffia
30cm (12 inch) square of fawn felt
wood shavings or sawdust

For the figures:
thin white card from food boxes
2.5cm (1 inch) diameter wooden or paper beads
coloured and white paper napkins
small rubber bands
20cm (8 inch) squares of felt: light green, dark green, black, bright blue, orange, grey-green
small pieces of coloured foil, or scraps of Christmas gift paper
beads, sequins and fringing for decoration
buttons and beads for kings' crowns and gifts
white tissue paper
12.5cm (5 inch) piece of florist's wire

Accessories:
salt dough for sheep
brown wrapping paper and card for making donkey
small piece of packaging twine for donkey's tail

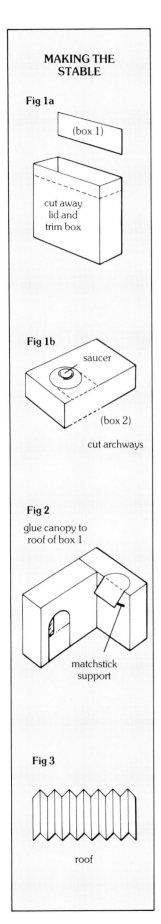

MAKING THE STABLE

Fig 1a

(box 1)

cut away lid and trim box

Fig 1b

saucer

(box 2)

cut archways

Fig 2

glue canopy to roof of box 1

matchstick support

Fig 3

roof

1 Cut the lid from box 1, then cut 2.5cm (1 inch) off the top. Tape the lid back on and then tape closed (Fig 1a).
2 On cornflake box 2, cut 2 archways (Fig 1b). Use a saucer to draw the curve. Glue the blue cellophane behind the archway.
3 Glue or tape box 1 onto the end of box 2. Glue sheets of white kitchen paper over the walls and roof of the stable. Glue the stable to the base card. Paint the walls white.
4 To make the canopy, cover one of the cut-out arch shapes with grey or brown gift wrap. Fold it across the middle (Fig 2) and glue or tape the curved end to the roof of the box 1 stable section. Colour 2 matchsticks for supports and glue to the outer edge of the canopy and to the stable wall.
5 Cut a small door shape from brown paper and glue to the stable wall next to the archway. Cut a 10cm (4-inch) diameter circle of gold paper and glue to the stable wall.
6 Cut a piece of pink crêpe paper 35 × 10cm (14 × 4 inches) and fold under the edges. Glue to the roof of the stable section with the arch. Cut a second piece of pink crêpe paper 25 × 10cm (10 × 4 inches), fold under the edges and glue to the other roof section.
7 Cut 2 strips 35 × 7.5cm (14 × 3 inches) and 25 × 7.5cm (10 × 3 inches) from the red patterned gift wrap and fold the strips along the length in accordion folds (Fig 3).
8 Glue the red paper tiles to the roofs, firmly at the ends and lightly under the folds.
9 Cut a star from white card and glue it to a matchstick. Apply a little adhesive to the star and dust it with glitter. Pierce a hole in the stable roof and glue the star into the hole (see picture).

Palm tree

10 Cut a 10cm (4-inch) square of card, roll it up tightly and tape the joint, to make the tree trunk. Glue coloured paper around it – or colour with pens. Glue the trunk to a 5cm (2-inch) square of card so that it stands up (Fig 4a).
11 Snip into the dark green felt all along one edge (Fig 4b). Wind the uncut edge of the felt around the top of the trunk, gluing as you go, and secure with a rubber band while it dries. Glue the palm tree beside the stable, pinning the base to the floor while it dries (see picture).

Crib

12 Cut the very small box down to 2.5cm (1 inch) deep and cover the sides with matchsticks broken to fit the depth of the box. Fill the crib with shredded raffia, or alternatively you could shred the discarded pieces of box.

Figures

13 All the figures are made on a cardboard tube base. Cut the pieces of card 6cm (2½ inches) deep by 10cm (4 inches) wide. Roll around a pencil to make a tube about 15mm (⅝ inch) across. Glue a bead to the top of each tube,

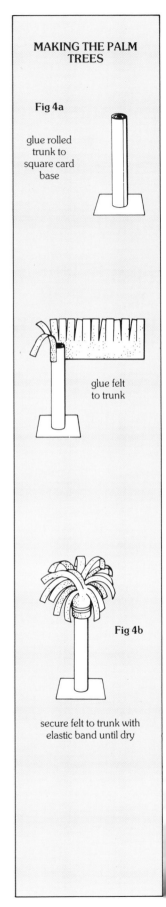

MAKING THE PALM TREES

Fig 4a

glue rolled trunk to square card base

glue felt to trunk

Fig 4b

secure felt to trunk with elastic band until dry

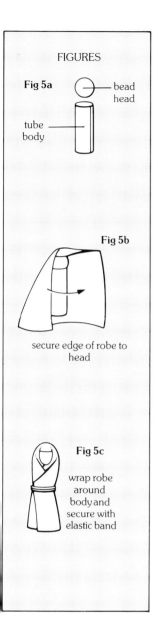

FIGURES

Fig 5a — bead head

tube body

Fig 5b

secure edge of robe to head

Fig 5c

wrap robe around body and secure with elastic band

so that the head looks downward (Fig 5a).

Robes for figures

14   These are made from coloured paper napkins.

Fold 1 edge under and arrange over the bead head (Fig 5b). Fold the sides forward and across the chest to the back. Secure with a rubber band (Fig 5c). Trim off level with the bottom of the tube so that the figure stands up.

Kings

15   Cut strips of foil or coloured paper to wrap around the tubes and glue or tape at the back.

Fig 6 for the shape) and secure around the kings with a rubber band. With a felt-tip pen, draw hair on the kings' heads, and 1 king should have a black face coloured in. Glue crowns made of leftover pieces of red or gold card or buttons to the heads. Decorate their robes with beads, sequins or fringing.

Mary

16   Mary is made from a smaller tube, 5cm (2 inches) high. Drape bright blue felt over the head bead, secure it with a rubber band, then turn the excess felt under the tube at the front. Trim to shape (see Fig. 7).

Hands

17   All the adult figures have praying hands. Cut strips of card, (or fold crêpe paper or napkins), to 5 × 2.5cm (2 × 1 inch). Fold once along the length and then once across the width (Fig 8a). Trim as shown by the dotted line (Fig 8b) and draw hands on the folded end. Glue the open ends to the sides of the figures (Mary's arms tuck under her robes). Glue the kings' gifts (beads, buttons, etc.) to the hands. Bend the end of the florist's wire over into a crook shape and tuck it in the brown shepherd's arms.

Baby Jesus

18   Make a short, narrow tube body, and glue a smaller bead on for a head. Wrap the baby in white tissue, and glue in place. Put the baby in the crib.

The sheep

19   These are modelled from salt dough. Mark the fleece with a sharpened matchstick. Ordinary clay can be used.

Donkey

20   Cut a piece of card 5cm (2-inch) square and fold it in half. Wrap a piece of brown wrapping paper around a small bead and secure with a rubber band. Wrap and glue more paper over and around the folded card, turning the edges under (Fig 9).

Cut 2 ears and glue to the head. Glue the head to the body. Colour a tiny piece of string with a felt-tip pen and glue it at the back of the donkey for a tail.

Finishing

21   Cut a fringed end on the fawn felt for the stable floor. Glue all the figures, animals and crib to the floor of the stable. Scatter sawdust and tie some raffia for straw.

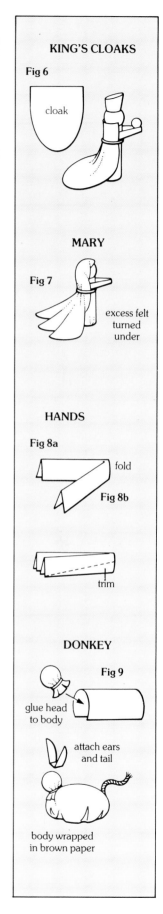

KING'S CLOAKS

Fig 6

cloak

MARY

Fig 7

excess felt turned under

HANDS

Fig 8a

fold

Fig 8b

trim

DONKEY

Fig 9

glue head to body

attach ears and tail

body wrapped in brown paper

ADVENT TREE

Hang up this big felt tree on the first day of December and discover a secret tucked inside a gift box every day until Christmas.

MATERIALS

75cm (29½ inches) of 1.8 metres (72 inch) wide dark green felt
51cm (20 inches) of 115cm (45 inch) wide Christmas print fabric
1 metre (39½ inches) of 1 metre (39½ inch) wide heavyweight polyester wadding
35cm (13¾ inches) of 115cm (45 inch) wide red polyester/cotton
25cm (10 inches) of 1 metre (39½ inch) wide mediumweight polyester wadding
25cm (10 inches) of 1 metre (39½ inch) wide lightweight polyester wadding
1 60cm (23½ inch) square red felt
8 metres (8¾ yards) of 1cm (⅜ inch) wide gold braid
70cm (27½ inches) gold elastic thread
matching thread (dark green, bright red, gold)
6 artificial fruits on wire stalks (from florist)
2cm (⅝ inch) wide gold sequin stars
pattern paper
scissors, tailor's chalk

1 Transfer the diagrams to the pattern paper. Using these as your patterns, cut the following:

from green felt 2 tree shapes, 1 with inverted V-shaped quilting lines marked with tailor's chalk
from heavyweight wadding 1 tree shape, 1 flowerpot rim shape
from red felt 2 flowerpot shapes, 1 flowerpot rim shape
from Christmas print 36 hearts
from red polyester/cotton 12 gift boxes
from mediumweight wadding 1 flowerpot shape
from lightweight wadding 18 hearts, 6 gift boxes
from ribbon 36 × 19cm (7½ inch) lengths, 1 × 68cm (26¾ inch) length
from gold braid 6 × 13cm (5 inch) lengths, 6 × 12cm (4½ inch) lengths

Tree

2 Match the heavyweight wadding tree to 1 felt tree. Pin and tack. Tack the chalk lines of the inverted V shapes on the felt side. Topstitch on the chalk lines to the quilt and pad. Tap the chalk marks away. With the topstitched side to the second felt tree shape, pin, tack and machine stitch 1 cm (⅜ inch) from the edges, starting and finishing at the base opening notches. Remove tacking, snip corners, turn to the right side. Lightly press. Rolling the seam to the edge, tack along all the edges to hold the tree shape flat. Leave

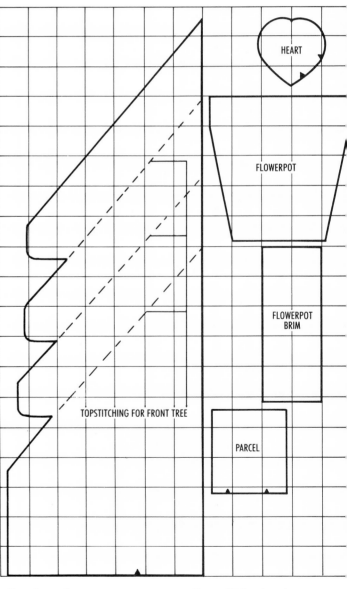

HEART
FLOWERPOT
FLOWERPOT BRIM
TOPSTITCHING FOR FRONT TREE
PARCEL

Scale   1 square = approx 5cm (2 inches)

the tacking until the hearts and gift boxes are positioned, but remove before the final pressing.

Flowerpot rim

3 Position the heavyweight wadding strip along 1 long edge of the felt rim shape and up to the centre. Sandwich the wadding by folding the felt over. Pin, tack and machine stitch along the long edges 1cm (³⁄₈ inch) from the 2 side edges, pushing the wadding toward the fold of the rim to form an open-ended "sausage" shape. Snip the protruding wadding from the side edges.

Flowerpot

4 With one red felt flowerpot shape and one mediumweight wadding flowerpot shape together, pin and tack around the complete shape. With the felt side of the padded pot shape uppermost, match the long raw edges of the filled rim to the top edge. Pin, tack and machine stitch approximately 5mm (¼ inch) from the top edge. With felt sides together, position the second pot shape over the rimmed pot. Pin, tack and machine stitch 5mm (¼ inch) down the sides and across the base of the pot. Remove the tacking. Trim the corners. Turn through to the right side. Lightly steam press. Slip machined top edge of the pot into 24cm (9½ inch) opening at the base of the tree, sliding in so that the turned under edges of the tree cover the original 5mm (¼-inch) turnings. Catchstitch the pot to the front and back of the tree, turning in the seam allowance on the tree opening. Remove the visible tacking.

Hearts

5 With right sides of printed heart shapes together and 1 lightweight wadding heart shape to 1 wrong side, pin, tack and machine stitch with 3mm (¹⁄₈ inch) seam, leaving the notched 4cm (1½-inch) openings. Turn through the opening to the right side. Catchstitch the opening together. Lightly steam press. Repeat to make 17 more hearts.

6 Take 1 19cm (7½ inch) long piece of ribbon, pin to the top centre of 1 heart, loop over the pin and catchstitch across the ribbon, leaving the long end free. Remove the pins. Repeat for the remaining 17 hearts.

Gift boxes

7 Arrange long braids down the box shapes

and short braids across the box shapes. Pin, tack and machine stitch in gold thread along the centre of the gold braid. Remove the tacking. Place 1 wadding box shape to the wrong side of the decorated box shape, pin and tack. With 1 red box shape to the braid/wadding shape and right sides of the fabric together, pin, tack and machine stitch 3mm (¹⁄₈ inch) from the edges, leaving notched opening at the base. Trim the corners. Turn through to the right side. Catchstitch the opening together. Lightly press. Repeat to make 5 more boxes.

To finish

8 Arrange the hearts and boxes on the tree as in the photograph, positioning 1 heart at the top, then a row of heart/box/heart and finally 4 rows of five each. Pin in position and handsew to the tree. Leave the top edge of the boxes and rounded tops of the hearts open for inserting small gifts. Match the remaining 18 lengths of red ribbon, one above each heart, and tack to the felt tree, turning 5mm (¼ inch) to neaten, corresponding to the ribbons on the hearts. Tie the bows. Cut the ends of the ribbon in a slant. Decorate the tree with sequin stars at the top, on each point, scattered across the tree and on some boxes. Add fruits between hearts and boxes. Sew the stalks in position. Tie the gold elastic thread around the base of the tree at top of the pot.

9 Fold the 68cm (26¾ inch) length of the ribbon in half and mark with a pin. Measure 13cm (5 inches) down each side seam from the top point of the tree and mark with tailor's chalk. Make a fold 3cm (1¼ inches) deep 13cm (5 inches) from each end of the ribbon and catchstitch the loop securely to each side of the tree. Cut slanted ends to neaten.

Other fabrics

An Advent tree could be made using gold lamé instead of green felt and be given silver lamé pockets. Alternatively, make an all-white tree covered in sparkling silver stars, or use red and green gingham checks.

SNOWMAN ADVENT CALENDAR

Twenty-five pockets to Christmas Eve. Fill the puddings, trees, leaves, robins and gift boxes with tiny gifts. His carrot nose, lumps of wood for eyes and dashing hat make this snowman very authentic.

MATERIALS

1.35 metres (1⅜ yards) of 90cm (36 inch) wide white felt

1.35 metres (1⅜ yards) of 1 metre (39½-inch) wide heavyweight polyester wadding

2 × 22cm (8½ inch) squares of felt in each colour: dark cypress green (holly), light pine green (tree), dark brown (pudding), leather brown (robin)

1 × 22cm (8½ inch) square orange felt

2 × 60cm (23½ inch) squares felt in each colour: scarlet, black

matching threads (red, green, orange, brown, black, white)

1 metre (39½ inches) of 3mm (⅛ inch) wide gold braid

75cm (29½ inches) of 3mm (⅛ inch) wide green double satin ribbon

2 large cube-shaped black buttons

5 gold star sequins, 15 small red beads, 5 small gold sequins, 25-30 1cm (⅜ inch) diameter assorted sequins

pattern paper

pencil, scissors, fabric adhesive, tissue paper

1 Transfer the diagrams to pattern paper. Using these as your patterns, cut the following:

from white felt 2 snowmen shapes, 5 icings

from dark cypress green felt 10 holly leaves

from light pine green felt 10 Christmas trees

from leather brown felt 10 Christmas puddings

from leather brown felt 10 robins

from scarlet felt 10 gift boxes, 5 robin breasts, 10 circles × 15mm (⅝ in) diameter, (berries), 2 strips 48×6cm (19×2⅜inch) (scarf)

from orange felt 2 carrot shapes (nose)

from black felt 2 hat shapes

from wadding 1 snowman shape, 1 hat shape trimmed on dotted line, 1 48 × 20cm (19 × 8 inch) length for hat brim

from gold braid 5 × 10cm (4 inch) lengths, 5 × 7.5cm (3 inch) lengths

2 Match pairs of felt boxes, puddings (not icing), robins, trees and holly leaves, topstitch together 1mm (¹⁄₁₆ inch) from the edge.

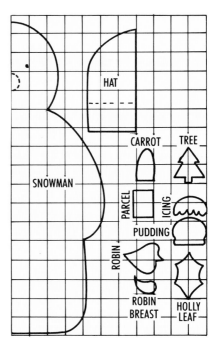

Scale 1 square = approx 5cm (2 inches)

shapes to join.

3 Decorate the pockets as follows.

Gift boxes

Pin and tack the vertical and then the horizontal lengths of gold braid to each box. Machine stitch through centre of braid to hold. Remove the tacking. Decorate each box by sewing on 1 gold star sequin.

Christmas puddings

Sew 3 small red beads to the top of the icing. Using the adhesive, attach the icing shape to the pudding as in the photograph.

Robins

Using the adhesive, attach the breasts to the robin shapes. Sew 1 gold sequin to each robin for eyes.

Christmas trees

Sew 5 or 6 large round sequins to each Christmas tree.

Holly leaves

Topstitch 2 machine lines down the center of each double-thickness holly leaf.

Using the adhesive, glue 2 felt berries to each leaf.

4 Position 24 of the felt shapes on 1 felt snowman as in the photograph. Keep back 1 robin for the hat decoration. Pin, tack and catchstitch each shape in place, leaving the tops open to form pockets.

5 Tack the wadding snowman shape to the back of the decorated felt snowman shape. With right sides together, match the decorated wadding snowman shape to the second felt shape, leaving the notched opening free. Back the wadding with tissue paper – tear away after machining. Pin, tack and machine stitch with 1cm (3/8 inch) turnings using a small zigzag stitch. Remove tacking. Trim the seams down to 5mm (1/4 inch). Carefully turn through to the right side, rolling out the felt shape to flatten. Pin and tack around the edges of the snowman to hold.

6 Pin and tack the trimmed wadding hat shape to 1 black felt hat shape. With felt shapes together, pin, tack and machine stitch with 5mm (1/4 inch) turnings, using a small zigzag stitch with the notched base open.

Trim the turnings on the curves. Remove the tacking. Turn through to the right side. Roll out the seam with fingers. Tack to hold. On the right side of the hat along the base edge, catchstitch the polyester wadding brim strip in position. Roll up the hat to form the brim and conceal the wadding. Catchstitch at the side seam. Catchstitch the remaining robin to the side of the hat.

7 Place the finished hat on the snowman's head, wadding-backed felt to front. Pin and catchstitch to the head at the side seams.

8 Pin and tack the 2 carrot shapes together. Machine stitch with 1mm (1/8 inch) turnings. Turn through to the right side. Using scraps of polyester wadding, stuff the carrot nose tightly. Catchstitch to the face around the base.

9 Sew on the button eyes.

10 Join the 48×6cm (19×2½-in) strips of scarlet felt on 1 short edge, taking a 5mm (1/4 in) seam. Fringe the ends by cutting into each end for 7cm (2¾ in) every 5mm (1/4 in).

11 Catchstitch each end of the green ribbon at the back of both shoulders and at 10cm (4 inch) intervals along the back so that the ribbon is secured at the back of the head and in the middle of the hat.

12 Matching the seam to the centre back of the snowman's neck, tie the scarf loosely.

THE CHRISTMAS TREE

O TANNENBAUM! O TANNENBAUM!

It is commonly believed that Queen Victoria's husband, Prince Albert, introduced the Christmas tree to England, bringing the custom with him from his native Germany. In fact it had been part of the festivities for many immigrant German families long before Prince Albert's day, and Queen Charlotte, the wife of George III, is reputed to have set up a Christmas tree at Windsor Castle as early as 1789. But the custom didn't capture the imagination of the public at large until Victoria and her husband gave it the royal seal of approval.

The Christmas tree was of course a particular source of delight to the children. In 1841 Queen Victoria wrote of her own tree at Windsor Castle:

Today I have two children of my own to give presents to, who, they know not why, are full of happy wonder at the German Christmas tree and its radiant candles.

In 1848 the *Illustrated London News* carried a charming portrait of the royal family, with by now six children, grouped around a twinkling fir. Victoria's subjects adored the royal family and aspired to make their own

home lives as like as possible to that of their dear queen, and so it isn't surprising that the Christmas tree rapidly became the focus of the seasonal celebrations.

The anonymous author of a booklet entitled *The Christmas Tree* forecast its brilliant future:

It now seems likely to become a naturalized plant. It is capable of adaptation to our national habits; and in less than a quarter of a century it will probably be familiar to all lovers of domestic observances, from the straits of Dover, to the Giant's Causeway, and John o'Groat's House; and even find its way to the wilds of Canada, and the banks of the Missouri and Columbia rivers.

Indeed as the century progressed the fashion for Christmas trees swept across Europe and America.

Quite where its origin is to be found is a bit of a mystery. It has been suggested that the Christmas tree was a descendant of the Paradise Tree, or Tree of Life, as it was represented in many medieval plays about Adam and Eve. Or its roots may lie in the pagan winter festivals, in which evergreens were used in fertility rites to ensure the coming of spring. But there is no record of decorated fir trees until about 1520, in

Alsace, and by 1605 the tradition was already established in Germany, where ". . . they set up fir trees in the parlours in Strasbourg and hang on them roses cut out of many-coloured papers, apples, wafers, gold foil, sweets, etc."

The lighted candles which gave the 19th-century tree its particular romantic appeal appeared in the 17th century, although legend has it in Germany that Martin Luther was the first to decorate a tree in this way. The story goes that he carried home a fir tree and illuminated it with candles to remind children of the starlit heavens from which Jesus Christ descended so long ago.

In Britain, both lights and evergreens had long since been associated with the season and were regarded as part of the old "Merrie England" Christmas tradition, so their happy conjunction in the Christmas tree assured its popularity.

Of course lighting a tree with candles had the disadvantage that they burned down very quickly, so the early tree tended to be an "occasion" in itself; it did not stand twinkling in the front parlour window for two weeks, as our modern trees do. And to this day it is traditional in Germany to decorate the tree in secret and only reveal it to the children in all its glory on Christmas Eve. So it was in Victorian times; the tree was adorned, the candles lit, and only then was the family or party guests summoned to admire it. The other obvious disadvantage was, of course, that candles constituted a fire hazard. In those times more fires were caused by candles than by anything else (particularly, so we are told, when people used them to look under the bed for burglars or chamber pots!) Party time was particularly hazardous, with girls in muslin dresses with their hair hanging loose, and cautionary tales abound. Under the headline *Fatally Burnt In Christmas Costumes* we read that ". . . fifteen children were set on fire, eleven of them fatally". In grand houses a footman would be employed to patrol the tree, armed with a wet sponge on the end of a long pole, to douse the candles as they burned down close to the branches.

It was also recommended that gelatine lights be used, rather than candles. These were like wax cups; each one contained in a little cup of coloured gelatine but since they had to be suspended below the branches rather than clipped to the top, there would still be a considerable danger of conflagration!

The risk of fire was overcome by the arrival of electricity, and the first electric tree lights became available in the late 19th century.

Edward Johnson, an associate of Thomas Edison, is said to have had the very first electrically lighted Christmas tree in New York City in 1882. And it was about 10 years after that that General Electric began manufacturing and selling Christmas tree lights.

In its early days the tree was adorned with simple handmade things: strings of popcorn and cranberries, small apples and nuts, wrapped homemade candies and paper-chains.

By far the greatest proportion of Victorian tree decorations were in fact small gifts or sweetmeats wrapped with exquisite care and ingenuity, and one suspects that the tree must have looked rather bare after they had all been distributed. But beforehand it was a thing of promise and enchantment. Here is

Martin Luther's 16th-century Christmas tree, as visualized in the Illustrated London News.

Dickens's description of a tree, In *Household Words*:

It was brilliantly lighted by a multitude of little tapers; and everywhere sparkled and glittered with bright objects. There were rosy cheeked dolls hiding behind the green leaves; and there were real watches (with moveable hands at least, and an endless capacity of being wound up) dangling from innumerable twigs; there were French-polished tables, chairs, bedsteads, wardrobes, eight-day clocks, and various other articles of domestic furniture (wonderfully made, in tin, at Wolverhampton) perched among the boughs, as if preparation for some fairy housekeeping; there were . . . witches standing in enchanted rings of pasteboard, to tell fortunes; there were tetotums, humming tops, needlecases, pen-wipers, smelling-bottles, conversation cards, bouquet-holders, real fruit, made artificially dazzling with gold leaf, imitation apples, pears and walnuts, crammed with surprises; in short, as a pretty child before me delightfully whispered to another pretty child, her bosom friend, "There was everything, and more".

But in the latter part of the 19th century more elaborate ornaments began to be imported from Germany. They were expensive, but they were all handmade and lovely to look at. There were fancy pieces with sparkling faux jewels in them, tiny dolls and stuffed toy animals. There were beaded balls and bells, gold stars and handsewn Santas.

At the turn of the century American ingenuity came on the Christmas scene. Companies here began to make paper ornaments, and soon large companies like Sears Roebuck & Co. began selling decorations for the tree by mail. World War I made it impossible to get German-made tree decorations any more, so there was plenty of incentive to build up the infant U.S. industry. By 1939 Corning Glass began manufacturing glass ornaments, and these quickly took the place of the German ones.

CHOOSING A TREE

There are a few clues to a tree's freshness that can help you choose a cut tree that won't disappoint you. When you spot a tree that you like, do these three things: First, tug at a bunch of its needles; they should not come off in your hand. Second, gently bend a branch; the more flexible it is, the fresher the tree. And then run your hand up and down the trunk to feel for sap. A fresh tree will still be a little sticky with sap.

As soon as you get your tree home, slice off the bottom of its trunk. You needn't take off a big piece; an inch or two is sufficient because you just want to break the seal that has formed when the trunk was last cut. Then stand the tree in a pail of water. Do this even if you don't plan to bring the tree indoors for a while.

When you are ready to move the tree inside, it is a good idea to maximize its ability to take up water by slicing off another inch or so of trunk. Place the tree in a pail or a tree stand that holds water, and water the tree each day; never leave it dry.

If possible, keep the room in which you have your tree cooler than you normally would. Even if you choose not to do this during the day, you can most likely lower the temperature at night. Raise the room's humidity with a humidifier, or place shallow pans of water near radiators and keep them filled. Try to keep the tree away from radiators, fireplaces and other heat sources.

"There was everything and more": toys galore for turn-of-the-century children.

Scotch pine is one of the most-valued trees for Christmas. Its long, slender needles contribute to the tree's graceful character. The dark blue-green needles stay green and remain on the tree even when it is dry.

Eastern white pine is a popular tree because it is full and bushy and has lovely thin needles that are often quite long and stay on the tree a long time.

Norway spruce can often be quite bushy, but its short dark green needles drop quicker than those on other trees.

A LIVE TREE FOR CHRISTMAS

Buying a live tree instead of one that has been cut is a lovely way of expressing the renewal and regrowth that is part of the spirit of Christmas. Once planted and growing in your garden it will be a constant reminder of a Christmas past.

Preparing the hole ahead of time

If you do decide to have a live tree this year, make that decision early if your soil freezes over winter. Some forethought will enable you to dig and prepare the hole for the tree well in advance of Christmas.

In October or early November choose your spot and estimate how big the roots of your Christmas tree will be. You may want to visit a nursery and take a look at container-grown or balled trees if you have no idea of their size. It is best to dig the hole twice as big and twice as deep as the rootball so that there will be plenty of room for digging in compost or peat moss and good topsoil (see page 44). Shovel the soil you remove for the hole into buckets or barrels and move it into a sheltered area so that it will not freeze, or pile it up next to the hole and cover it with a thick layer of leaves or other mulch covered with black plastic weighted down at the corners. Also cover the hole with a good layer of leaves so it doesn't freeze.

Buying the tree

If you have your heart set on a large Christmas tree, a live tree may not be for you. Live trees, because they must have their roots intact, cannot be very big when you buy them. And the larger the tree, the greater the risk that it will not survive the shock of being dug up, kept in the warm, dry house environment, and then replanted outdoors.

The best survival rate is with the more expensive container trees rather than those balled and wrapped up in sacking or the heavy-duty plastic that many nurseries are now using. This is because container trees are grown right in their containers almost from the start and then sold this way. The roots need not be disturbed until you are ready to plant the tree out.

Whatever live tree you decide upon, check it over carefully first, looking for no dead needles or branches. If it has recently been heavily pruned you can be pretty sure that it was pruned to remove diseased or dead parts. Rootballs should feel moist and solid, with no crumbling soil indicating that it has been left to get too dry.

Purchase your tree at least a week or two before Christmas. This is so that you can condition the tree in a cool basement or garage before bringing it into the house for a week at Christmas. While the tree is resting in a cool place, keep the container or rootball moist but not wet, and spray the needles with water daily.

Balsam fir is best known for its distinctive and pleasant fragrance. Its flat, dark green needles have more of a shine than those of most trees and stay on the tree for a long time. Branches are not as regular as those of other trees: there are often spaces between, giving the tree an irregular shape.

The blue spruce's short, sharp and densely growing bluish needles drop more quickly than those of most other conifers. The shape of the tree is quite symmetrical.

Douglas fir is the most common tree sold for Christmas. The short green needles stay on the tree a long time, and the tree itself is very symmetrical in shape.

Bringing it indoors

Keeping the tree indoors for more than a week, where the air is dry and temperature warmer than the tree would like, will reduce its chances of survival outdoors again. It is best to keep the room temperature no greater than 23°C (70°F) and cooler at night if possible. Place a balled tree in a large bucket or sealed barrel so that you can keep the roots watered without getting water over your floor. Container trees should also be in a bucket or barrel or have a large tray underneath to catch water. It won't be very easy to spray the needles with water once decorations are in place, but be sure to water the roots daily as you did during conditioning.

Moving it outdoors for planting

After Christmas place the tree back into the cool garage or basement for more conditioning to get it ready for planting outdoors in the garden a week later.

At planting time, remove the leaves from the hole (Fig 2) and water it well. Then gently remove the container or sacking and place the tree in the hole, being careful not to lift it by its trunk but rather by the roots. Gently loosen the compacted roots with a garden fork. Place compost or peat moss mixed with the soil originally in the hole under, if necessary, around and over the roots, tamping it down as you go. Leave a slight depression at the soil line so that water will not run away from the tree as you water it well now (Fig 3). If your winter is dry, water the tree regularly this season.

NON-EDIBLE TREE ORNAMENTS

Here are several ideas for tree trims made from things easily and inexpensively bought and from scraps and packaging normally available around the house.

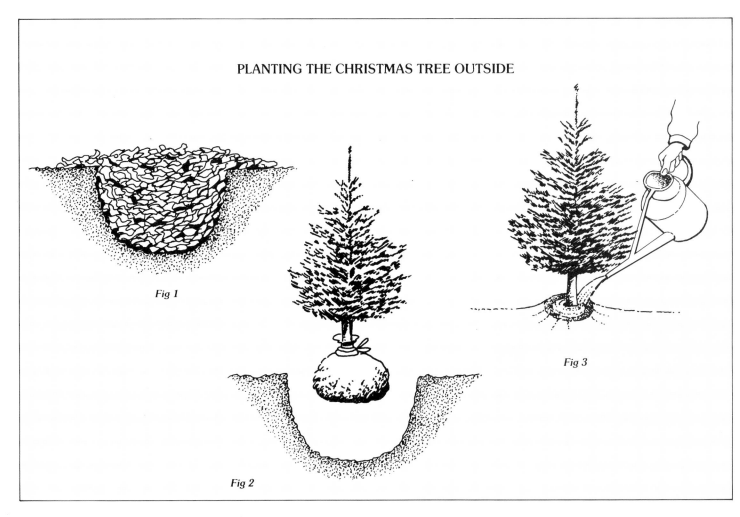

PLANTING THE CHRISTMAS TREE OUTSIDE

Fig 1

Fig 2

Fig 3

Cranberry and popcorn streamers

Buy or make your popcorn a day in advance so that it has a chance to get a little stale. Fresh popcorn, while great to eat, breaks more easily as it is pierced. Thread your needle with heavy-duty thread or even nylon thread, and sew away, alternating fresh (not cooked) cranberries with the popcorn for contrast if you like.

Miniature christmas wreaths

Attach dried or silk flowers in a little cluster on 1 side of a 5cm (2 inch) diameter wood or plastic curtain ring, opposite the metal hook or eyelet, with dabs of glue. If flowers have long wire stems, wrap these around the ring first, then glue down the flowers.

Take a length of 2.5cm (½ inch) wide lace ribbon and tie it into a bow. Glue it to the ring at the metal hook or eyelet, leaving the hook or eyelet open for a string hanger.

Run some decorative string through the hook or eyelet and tie it into a long loop so that it can be hung on the tree.

Santa Claus

Cut half circles of coloured or white card. Cover the white card with gaily coloured paper or colour with felt-tipped pens or children's painting pens. Glue or staple into a cone. Glue on a piece of a cotton ball for a beard and a bead for a nose. Thread a hanger through the point of the cone.

Teazels and cones

Collect teazel heads and fir or pine tree cones and dry them. Paint gold and, before the paint has dried, sprinkle with glitter.

Pierce a hole in teazel stems for the thread hanger, wind the thread through the cones.

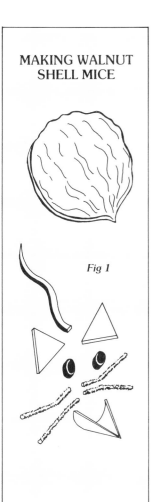

MAKING WALNUT SHELL MICE

Fig 1

Walnut shell mice

Cut out 2 small, light pink felt triangular ears and a thin, long tail. Cut 2 small eyes from black felt. Then glue them all onto half of a walnut shell in the appropriate places.

Make a nose by cutting out another light pink felt triangle and shape it into a small cone as you glue it on. Add whiskers by gluing on 2 short pieces of white pipe cleaners on either side of the nose (Fig 1).

Tie a thin piece of ribbon around the mouse's middle and make a loop out of the ends so that you have a hanger (Fig 2).

Pretty bows

Little bows made from pretty ribbons of all kinds simply pushed between the needles on the tree make lovely fillers between other, more elaborate ornaments. Keep to a single color theme, or mix colors and types of ribbons. Place a lacy ribbon over a wide satin ribbon and together tie them into a double bow. Solid coloured ribbon is an obvious choice, but don't overlook dotted and plaid ribbons, too.

Small gift boxes

Let children wrap up little boxes of all kinds with leftover scraps of wrapping paper or any sort of craft paper. Foil paper is particularly good because it folds and wraps around small boxes easily. Film boxes and little guest soap boxes are just the right size. Dress them up with pretty ribbons and bows, with glitter or dried flowers.

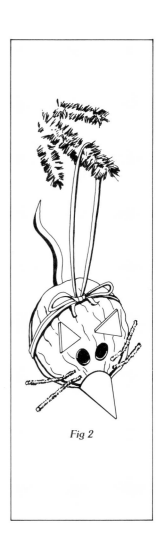

Fig 2

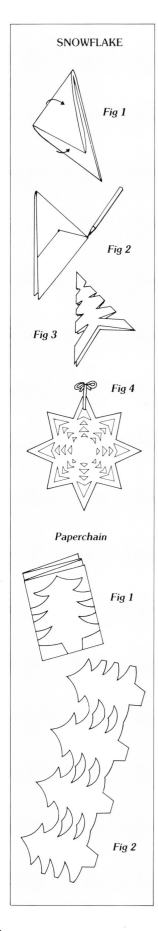

SNOWFLAKE

Fig 1

Fig 2

Fig 3

Fig 4

Paperchain

Fig 1

Fig 2

Felt cut-outs

Use Christmas pastry cutters or shapes you have cut out yourself as templates. Children can use them to trace out shapes on felt, and if they are old enough, cut them out themselves. Then decorate with felt-tip markers, glitter, little pieces cut out of felt, buttons, or pregummed stars and hearts. Jolly snowmen, candy canes, gingerbread men and women, stars, Christmas stockings, rocking horses and toy soldiers are all simple and popular shapes.

Snowflakes

Cut squares from white or silver craft paper. Fold them in half and then in half again (Fig 1). Draw a 'v' shape from the longest side to the opposite corner (Fig 2).

Cut several small pieces out of the folded-up shapes (Fig 3). Unfold and see the cut-out snowflakes that have been created. Run ribbons through one of the holes near an edge to make a hanger (Fig 4).

Paperchains

Cut a long 7.5cm (3 inch) wide strip of coloured craft paper, crêpe paper or tissue paper. Accordion-fold the paper. Using a pastry cutter or drawing freehand, make a shape such as a snowman, star, Christmas tree or bell on the top fold, allowing the shape to extend about 5mm (¼ inch) beyond the fold on both sides (Fig 1).

Cut along the shape through all the folds and open up (Fig 2). Several cut-out strips can be joined together to form a long paper chain.

Stuffed fabric chains

Make a template or use a pastry cutter to trace simple shapes on cotton or satin fabrics in solid colours or a small checked print (Fig 1). Hearts, gingerbread men or women, bells and even simple wreaths are good shapes. Avoid shapes that have points like stars; they will be difficult to stuff. Cut at least two of each shape 5mm (¼ inch) larger all around than you want them to be when finished (Fig 2).

Stitch right sides of 2 shapes together, leaving a 5mm (¼ inch) seam allowance. Leave a small opening along 1 edge (Fig 3). Trim the corners and clip the curves (Fig 4).

Turn the shape right side out and fill with stuffing until it is puffy. Close the opening with slipstitches (Fig 5). Sew the shapes together for a stuffed fabric chain, alternating shapes and colours if you wish.

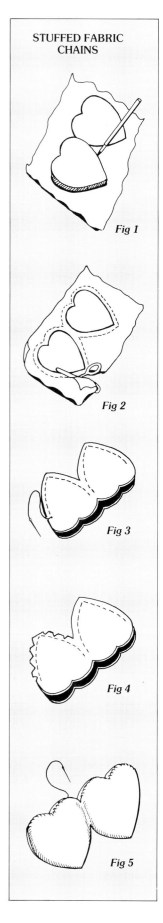

STUFFED FABRIC CHAINS

Fig 1

Fig 2

Fig 3

Fig 4

Fig 5

Lace and roses

These make very pretty tree decorations and the entire tree can be dressed with them. Use inexpensive nylon lace and gift ribbon or woven ribbon to make the flowers. Sew approximately 90cm (1 yard) of frilled lace into a circle (see photo). Sew ribbon roses to the middle of the lace circle. If you like, you can add fabric leaves. Add loops of narrow ribbon and a ribbon hanger.

This ornament can also be made with a paper lace doily, by gluing the doily to a circle of card, pleating the doily as you work.

Stars

Cut star shapes from white polystyrene trays, dab with a little adhesive and press into glitter. Pierce a hole on 1 point and thread through white or gold string for a hanger.

Silver bell

Cut 1 section from a clear plastic egg box. Pierce a hole in the top. Cut a piece of aluminum foil and push it inside the bell, with about 5mm (¼ inch) hanging over the edge. Cut the edge into points. Dab on a little adhesive and dip in green glitter. Push a shanked button inside the bell so that the shank protrudes from the top: tie narrow ribbon through the shank for a hanger.

Gold bell

Cut 1 section from a polystyrene egg box and cut another piece approximately 1cm (½ inch) square.

Cut a slit in the top of the bell, pierce a hole in the square piece and push the piece through the slit in the bell, hole end uppermost. Paint or spray gold. Dab adhesive on the mouth of the bell and dip in gold glitter. Thread gold twine through the hole to hang.

Choirboys

Cut circles of gift wrap foil, drawing around a cup or bowl to get the shape. Cut the circles in half, overlap the edges and glue or staple to make a cone. Cut a circle from a white paper doily. Glue over the foil cone. Draw eyes and a mouth on the circle. Dab a little adhesive around the edge of the circle and dip into glitter. Tie a narrow ribbon or a piece

Lace and roses bouquet, ideal for hanging on the Christmas tree, or as a gift for a close friend.

of thread around the choirboy's neck. The arms are sections of white doily glued at the sides and at the "hands"

Silver star

Collect some foil bottle tops and nightlight foil holders. Wash clean, press flat and cut into the edges. Lay the foil right side down on a soft surface (2 or 3 layers of kitchen paper will do). With a cocktail stick or a blunt pencil draw a design in the centre of the star. On the right side, this will make a raised design. Decorate with beads or glitter.

Lanterns

These are best made either wtih double-sided gift wrap foil, or with freezer foil. Strips from colour pages from magazines also look effective, but mount the pages on dark-coloured paper first. Cut a strip about 30cm (12 inches) long by 7.5cm (3 inches) deep. Fold lengthwise and snip into the folded edge. Open the paper out and overlap the short ends, staple or glue. Push the ends together to open the lantern. Make a hanger with foil or with thread or ribbon.

MAKING THE
ROUND LANTERNS

Fig 1

glue

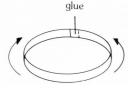

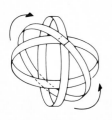

Round lanterns
Make these either from foil or coloured magazine pages mounted on a dark-coloured paper with spray-mount. Cut 4 × 20.5cm (8 inch) strips of foil or paper, 1cm (½ inch) wide. Join the ends of one to make a ring. Glue each strip in turn (Fig 1) until the 4 strips make a ball. Make a thread hanger.

Ribbon balls
Woven or gift ribbons can be used to decorate foam balls. Choose balls about 5cm (2 inches) in diameter. Cut ribbons and secure into the ball with dressmaker's pins (the kind that have coloured glass heads). The ribbons can be laid over each other or interwoven. Fasten a hanger with a pin. The coloured pinheads become part of the decoration.

Mini Christmas crackers
Make these over long sweets, toffees etc. Roll the sweet in stiff paper (such as writing paper). Cut a piece of crêpe paper to go around the wrapped sweet and to about twice the length. Secure with a touch of glue. Fringe the ends of the crêpe paper (Fig 2), then wind a piece of strong thread around the cracker, just at the end of the stiff paper. Pull the thread ends away from each other to pinch in the ends of the cracker. Decorate with scraps of foil or Christmas wrapping paper.

Golden rings
Use inexpensive plastic curtain rings of different sizes. Wind gold crochet thread closely around the rings (or use gift ribbons), finally knotting the ends together to make a hanger.

Christmas trees
You can make these of any shape – balls, diamonds, cones, etc. Use gift wrap foil or paper cut from magazine pages. Draw the shape on the foil or paper. Fold down the middle and cut out. Use this as a template to cut out two more shapes. Glue the 3 shapes together (Fig 3) to make the "Christmas tree".

Velvet bells
Push pipe cleaners or wires into velvet tubing (or satin, if you prefer). Twist into shapes – bells, trees, stars, fleur de lys – wire on some pretty beads for extra decoration and use gold twine as hangers.

MAKING THE MINI
CRACKERS

Fig 2

*roll sweet in
crêpe paper*

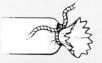

*pinch ends
with strong
thread*

**MAKING THE
CHRISTMAS TREE**

Fig 3

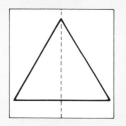

*cut out × 3 shapes
using template*

*glue 3 shapes
together inserting
gold thread to hang*

SALT DOUGH MODELLING

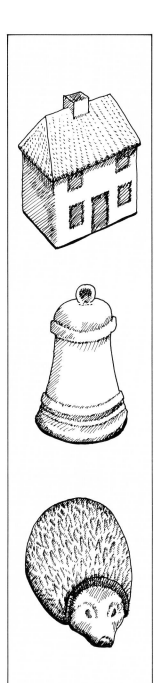

MATERIALS

560g (1¼ lb) flour
225g (8 oz) table salt
335ml (12 fl oz) cold water

1 Heat the oven to 150°C (300°F), Gas Mark 2.
2 Mix the flour and salt. Add the water gradually to make a stiff dough. Knead thoroughly until a smooth, puttylike substance is achieved.

Working with salt dough

Salt dough dries out after an hour or two but you can make it flexible again by adding a little water on the fingertips and rekneading. You can keep it in a plastic bag in the refrigerator overnight.

3 Roll salt dough with a floured rolling pin and cut out shapes using pastry or biscuit cutters, a knife point or a knitting needle. Roll balls or thick rolls between the palms. Flatten shapes under the hand. Roll thin strips under a fingertip on a floured surface. Make disks by flattening small balls. Mark designs with kitchen tools, a knife point, graters, sieves, etc. Join pieces by dampening the surface with cold water.

4 Work the shapes on a baking sheet or on a piece of aluminum foil so that they can be easily transferred to the oven. If you are planning to add beads, buttons and so on make an impression with them in the raw dough before baking, remove them, and then glue the decoration into the baked indentation afterward. Pierce holes for hangers before baking. Make a selection of items: bells, sheep, snowmen, animals and houses.

5 Leave shapes to dry out for about 15 minutes before putting into the oven.

Baking ornaments

6 Salt dough takes about 2-3 hours to harden. If you want a shiny, brown finish, brush with a little condensed milk or a milk and sugar mixture. Thicker pieces, such as sheep for a nativity scene, will take longer to bake and should be turned over halfway through baking.

Finishing

7 After the pieces have cooled they can be painted with poster paints and then varnished for a permanent finish. To create sparkle, dip the pieces in glitter while the varnish is still wet. Small shapes can be glued to larger shapes to create interest.

CHRISTMAS CONES

Fir cones look delightful in autumnal arrangements, but don't neglect their Christmas decoration value.

Spray cones with gold or silver paint. Make a ribbon loop and fix it to the cone with wire. Then attach smaller multiple ribbon loops to the cone with stub wires, leaving short lengths of ribbon that can be split into "tails" (*above*). Tuck any leftover wire under the hard "scales" at the top of the cone, and hang the cones by their ribbon loops on Christmas tree branches (*below*) for a festive display.

Give sprayed cones an extra festive touch by sprinkling a little gold or silver glitter over glued patches (use a paintbrush to apply the glue in a thin coating). Shake off excess glitter onto a sheet of paper.

CHRISTMAS TREE BAUBLE

Make a ribbon loop wide enough to hang over a branch of the tree. Bind the ribbon ends together with ordinary wire, leaving a long tail of wire (*above left*); insert the wire tail into the centre of the foam ball. Begin covering the foam ball from the base of the ribbon: attach stub wire to each of the ingredients – the berries, nuts, flowers and holly – and insert them in the foam ball in turn, so that you build up a variety of colours and textures (*above right*).

To make tiny bows for eye-catching areas of colour, split the ribbon into thin strips. Hold the ribbon at a single point, loop it 3 times and then bind it with reel wire. Leave a ribbon "tail" on each bow and twist stub wire around the tail. Insert the bows by their stub wires randomly in the foam ball.

EDIBLE ORNAMENTS

Christmas tree decorations can, of course, be edible; indeed the old German tradition was to decorate the tree almost exclusively with gilded nuts, fruit and gingerbread. *Weinachts-kuchen*, exquisite little cakes and biscuits, like petits fours, are still enjoyed by German families at Christmas. Pretty biscuits to hang on the tree can be made by cutting a simple gingerbread mix into different shapes (stars, moons, bells, holly leaves, etc.). Make a hole with a skewer at the top of each one, bake, and then decorate them with coloured icing, silver balls and dried fruit. They can then be suspended on the tree by a piece of ribbon or cord passed through the hole.

Barley sugar twists make wonderful edible baubles, hanging like icicles from the branches and catching the light as they turn; here is a traditional recipe:

Take twelve ounces of loaf sugar, a quarter of a pint of water, and half the white of one egg. Boil all together. When it commences to candy, add one teaspoonful of lemon juice. Boil it quickly till it again begins to candy, butter a dish and pour the mixture quickly over it. As it cools cut it into thin strips, and twist it in the form of sticks.

Sticky sweetmeats individually wrapped in foil, and hung on a piece of ribbon, can take the place of glass balls. The only problem is that the gilded fruit, the nuts and the sweetmeats were supposed to be left on the tree until Twelfth Night, when they would be consumed as the final treat of the Christmas season. It is difficult to believe that they would last so long!

GINGERBREAD BISCUITS

These flavourful biscuits are "sturdier" than most biscuits and therefore good for tree hanging. Makes about 1 dozen large or 2 dozen small biscuits.

INGREDIENTS
50g (2 oz) butter or margarine
75g (3 oz) well-packed light brown sugar
170g (6 oz) black treacle
550g (1 lb) flour
1 teaspoon baking powder
$1/4$ teaspoon cinnamon
$1/2$ teaspoon ground ginger
$1/2$ teaspoon ground nutmeg
$1/2$ teaspoon salt
55ml (2 fl oz) water

ICING
icing sugar
water
food colouring

METHOD
1 Preheat the oven to 180°C (350°F), Gas Mark 4 and grease baking sheets.
2 Beat butter with brown sugar until creamy. Beat in molasses.
3 Sift together flour, baking powder, cloves, cinnamon, ginger, nutmeg and salt.
4 Add and blend dry ingredients about 2 tablespoons at a time to the butter-sugar mixture together with the water.
5 Roll out the dough to about a 5mm ($1/4$ inch) thick and cut out shapes with the cutters of your choice.
6 Lift them carefully with a spatula onto greased baking sheets. Decorate the biscuits, if you wish, with raisins or pieces of dried fruit or nuts or small candies.
7 Bake for 5 minutes and test for doneness. If dough springs back after you've gently pressed down on it, it is done; if not, bake for a few more minutes until it does.
8 Remove to wire racks and cool, then ice, if you wish.
9 For icing, mix together the sugar, a few drops of water and colouring to make a paste and paint it onto the biscuits with a small paintbrush or cocktail stick.

SCANDINAVIAN CHRISTMAS TREE BISCUITS

These biscuits will remind you a bit of gingerbread biscuits, but the cardamom and almond flavours make them distinctive. Makes about 30.

INGREDIENTS
75g (3 oz) black treacle
100g (4 oz) butter or margarine
4 cardamom seeds
50g (2 oz) caster sugar
2 tablespoons ground almonds
200g (7 oz) plain flour
½ teaspoon bicarbonate of soda
½ teaspoon cinnamon
½ teaspoon ground ginger
1 egg yolk

ICING
75g (3 oz) icing sugar, sifted
about 1 tablespoon warm water

METHOD

1 Preheat the oven to 190°C (375°F), Gas Mark 5 and grease baking sheets.
2 Melt the treacle and butter or margarine in a pan.
3 Split the cardamom seeds open and crush the kernels finely. Add to the melted mixture with the sugar and almonds.
4 Sift the flour, bicarbonate of soda and spices into the mixture, add the egg yolk and work together to form a smooth dough. Cover and chill for 20 minutes.
5 Roll the dough out thinly on a lightly floured surface or between 2 sheets of cling film to about 5mm (¼ inch) thick. Using Christmas biscuit cutters, cut into shapes about 5-6cm (2-2½ inches) in diameter.
6 Place on greased baking sheets and bake for about 10-12 minutes or until just firm to the touch.
7 Immediately make a hole at the top of each biscuit with a skewer. When firm enough to move, remove to wire trays and leave until cold.
8 For the icing add sufficient water to the icing sugar to give a smooth spreading consistency. Place in a piping bag fitted with a small plain nozzle (size 2 or 3) and pipe a line around each biscuit about 5mm (¼ inch) from the edge; alternatively pipe small stars. Leave to dry and store carefully in an airtight container.
9 Carefully thread a piece of wool or coloured string through the holes in the biscuits, tie firmly and hang on the Christmas tree. If they are to be eaten they must be removed from the tree after several hours, but they may be left there indefinitely for decoration.

TRADITIONAL SAND TARTS

These Christmas favourites can be hung on the tree, but be careful when stringing them up because they are more delicate than gingerbread biscuits. They will only stay fresh on the tree for a few days. Makes about 5 dozen biscuits.

INGREDIENTS
170g (6 oz) butter or margarine
285g (10 oz) caster sugar
1 egg
1 teaspoon vanilla or almond essence
1 teaspoon cinnamon
450g (1 lb) plain flour
¼ teaspoon salt
1 egg white
sugar

METHOD

1 Beat the butter or margarine and sugar until creamy. Add the egg, and vanilla or almond extract. Then gradually add the cinnamon, flour and salt until well mixed. The dough will be stiff.

2 Cover the dough and chill for at least 1 hour.

3 Preheat oven to 200°C (400°F), Gas Mark 6. Grease baking sheets.

4 Roll the dough very thin and cut out shapes with biscuit cutters. Press a piece of looped ribbon on the bottoms, if desired (see the box, For Tree Ornaments). Then place on greased baking sheets.

5 Beat the egg white until frothy and brush it on the tops of the biscuits and sprinkle sugar over it.

6 Bake about 7 minutes, being careful not to get them too brown.

7 Remove to wire racks and cool.

FOR TREE ORNAMENTS

Before you bake the biscuits either put holes in the tops for stringing a ribbon through later, or bake a ribbon loop right into the biscuits.

To make a hole, break the tip off wooden matchsticks and pierce a hole in the top of each biscuit with the wooden sticks that remain, leaving them in place until the cookies are baked. When cool but not hard, remove the wooden sticks and you will have holes through which you can run ribbons for hanging on the tree.

To bake a ribbon loop right onto the biscuits, cut lengths of ribbon and turn in half to make loops. Press both ends of the loops firmly into the backs of the biscuits before you put them on the baking sheets. Bake and cool as usual, and when you remove the biscuits from the baking sheets they will be ready for hanging.

Decorations you have made yourself add individuality and interest to the Christmas tree.

Ribboned sugar sticks

Wrap contrasting-coloured thin ribbon around cellophane-wrapped sugar stick, fastening it with small drops of glue as you work your way up the stick. When you reach the curve, tie a bow, fasten it with a drop of glue, and make a long loop for a hanger.

Shiny wrapped sweets

Wrap sweets in gift wrap foil and tie with a big ribbon bow.

GIFTS TO MAKE

 ## THE SPIRIT OF GIVING

Christmas would not be Christmas if there was no Santa Claus. Nor would it be the same if we did not give presents to our families and friends. But these traditions only developed during the 19th century. The giving of presents had been a New Year custom before then, but even that was in decline. But when we come to Dickens' *A Christmas Carol*, published in 1843, present-giving seems to be the order of the day. The Spirit of Christmas Past takes Scrooge to see the family of the girl he might have married, just as father returns:

. . . attended by a man laden with Christmas toys and presents. Then the shouting and the struggling, and the onslaught that was made on the defenceless porter! The scaling him with chairs for ladders to dive into his pockets, despoil him of brown-paper parcels, hold on tight by his cravat, hug him round his neck, pommel his back, and kick his legs in irrepressible affection! The shouts of wonder and delight with which the development of every package was received!

As with the Christmas tree, England's Prince Albert may well have had a hand in popularizing the custom of present-giving; his biography says that the Prince thought Christmas day was "a day for the exchange of presents, as marks of mutual affection and good-will". But when the magazine *Punch* wrote about Christmas shopping in 1849, it was to describe the grocers, confectioners, the poulterers and other purveyors of Christmas fare, not presents. As the century progressed, however, the present industry mushroomed, until by 1887 one trader was offering no less than 100,000 gift ideas, and magazines were full of advertisements and articles on the subject.

But as the festive season centred so much on children, it was, then as now, toys which were most heavily marketed. For girls there were dolls, such as Miss Dolly Daisie Dimple, the Barbie doll of her day, advertized as "the Craze of the Season", who came with a trunk full of clothing. And then there were the dolls' houses, perfect in every detail of decor and furnishing. For boys there were trains, boats and carriages, often the most exquisite working models, and toy soldiers.

But of course presents didn't need to be extravagant and expensive. The delightfully named A.A. Strange Butson writing in the children's magazine *Little Folks* maintains that "nearly everyone values more a gift that has been specially made for them than the smartest bought thing". The expectation was clearly that little girls were very deft with their needles, and could turn their hand to embroidered aprons, or "a warm quilted cape of some dark silk edged with fur" for grandmama. Boys meanwhile were expected to be skilled at fretwork, making for papa a writing case or for mama ornamental picture frames.

While some of Butson's suggestions seem outdated now, others have aged well; they make charming and often practical gifts even today. A jar of homemade jam, lemon curd or mincemeat makes a lovely little present on its own, or it can be tucked into a wicker basket or decorative tin with other gifts. Lavender bags, for sweet-scented drawers, can be made from scraps of fabric and ribbon and stuffed with dried lavender or a pot pourri.

There are, of course, many other gifts that can be made at home for Christmas giving. There are fairly easy things to make, like lacy pincushions and pillows and dried flower bookmarks. There are more elaborate presents such as appliquéd holiday tablecloths and placemats, decorated boxes and flower-scented candles. And there are edible treats like fancy sweets and flavoured vinegars, oils and butters. These and other ideas for gifts are presented in the pages that follow.

This charmingly evocative illustration by Charles Robinson captures the delights of Christmas morning.

SANTA CLAUS, THE SPIRIT OF CHRISTMAS

Santa Claus was quite unknown before the nineteenth century, although "Old Father Christmas", "Sir Christmas", even plain "Mr Christmas" had been a symbol of the season for centuries, popping up in mummers' plays, medieval carols and Elizabethan masques. He is said to be based on St Nicholas, who had been a bishop noted for his benevolence in fourth century Asia Minor, but his origins go back even further. St Nicholas was coopted in by the Church to give Christian respectability to the old pagan custom of midwinter present giving. After the Protestant Reformation in Europe, however, the worship of saints was frowned upon, and veneration of St Nicholas's saintly qualities was replaced by an emphasis on merry twinkling joviality.

The tradition of hanging up stockings definitely owes its origin to St Nicholas, who was reputed to be enormously rich, and much given to distributing largesse among the deserving poor. One recipient found a bag of gold in a stocking she had hung up to dry in front of the fire; St Nicholas had evidently thrown it down the chimney.

In the early nineteenth century the bringer of gifts and good cheer was usually known as "The Spirit of Christmas", and was portrayed as a rather bacchanalian old chap with a glass in his hand. Even in the 1860s and 70s, Christmas card designers couldn't agree about his appearance: sometimes he had a beard, sometimes he didn't, and he wore a variety of clothing, by no means always red, though he usually had a sprig of holly in his hair.

It was in fact Americans who created the standard image, and gave him the alternative name Santa Claus, from the Dutch-American name for St Nicholas. The illustrator Thomas Nast came up with the definitive physical image in his drawings for *Harper's Weekly*: the flowing beard, the portly figure in a red suit and cap.

By far the most enduring image of Santa Claus comes from Clement Clark Moore's 1822 poem *A Visit from St Nicholas*, more popularly known as *The Night Before Christmas*. Moore describes Santa as a jovial old man who "was dressed all in fur from his head to his foot/ . . . with a little round belly/ That shook, when he laughed, like a bowl full of jelly . . ." That was quite a transformation from the ascetic bishop of fourth century Asia Minor!

PRETTY THINGS OF SILK AND LACE

Romantic gifts, using lace, satin and silk fabrics, lustrous ribbons and fragrant pot pourri can be as original and special as you care to make them. Look for pieces of antique lace in specialist shops, or colour new cotton lace by dipping it in tea. The creamy look of dipped lace harmonizes with pastel-coloured fabrics.

Lace sachets

Antique shops often have old lace mats or crocheted doilies that can be used to make herb or pot pourri sachets with very little sewing. The rectangular sachet in the picture is made from an old wineglass mat.

Measure the mat and cut two pieces of thin fabric to the same shape and dimensions. Pin, baste and machine stitch the pieces together, right sides facing, leaving one short end open for filling. Pour in the herbs or pot pourri (see Chapter 5) and turn in the edges of the open seam, slip-stitching to close.

Sew the lace mat to the filled sachet. Make a ribbon rose for one corner and trim with 3mm (⅛ inch) wide single-faced satin ribbon. Thread a needle with matching thread and knot the end. Roll one end of the ribbon into a tight tube – about five turns. Oversew the end of the tube. Leave the needle and thread hanging. Hold the "rose bud" in one hand and with the other, fold the ribbon end away from you, making a diagonal fold (Fig 1). Turn the "bud" onto the fold and keep turning the bud until the ribbon lies straight (Fig 2). Oversew the bottom end of the rose.

Make another petal in the same way and oversew the bottom end. Make a third petal and sew. With the last 25mm (1 inch), bring the ribbon end down to the bottom of the rose, gather and sew. Use the same thread to sew the rose in place.

Tiny roses can be made with narrow ribbon for decorating sachets. The circular, pale green sachet is made from a small piece of embroidered organdy that has been edged with 25mm (1 inch) wide insertion lace and then 25mm (1 inch) wide lace edging. The filled sachet underneath is made from pale green moiré taffeta. Finish the sachet with a stitched bow of 3mm (⅛ inch) wide green ribbon.

Herb sachets filled with sweet-smelling combinations can also be made from pieces of ribbon weaving, but instead of hand weaving and pinning ribbons, ribbons are woven with a darning needle.

Pincushions

Use crocheted doilies for making pincushions, making them as you do for sachets, but stuffing the "pad" with polyester filling.

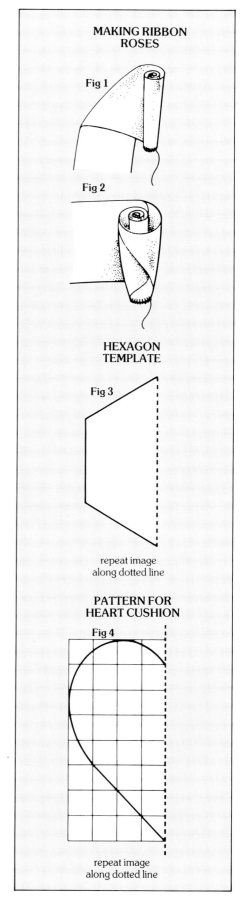

MAKING RIBBON ROSES

Fig 1

Fig 2

HEXAGON TEMPLATE

Fig 3

repeat image along dotted line

PATTERN FOR HEART CUSHION

Fig 4

repeat image along dotted line

Clockwise from top: Satin pillow; Covered coathanger; Rose-trimmed heart cushion; Taffeta sachet; Handkerchief sachet; Patchwork pincushion; pink pincushion; rectangular pot pourri sachet.

Pink pincushion

Press a plastic bowl into a block of florist's dry material oasis so that the bowl is filled, then cut the block off level using a sharp knife. Cut a circle of bright fabric 12mm (½ inch) larger than the circumference of the bowl, place it on top of the filling and push down the inside of the bowl using a knife tip.

Cover with a scrape of lace or net, and push this down inside the bowl also. Glue a strip of gathered lace edging around the bowl, and then finish with a strip of lace insertion. Trim with a 20cm (8 inch) wide ribbon sewn into a bow.

Patchwork pincushion

Using a 2.5mm (1 inch) hexagon template (Fig 3) (see page 56), cut 14 fabric shapes and 14 backing papers.

Mount the fabric on a backing paper. Sew 6 hexagons around 1 hexagon, right sides facing, using small oversewing stitches. Make two "rosettes" of patchwork in the same way. Remove the backing papers and place the two rosettes of patchwork together. Machine stitch together, or hand sew, using back stitches, all around the rosette shape, leaving sides of two adjoining patches open.

Turn the pincushion to the right side and fill with cotton wool or polyester filling. Oversew the open seam. Sew on looped, narrow ribbons.

The same technique can be used to make a perfumed sachet.

Handkerchief sachet

The sachet in the picture is made with an antique silk embroidered handkerchief but new, lace-edged handkerchiefs could be used, or cut a 30cm (12 inch) square of a delicate fabric and edge it with lace.

Cut a square of thin fabric in a pale cream (or white) 12mm (½ inch) smaller than the handkerchief. Finish the edges with machine stitching, or hand hemming.

Place the square on the wrong side of the handkerchief. Catch it to the handkerchief at the corners only. Fold 3 corners of the handkerchief to the middle (like an envelope) and catch them together with tiny stitches. Sew a ribbon bow to the outside of the sachet.

Covered coathanger

Pad a wooden coathanger with strips of thin polyester until the coathanger is rounded and the wood can no longer be felt.

Measure the length and circumference of the padded coathanger. Cut a piece of polyester satin fabric to the measurements plus 2.5cm (1 inch). Snip a hole in the middle of the satin and slip the cover over the hanger hook, right side out. Turning in the edges as you sew, slipstitch the cover around the coathanger, rounding off the seam at the lower edge and the ends. Cut a piece of wide lace insertion to three times the length of the hanger. Gather the lace 12mm (½ inch) from one edge. Sew the lace along both sides of the hanger, along the bottom edge. Join the short ends of the lace with running stitches.

Thread a long, sharp needle with 1.5mm (¹⁄₁₆) inch wide ribbon. Take the needle through from one side of the hanger to the other, leaving a long end of ribbon. Bring the needle back through, 3mm (⅛ inch) away. Knot the ribbon ends together or tie a small bow. Work knots at intervals along the hanger to produce a "quilted" effect. Finish the hanger by winding 12mm (½ inch) wide ribbon around the hook, sewing the ends together to secure. Tie a matching bow.

Rose-trimmed heart cushion

This pretty cushion, only 20cm (8 inches) long, is filled with polyester padding, and a sachet of fragrant herbs or pot pourris is tucked inside, making it a charming bedroom accessory. Fig 4 on page 56 is a pattern for a heart shape. To make a pillow of the same size, 1 square = 2.5cm (1 inch).

Make an 20cm (8 inch) deep sachet from sprigged fabric and, before making up into a cushion, cut lengths of narrow green ribbon and pin them across the sprigged heart shape, approximately 2.5cm (1 inch) apart. Pin lengths of ribbon diagonally across to make a lattice pattern of ribbons (see picture). Catch the ribbons to the fabric at the intersections with cross stitches, using green embroidery cotton. Work a small pink French knot in the centre of each cross stitch.

Add ribbon roses (see page 56). Finish the roses with yellow French knots for stamens.

Work green satin-stitched leaves around the roses and finish the cushion front with 20cm (8 inch) strands of embroidery thread, threaded through the fabric so that 10cm (4 inch) lengths hang. Tie a small bow of pink ribbon and sew over the strands.

Trim the cushion with ribbon bows and loops. Make up the cushion by machine stitching back and front together, right sides facing, leaving a gap in the seam at the top of the heart for stuffing with cotton wool and a sachet of fragrant herbs. Close the seam with slip stitches, tucking in loops of green and pink ribbon. Trim with guipure.

AN APPLIQUÉ TABLECLOTH

This delicate white voile tablecloth and its six napkins will enhance any holiday setting and is an *especially* attractive background for Christmas dinner itself. The edges are bound with a self-border and corners are decorated with white voile Christmas trees that are appliquéd and topstitched in position. This cloth is suitable for a table measuring 2 metres × 90cm (6 feet 6 inches × 36 inches).

MATERIALS

4.5 metres (5 yards) of 148cm (59 inch) wide white polyester/cotton voile
matching thread (white)
pattern paper
scissors, pencil

1 Transfer the diagrams to the pattern paper. Using these as your patterns, cut the following: 2.4 metres × 148cm (94½ × 59 inches) for tablecloth, 6 53cm (20¾ inch) squares, 7 large trees, 8 small trees.
2 Turn a 10mm (⅜ inch) hem twice on both long sides and then both short sides of the tablecloth. Pin and tack to hold. Press. Keeping to the wrong side and placing right sides together, fold a 5cm (2 inch) hem on each side and form a mitre by bringing the corners up together, creating a line from the inner hem edges out to the pointed corner. Pin, tack and machine stitch the mitre seam with 10mm (⅜ inch) turnings. Remove the tacking. Trim seam and press the seam open.

Satin cushion

This is made with a bobbin lace tray cloth, dyed in tea to produce a soft, creamy colour.

To dye lace with tea, pour boiling water over 2 teabags and then add 1 tablespoon of vinegar. Remove the teabags when the liquid is fairly dark. Steep the lace in the tea, squeezing it out periodically to check the colour. Rinse and dry. Spray starch to stiffen the lace before mounting over a satin cushion. Thread narrow, cream-coloured ribbons through the lace, tying bows at the corners of the central panel. A sachet of fragrant herbs could be sewn in the pillow.

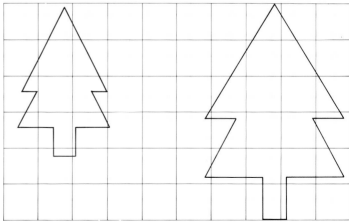

Scale 1 square = approx 5 cm (2 inches)

Repeat for the other corners. Turn each corner to the right side, pointing out the corners to form a 5cm (2 inch) hem. Steam press. Pin and tack along the inner hem edge and the folded edge to hold.

3 Set the machine on an approximate stitch width just under a 3mm (⅛ inch) satin stitch and work on the front of the tablecloth. Topstitch the edges of the hem to hold. Remove tacking, press on wrong side.

4 Working on the wrong side of the tablecloth, position 3 large and 2 small trees centrally, turning no hems. Pin and tack the edges of the trees to the tablecloth. Position 4

large trees at the corners as photograph. Pin and tack the edges to hold. Using the 3mm (⅛ inch) satin stich, carefully topstitch around the trees. Press on the tree side.

5 To make the napkins, repeat the hem edge as for the tablecloth, but turn a 7cm (2¾ inch) mitred hem.

6 Working on the wrong side of the napkin, position 1 small tree to the left of centre so that the tree sits to the right on right side of the napkin. Turning no hem, pin and tack. With a 3mm (⅛ inch) satin stitch, topstitch carefully around the tree shape. Remove tacking and press.

A CHRISTMAS APRON

This practical and attractive bright red and green PVC apron will make the cook feel especially festive this Christmas. It has a decorative detachable band of berries, leaves

and seedheads, and a roomy pocket. You could use the pattern given here to make a plain PVC apron for wearing the rest of the year.

MATERIALS
70cm (27½ inches) of 120cm (48 inch) wide berry print cotton-backed PVC
2 metres (2¼ yards) of 2.5cm (1 inch) wide woven cotton tape
24cm (9½ inches) of 2cm (¾ inch) wide green velcro matching thread (red)
scraps of green PVC
seedheads, artificial berries, fir cones
pattern paper
51cm (20 inches) of 3mm (⅛ inch) ribbon
cellophane tape, ballpoint pen, teflon foot

1 Transfer the diagrams to the pattern paper then cut the following:
from printed PVC 1 apron shape, 1 oblong 28 × 119cm (11 × 7½ inches) for pocket, 1 decorative front band

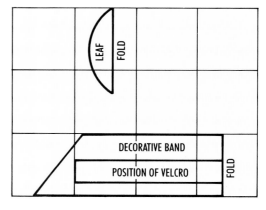

Scale 1 square = approx 5cm (2 inches)

Scale 1 square = approx 5cm (2 inches)

from woven tape 3 × 66cm (26 inch) lengths (check head loop and side ties against your personal measurements)
from green PVC 6 leaf shapes

2   Fold 15mm (⅝ inch) turning across the hem edge, hold with cellophane tape. Topstitch 10mm (⅜ inch) from the edge. Position the side tapes as in the diagram, hold with cellophane tape. Fold a 15mm (⅝ inch) turning, enclosing the tape ends. Topstitch the sides 10mm (⅜ inch) from the edge.

3   Position the neck tape as in the diagram, hold with cellophane tape. Fold a 15mm (⅝ inch) turning across the top edge enclosing the tape ends and hold with cellophane tape. Topstitch across the neck edge. Remove all cellophane tape.

4   Fold a 15mm (⅝ inch) turning across the top and bottom of the pocket oblong, hold with cellophane tape. Topstitch close to the edge. Repeat for both side edges. Remove cellophane tape. Position the pocket as in the diagram. Hold with cellophane tape and topstitch along both sides and bottom 5mm (¼ inch) from the edge, leaving the top edge open. Remove cellophane tape.

5   Tear apart the 24cm (9½ inch) length of velcro. Position the loop half centrally on the right side across the top of the apron and follow diagrams 1-3.

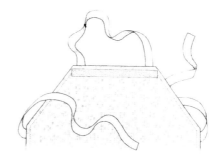

1. Tear velcro apart. Position it along the top of the apron, so it sits in the centre. Tack and topstitch to hold.

2. Place the wrong side of the other piece of velcro to the wrong side of the PVC band. Tack and topstitch.

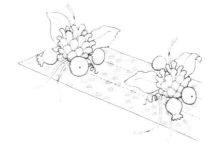

3. Arrange the leaves, berries, seedheads, fir cones and ribbon on the band and catchstitch to secure the velcro to the apron.

A CHRISTMAS TABLE SET

This set of delightful, easy-to-make Christmas table decorations is made from printed cotton-backed PVC bound in brilliant red bias binding. The round place mats and wineglass mats are decorated with bright red berries, shiny green leaves, seedheads and fir cones. If you have some spare fabric, improvise and make a rectangular mat for the centre of the table.

MATERIALS FOR 4 SETS

(70cm (27½ inches) of 120cm (47 inch) wide berry print cotton-backed PVC

70cm (27½ inches) of 130cm (51 inch) wide green laminated PVC [or 45cm (17¾ inches) of 45cm (59 inch) wide cotton-backed PVC]
70cm (27½ inches) of 82cm (32¼ inch) wide craft-quality vilene
9 metres (10 yards) of 2.5cm (1 inch) wide red cotton bias binding
2 metres (2¼ yards) of 3mm (⅛ inch) ribbon
1 metre (1⅛ yards) of 18mm (¾ inch) wide dark green velcro
various minifruits on stalks (from florist's)
4 pine cones
matching thread (red, green)
pattern paper
scissors, pencil, ballpoint pen

1 Transfer the diagrams to the pattern paper and use these as your patterns. Cut the following:

Placemats

from cotton-backed PVC 4 mat circles, 4 mat crescent strips
from laminated PVC 4 mat circles, 24 leaves
from vilene 4 mat circles
from velcro 4 × 16cm (6¼ inch) lengths
from bias binding 4×108cm (42½ in) lengths

Coasters

from cotton-backed PVC 4 coaster circles, 4 coaster crescent strips
from laminated PVC 4 coaster circles, 8 leaves
from vilene 4 coaster circles
from velcro 4 × 18mm (¾ inch) lengths
from bias binding 4 × 37cm (14½ in) strips

Napkin rings

from cotton-backed PVC 4 napkin ring strips
from cotton-backed PVC 4 napkin ring strips
from laminated PVC 4 napkin ring strips
from vilene 4 napkin ring strips
from velcro 4 × 4cm (1½ inch) lengths
from bias binding 8 × 25cm (10 inch) lengths, 8 × 7cm (2¾ inch) lengths

2 Tear a 16cm (6¼ inch) length of velcro in half and position the wrong side of the loop half to the right side of 1 print PVC placemat shape. Pin, tack and machine stitch, using red thread. Pin, tack and machine stitch the hook half to the wrong side of 1 large crescent strip. Repeat for the other mats.

3 Tear a 18mm (¾ inch) length of velcro in half and position the wrong side of the loop half to the right side of 1 print PVC coaster shape. Pin, tack and machine stitch. Pin, tack and machine stitch the hook half to the wrong side of a small crescent strip. Repeat for the other coasters.

4 Tear a 4cm (1½ inch) length of velcro in half and position the wrong side of the loop half to the right side of 1 printed PVC napkin ring (see photograph). Position the wrong side of the hook half on the right side of the plain PVC strip to correspond. Pin, tack and machine stitch. Repeat for the other napkin rings.

5 Sandwich circles of vilene between the wrong sides of the corresponding circles of laminated and print PVC placemats and coasters.

6 Sandwich strips of vilene between the wrong sides of the corresponding napkin ring strips of laminated and print PVC. Make sure velcro strips are at opposite ends of each ring.

7 Pin and tack 15mm (⅝ inch) from the edges through 3 thicknesses on all mats, coasters and napkin rings.

8 Open out a 108cm (42½ inch) length of bias binding and place the raw edge to the curve of the tacked triple-layer placemat. Working on the crease and curving the binding as you go, pin, tack and machine stitch. Turn the folded edge of the binding to the laminated side and catchstitch.

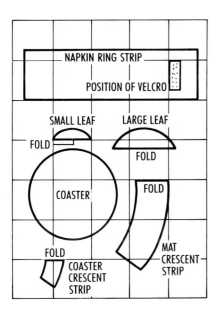

Scale   1 square = approx 5cm (2 inches)

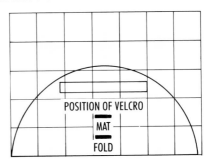

Scale   1 square = approx 5cm (2 inches)

9 Repeat for coasters, using the 37cm (14½ inch) lengths of bias binding.

10 Open out 7cm (2¾ inch) lengths of binding and fold over the raw edges on the short ends of each napkin ring strip. Pin, tack and topstitch on the folded edge.

11 Open out the 25cm (10 inch) lengths of binding and place the raw edge to the long sides of each strip. Pin, tack and topstitch on the folded edge, tucking in at end to neaten.

Catchstitch to secure.

12 Fold each PVC leaf lengthways, make a tuck at the base to form a central vein, and topstitch down the fold for the spine. Position the leaves spine down and arrange them on strips. Catchstitch to the strips at the stem and oversew the stalks of fruit in place. Use 6 leaves in pairs on each mat and 2 leaves on each coaster. Using ribbon, tie a cone around the centre set of the leaves on each mat.

PERFUMED FLORAL CANDLES

Candles are surprisingly easy to make at home, and once the basics have been grasped, you can go on to create more individual versions. In no time at all, you'll find that you are making candles to burn and work magic all over the house – in the hall, livingroom, bedrooms and even the bathroom. The colour of your candles and the type of dried flowers used to decorate them can be chosen to tie in with the colour scheme of the room in which they will be used.

The main ingredients

The main ingredient used in making candles is paraffin wax. This can be bought at craft shops or department stores in either easy-to-use granules, or in blocks, which have to be broken up.

Stearin (stearic acid), which is also widely available, is the second main ingredient added to the wax for a number of reasons. It makes the candles harder, burn for slightly longer, makes them easier to release from the moulds by causing the wax to shrink slightly, and minimizes the drips. Use 1 part stearin to 9 parts wax. Add too little stearin and the result will be a soapy candle; too much, a brittle one.

The wick

Care should be taken when buying a length of wick for your candles. Wicks are available in a number of sizes; the greater the intended diameter of the candle, the thicker the wick is needed. Cut your wick to the required candle length by measuring it against the side of the mold. A wick that is too small for a candle will not burn evenly, and a shell of unburned wax will build up and eventually extinguish the flame. If a wick is too large, on the other hand, the flame is likely to be very smoky.

MAKING FRAGRANT PRESSED-FLOWER CANDLES

MATERIALS

1. 2 saucepans (one larger than the other)
2. bucket or bowl of cold water
3. thermometer
4. 1 lb white paraffin wax
5. 4 oz stearin
6. wick rod pack
7. candle mould
8. blue tacky clay (mould sealer)
9. transparent glue
10. small paintbrush
11. wooden spoon
12. wooden stick to secure wick
13. pressed flowers and foliage candle dye pack (optional)
essential floral oil (optional)

MAKING THE CANDLES

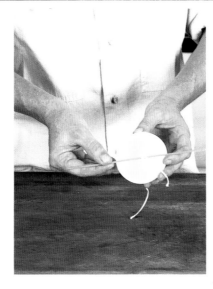

1 Make sure the mould is clean. Then cut a length of wick at least 15cm (6 inches) longer than the mould. Make a hole in the bottom of your mould (if it is home-made) and poke your wick through the hole using a wooden stick, leaving a long end. Seal the hole underneath the mould with blue tacky clay.

2 Next use the wooden stick to secure the wick. Lie the stick across the top of the mould and wind the wick around it to hold it in place. The wick should be tied loosely but not so much that it bends in the middle. Leave the mould in a warm place in preparation for the wax. This improves the finish of the candle.

3 Fill the large pan with water and place it over the heat. Place 550g (1 lb) of paraffin wax (this amount will make about 6 candles), in the smaller pot and insert in the larger pot to melt. Keep on a low heat.

4 Test the temperature of the wax as it melts with the thermometer. Check the level of the water in the larger pot from time to time and fill up when necessary. Don't leave wax once it is on the heat. Add the stearin (and dye if required) to the pot as the wax is melting. Add essential oils now for scented candles.

5 Remove the wax from the heat when it reaches 32°C (90°F). Do not allow it to get any hotter. Carefully pour the wax into the mould, making sure that it is held on a tilt (otherwise air bubbles will form in the wax), and keep the wick dead centre.

6 Once full, place the mould in a bowl of cold water to cool down the wax so that it sets hard. Place your mould in the refrigerator to speed up the process. Your candles should be ready in an hour. Once set, remove the blue tacky clay and slide the candle out of the mould. If the candle sticks, run the mould under hot water.

DECORATING CANDLES WITH PRESSED FLOWERS

1 To level off the bottom of the candle, rub it around a warm, empty pot or slice it away with a sharp knife. To decorate your candles, position the flowers and leaf material on the candle in your desired pattern and attach them with transparent glue.

2 Next, dip your candle quickly in and out of a warm pot of wax (without added stearin), holding it by the wick. This seals the flowers in the right position. Leave in a warm, dry place for several days to harden. Cut the wick to the required length.

Candle moulds

Flexible candle moulds can be bought in a wide range of shapes and sizes, however, it is also possible to improvise. Suitable containers should be able to withstand the temperature of the hot wax (test with hot water before starting on the candle-making operation) and have a small hole in the centre of the bottom – pierced or drilled through the base – for the wick to pass through. Fruit juice and milk cartons and some plastic yogurt cartons make good improvised moulds.

To make coloured candles, simply add candle-making dyes that are specially designed for the purpose; 1g (.035 oz) of dye will colour 500g (1 lb) of white wax. Dyes for colouring candles can be bought as sticks, disks or, occasionally, as a powder or liquid. Wax dyes are concentrated so add them carefully – it is easy to add some more, impossible to remove too much. Sprinkle or pour the dye into the melted stearin so that it is completely dissolved before adding it to the wax.

Multicoloured candles

To create a straightforward multicoloured, layered appearance, pour a small amount of different coloured wax into the mould at a time, allowing each layer to set before adding the next. To give the layers an attractive "twist", carefully lay the mould slightly on its side so that the wax sets on a slant. In this way, each layer can be set at a different angle.

Fragrant candles

To perfume your candles, use fragrant dried flowers or, if these are not available or their scent needs a boost, a few drops of essential floral oil. These should be added to the wax just before it is poured into the mould.

Decorating with dried flowers

Give your finished candles a personal touch by decorating them with pressed flowers and foliage. Arrange them carefully on the surface of the candle. Use a pair of tweezers or the end of the paintbrush to pick up the flowers and a small paintbrush to dab on clear glue.

FINISHING CANDLES

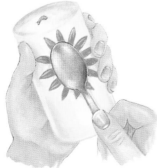

1 As an alternative to gluing your flowers in position, try sealing your flowers in place with the back of a heated spoon.

2 For a truly professional finish to your candles, polish them to a shine with a soft cloth and a drop of cooking oil.

This attractive pressed flower design decorates a simple bookmark. Gift tags and cards can be made in a similar way. You will need pressed flowers and foliage, a sheet of rather thick paper or thin card and a short length of ribbon in a toning colour, clear-based glue, self-adhesive transparent plastic, a paintbrush or blunt-ended tweezers, a pair of scissors and a hole punch. Cut a rectangular piece of card large enough for your design – leaving enough space around the edge for a border. Using a paintbrush or tweezers (so as not to damage your flowers) carefully arrange the pressed flowers on the card, leaving a space at 1 end where the ribbon is to be attached.

To fix the flowers in position, apply the glue sparingly to the underside of each flower, leaf or stalk, and using a brush or tweezers, slide or position them in place. To protect your finished design, cover it with self-adhesive transparent plastic. Take care when using such plastic, as it creases easily and can form unsightly air bubbles. Finally, punch a hole in the card and thread through and attach a small length of ribbon.

PRESSING SMALL FLOWERS

1 Flowers with single blooms such as pansies and geraniums require little preparation. Cut off unwanted stalks and foliage and flatten the flowers by pressing them *gently* with your fingertips.

2 Arrange the flowers on the blotting paper, making sure that they do not overlap. Separate out any overlapping geranium petals (handling gently to avoid bruising), so that they lie as flat as possible.

3 Fold over the blotting paper and place in the flower press. Flat flowers dry more quickly than bulky flowerheads and can be ready within 4 weeks if placed in a warm, dry place.

FRAGRANT POMANDERS

Pomanders – enhanced by pot pourri – are rewarding to make and give at Christmas time. Originally pomanders were jewelled metal caskets containing ambergris (the word pomander combines two French words *pomme*, apple and *ambre*, amber to mean apple of amber). Ambergris, still the basis of many perfumes, was thought to ward off infection and cleanse the air of unsavoury odours.

Traditional orange pomanders are a delightfully fragrant way to hold the scents of summer and autumn. Use them to perfume rooms or wardrobes. You could also use a lemon or an apple as a base.

MATERIALS

1 medium-sized orange or lemon
2 50g (2 oz) whole cloves
3 1 teaspoon orris root (The delicately perfumed, ground dried root of *Iris florentina* is used to fix other scents. Available from a few chemists; some will order it but you may have to purchase a large quantity.)
4 1 teaspoon ground cinnamon (for oranges and apples, ground cloves for lemons)
5 adhesive tape to divide the fruit visually into quarters
6 pins
7 skewer or tapestry needle
8 90cm (1 yard) narrow satin ribbon
9 scissors; 50 g (2 oz) pot pourri; tissue paper; an old toothbrush.

1 Wind the tape around the fruit, top to bottom to mark out 4 quarters.

2 Stud the fruit with whole cloves covering all 4 marked-out quarters. (It may help to pierce a hole for each clove with the skewer or tapestry needle.) Pack the cloves as closely as you like.

3 Place the fruit in a large bowl and shake over the orris root and cinnamon or ground cloves. Roll the fruit in the powder and scoop the powder up to pour over the fruit until it is covered evenly with the spicy powder.

4 Place the fruit in another bowl, this time containing pot pourri. Roll it in the petals, then remove it and wrap it in tissue paper. Place the fruit in a dry, dark place to dry out thoroughly.

5 After about 3 weeks remove the fruit from its wrappings, remove the tape, and, using a toothbrush, dust off any loose spices or petals.

6 To decorate the pomander, cut a piece of ribbon to fit along one of the circular channels of cloves. Pin this piece of ribbon in place, then encircle the remaining channel with a piece of ribbon long enough to tie into a bow or loop.

DECORATING WITH DÉCOUPAGE

Découpage is the art of cutting out pictorial images and using them to cover household objects that are then varnished many times to produce a smooth, tough, durable finish that has the appearance of lacquer. The intricate pattern shines through the varnish, giving it a hand-painted appearance.

The word découpage is derived from the French word 'découper' which means to cut out. The practice first became popular in 17th-century Italy and spread throughout Europe during the 18th century. Originally inspired by imported Oriental furniture, exponents of the art used hand-coloured engravings and prints which they pasted onto tables, cabinets and screens and covered with layers of lacquer. Découpage regained popularity in Victorian times when ladies saved their Valentine and greeting cards and magazine cuttings to decorate boxes, table tops, trays, and all manner of trinkets.

Materials you will need

Any picture or patterned paper can be used for découpage, and a floral design is especially charming. Suitable flower motifs can be cut from wrapping paper, old and reproduction prints, cards, calendars and decorative seed and bulb packets. It is best to use paper that is not too thick and is printed on 1 side only, although magazine images can be used, as long as you do not sand them down, as this destroys the paper.

When cutting out your images you will need a pair of good-quality paper scissors and a scalpel for the intricate flower shapes. In addition, a water-soluble adhesive, such as standard wallpaper paste or any transparent nontoxic craft glue, will be needed to stick down the motifs in your chosen design.

Varnishing is an integral part of the découpage process, and the varnish you will require will depend on your chosen base material. If you are covering wood, choose a clear or tinted polyurethane-based gloss varnish that will dry relatively quickly and has a hard finish. The coloured varnishes will give a more authentic appearance to your covered objects. Clear and coloured gloss varnishes are available from DIY shops. For glass, metal and plastic surfaces use an acrylic gloss varnish, available from craft shops.

You will need 2 good-quality brushes, one each for gluing and varnishing and designed specifically for these purposes. Use 2.5-5cm (1 to 2 inch) brushes for medium to large objects and 15mm (½ inch) ones for intricate objects such as trinkets and jewelry. Always keep some white spirit on hand to clean the varnish brush between applications. Other necessary equipment includes a clean damp cloth or sponge for wiping away excess glue or paste and medium and fine grade sandpaper for preparing the object and smoothing the varnish between coats.

Traditional techniques

The traditional art of découpage uses wood as its base material. Once you have glued down your floral motifs, cover the whole surface of the object with a thin coat of tinted varnish, using as little as possible on the brush. Lift up the brush at the end of each stroke, brushing the varnish out carefully to avoid unsightly streaks or runs. Leave to dry completely – this will take 6 hours or more. Gently rub down with fine grade sandpaper after every third coat of varnish to smooth the surface. Display pieces will need fewer coats of varnish than practical objects which may need up to 20 applications. To assess whether you have applied enough coats of varnish, run your finger over the dry surface to check that it is smooth. When you are satisfied with the finish and the varnish is completely dry, rub down once again with a fine grade sandpaper. The surface will now look dull and opaque. Polish it with wax polish and the colours of the paper motifs will glow through the varnished surface as though they have been hand painted.

Objects to decorate

Wood is a popular choice for découpage: wooden boxes, trays, brushes and frames are all suitable. If you want to be more ambitious, old furniture, too, can take on a new, decorative life. Adapted modern techniques work well on glass, plastic, metal and china; for example, glass or plastic door finger plates, metal trays and wastepaper containers.

COVERING YOUR BOX WITH DÉCOUPAGE

MATERIALS

1 floral print wrapping paper
2 wooden box 30 × 15cm (12 × 6 inches)
3 scrap paper
4 nontoxic transparent glue
5 brush for gluing
6 scissors
7 container for white spirit
8 brush for varnishing
9 white spirit
10 clear varnish
11 tinted varnish
12 medium and fine grade sandpaper

1 Using medium grade sandpaper, rub down a wooden box to smooth any rough surfaces. This allow the varnish to lie properly on the surface. Apply clear varnish to the box inside and out to prevent the paper design from coming away from the wood. Allow the varnish to dry – this will take at least 6 hours. Once dry, use fine grade sandpaper to rub down the varnish very gently.

2 Take a selection of attractive floral wrapping papers. You can use gift wrapping left over from a celebration, pictures of flowers taken from magazines, or buy fresh paper images. However, magazine paper is not ideal as it tends to disintegrate when sanded. Cut out approximately 100-130 flowers, trimming carefully around the printed edges. Make sure that you gather flowers of all sizes.

3 Divide your flower cut-outs into types and colours. Start with the largest blooms and paste the back of the paper motifs using newspaper or an old magazine to protect your work surface. Place the glue-covered flower onto the box, smoothing out any air bubbles. Cover most of the exterior surface area. You may wish to plan your flower pattern before you start gluing.

4 Select the middle-sized flowers and glue them onto the box so that they overlap the larger flowers. As you stick the flowers down, leave some of the edges unstuck so you can slip other flowers underneath. Where you have a sharp angle, for example a horizontal paper edge meeting a vertical one, cover this with a paper flower so the paper does not lift off the box once it is varnished.

5 Use the remaining smaller flowers to build up the pattern and to mask any gaps in the design. Ensure that none of the bare wood is visible on the outside of the box. Trim the flowers at the top edge of the box or use straight-edged paper flowers and position these flush with the box top. Check for any rough flower edges; either paste these down or obscure them with other flowers.

6 Once the whole of the box is covered, varnish it inside and out with tinted varnish and leave to 1 side to dry. Use white spirit in an old container to clean the brush. When the varnish has dried, sand it down with the fine grade sandpaper. Varnish the outside of the box again, allow to dry and sand down slightly. Repeat up to 20 times until you have a satisfactory smooth finish.

FLOWER AND HERBAL GIFTS FOR THE LARDER

Take advantage of fragrant fresh flowers and herbs to make edible treats for your larder. You don't need to be a great cook to create these delicious flavours, as no cooking is necessary. Simply impregnate standard kitchen ingredients, such as oil, vinegar, butter and sugar, with the perfume of flowers, such as marigolds, violets, honeysuckle, lavender, roses, jasmine, clove pinks, freesias, orange, and the flavours and aromas of herbs like basil, chives, dill, garlic, mint, rosemary and tarragon.

Choosing the flowers and herbs

Only use fragrant flowers and herbs that you know are edible. The plants must not have been sprayed with insecticides or fungicides or have been growing near a road where they absorb toxic fumes.

To gain the most fragrance, pick flowers and herbs early in the morning or in the cool part of a sunny day. Flowers should be cut either just before they are in full bloom or at the height of bloom. They must be dry before you use them; discard any damaged petals and leaves and shake off any insects. Small flowers, such as chives, violets and lavender, can be used whole with just the stamens and green calyx at the base of the flowers removed. Use only the petals from larger flowers, such as clove pinks, marigolds and roses.

Flavoured vinegars and oils

Add zest to wine vinegar and olive oil by infusing them with a handful of chive flowers or sprigs of herbs. Use only white wine or distilled white vinegar because strong-tasting cider vinegar kills delicate flavours. Choose mild, pure olive oil or bland vegetable oil – use the scented oil for frying as well as dressings. Winter salads dressed with these infusions will smell and taste of summertime. See the step-by-step instructions here for details on making chive flower vinegar – herbal oil can be made in the same way.

Bottles and jars of oils and vinegars containing flowers and herbs displayed along a windowsill, either during or after preserving, also make practical and attractive kitchen decorations.

Flower honey

Transform an inexpensive blended, but mild-flavoured, honey into a luxurious preserve for spreading on bread, toast and tea breads, stirring into oatmeal and milk puddings; accompanying pancakes, waffles and doughnuts, and for using in cake and biscuit mixtures.

Melt 550g (1 lb) honey in the top of a double boiler over hot water, stirring occasionally with a wooden spoon. Lightly bruise 225g (8 oz) of fragrant flower petals, then add to the honey and continue to warm gently for half an hour. Remove from the heat, cover and leave in a warm place for a week, giving an occasional stir. Place the honey in the top of a double boiler over hot water again and reheat gently. Strain through a muslin-lined sieve into clean jars. Cover, label and keep in a cool place for a few days before using or giving it as a present.

Flower sugar

Use flavoured sugar when baking cakes and puddings; in sweet sauces; sprinkled on raw and cooked fruits; to flavour cream, yogurt, soft cheeses; to serve with puddings; to decorate cakes and biscuits – almost everywhere you use ordinary sugar.

Mix 550g (1 lb) of flowers or petals with 225g (8 oz) of sugar for a strongly flavoured sugar or equal quantities for a mild one. Grind together with a mortar and pestle until the mixture is very fine. Spread on a baking sheet lined with foil and leave for 2 hours in a cool oven until the sugar has absorbed the moisture from the petals or flowers and is completely dry. Leave until cold, then pack loosely into clean jars and close with an airtight top. Label and keep in a cool, dark place.

Attractive bottles of flavoured vinegars and oils add zest to marinades and salad dressings; they make delightful gifts or decorations for a kitchen shelf.

MAKING CHIVE-FLAVOURED VINEGAR

MATERIALS

1   bowl
2   strainer
3   muslin
4   1 cup white wine or white distilled vinegar
5   measuring cup
6   mortar and pestle
7   glass bottle
8   cup
9   paper labels
10 a handful of chive flowers
11 airtight stopper
12 spoon
13 airtight jar
14 kitchen paper
15 scissors

DECORATING LABELS

Floral and herbal flavoured honey, butter, sugar, vinegar and oil make charming gifts to give to family and friends. Transform a simple jar into a special present for any occasion by decorating your labels with drawings of the appropriate flower or herb or by attaching pressed flowers or herbs to them. To personalize the gift even more, write clearly on the labels details of the ingredients, the date the gift was made and its storage life.

To continue the natural theme, wrap the gift with paper which is printed with flowers or plants. Alternatively, adorn the wrapping paper or container with sweet-scented fresh or dried flowers or herbs tied around the neck or tuck one into the packaging ribbon.

1 Gather the chive flowers when they are at their most fragrant. Shake to dislodge insects and wash the flowerheads gently with a light sprinkling of clean water and toss them on kitchen paper to dry. Allow about 4 tablespoons of fresh flowers to each 225ml (8 fl oz) of white wine or white distilled vinegar. Carefully remove any blemished stalks or damaged petals with a pair of sharp scissors.

2 Lightly bruise the prepared chive flowerheads with a clean, dry mortar and pestle or by pressing them firmly with the back of a kitchen spoon. This helps release the fragrant oils from the petals and releases the flavour, allowing it to impregnate the vinegar. Thyme and other flowering herbs or nasturtium buds would be suitable alternatives to use in vinegar or oil.

3 Place the bruised chive flowerheads in a clean, dry, wide-necked jar. Measure the required amount of the vinegar into a measuring cup and pour it slowly over the herb flowerheads. Close the lid of the airtight jar and make sure it is sealed securely against leakage when the jar is being shaken vigorously, or evaporation when the prepared liquid is standing in the sunlight.

4 Shake the jar to mix the flowerheads thoroughly with the vinegar. Leave the jar on a warm, preferably sunny, windowsill for several weeks. Shake the jar briefly every day so the chive flowers shed their fragrant and tasty oils into the vinegar. Taste the vinegar to check that it has reached the required taste and strength. If not, leave it on the windowsill until it is ready.

5 Place the clean, dry strainer over the bowl. Drape the muslin over the strainer, ensuring that it covers both the strainer and the bowl so that any stray drips are caught. Slowly strain the scented vinegar into the bowl – if preparing flavoured oil, take care to empty the jar completely. Carefully lift the muslin off the strainer and discard the saturated flowerheads as well as any residue.

6 The vinegar may have taken on a coral pink tinge and the flowers will have imparted their scent and flavour. Place a few fresh chive flowerheads into a clean bottle and pour the scented flower vinegar over them. Seal the bottle with an airtight and acid-proof stopper, label and store in a cool place. To sample them at their best, consume flavoured oils and vinegars within 3 months.

Herb butter

This special butter makes a lovely gift for someone you know who loves to cook – or to eat! It is delicious on pasta, baked or boiled potatoes, steamed vegetables and grilled fish. To fully enjoy its flavour and fragrance it should be eaten within a few days, or it can be frozen for up to 1 month.

Put 225g (8 oz) fresh basil leaves, 1 large sprig of parsley and about a 30cm (12 inch) shoot of chives in a food processor and mince finely. Add 225g (8 oz) softened unsalted butter and blend until creamy and all is mixed together.

Scrape out of the processor bowl into a large ramekin or other decorative container. Or scrape onto a wooden board, cover and refrigerate for about 30 minutes or until the butter is firm enough to handle. Then roll into a log.

Cover with cling film or aluminium foil and store in the refrigerator or freezer.

BASKETS OF BOUNTY

Delicious festive foods are, for most people, the best Christmas present to receive. Delicacies, or unusual foods that might not be eaten at other times of the year, are welcomed at Christmas.

Christmas is a time when, traditionally, feasting with family and friends is perhaps more important than at any other time of the year. It's the season for rich warming foods, Christmas puddings and cakes, pies and pâtés, rich sauces and desserts. Gifts of food, chosen carefully, can provide the extra items for Christmas that everyone can appreciate, and put the finishing touch to any entertaining they might be planning.

The traditional Christmas hamper, bursting with festive foods, is an alternative way of presenting a gift of food, and there is no reason why a hamper should not include both purchased foods and some delicacies cooked in your own kitchen. The wide range of foods available in modern supermarkets makes the planning of Christmas hampers comparatively simple and the expenditure can be spread over the weeks up to Christmas, choosing items along with your own pre-Christmas shopping. The baskets here have been planned for different life styles, from young people living alone to older, retired people, and will provide some ideas for the contents of your own hampers.

A Christmas hamper can contain several kinds of food, or just one or two, depending on the amount of money you want to spend.

A Christmas basket overflowing with good things

If just one or two items is the aim, choose related foods, such as a special cheese packed with a box of oatcakes, or cheese with a bottle of port. Christmas cake and a bottle of sherry make a good combination, and so do a selection of biscuits and a caddy of special tea. Pretty – or useful – baskets make good hampers and there are different kinds available. Small round or oval baskets can be purchased quite cheaply and these are ideal for gifts such as a selection of cheese, or one or two small packets of foods. Larger baskets, intended as fruit baskets, can sometimes be found in craft shops, and of course, there are bread baskets and shopping baskets in household departments and shops. Plastic storage baskets, which can be purchased at office supplies some large hardware stores look surprisingly attractive dressed with bright ribbons.

Pack the gift foods in white or coloured tissue paper, arranging the paper as a kind of "nest" for the boxes, jars and bottles.

FOR AN OLDER PERSON LIVING ALONE
Shortbread fingers
Small fruit cake
Gingerbread
Comb honey
Salmon bisque
Potted beef or salmon
Oatcakes
Boxed cheese with herbs
½ bottle of red wine
Chamomile tea
Speciality soap

FOR A SINGLE PERSON
Cream of pheasant soup
Cured turkey breast
Asparagus spears
Apricot or peach chutney
Home-made jelly
Stuffed figs
Black cherries
Christmas pudding
Brandy or rum butter
Cognac truffle chocolates
Bottle of sparkling dry white wine

FOR A SMALL FOOD BASKET
Fruit cake
Speciality coffee or tea
Lemon marmalade
Shortbread biscuits

FOR THE HOSTESS
Packets of assorted cocktail mats
Cocktail sticks
Spiced nuts
Paper guest towels
Small candles
After-dinner chocolates
Pretty paper serviettes

FOR A FRIEND WHO LOVES TO COOK
Assorted, unusual herbs or spices
Walnut oil
Herb vinegar
An unusual kitchen gadget
Whole grain mustard
Peach chutney
One of the newest paperback cookery books
Sun-dried tomatoes

FOR THE TEACHER
Crisp apples
Apple chutney
Apple brandy
Apple marzipan fruits
Box of biscuits
Packet of speciality tea

FOR A FRIEND WHO LIKES TO TRAVEL
Spiced nuts
Fruit gums
A new paperback travelogue, for armchair travelling
Assorted guidebooks or maps of interesting places to visit
A travel journal
Foreign cookery book

FOR SOMEONE WHO LIKES SNACKS
Gourmet popping corn
Taco dips
Spiced nuts
Pickles
Cheese dip
Water biscuits
Muesli health bar

SWEET AND SPICY GIFTS

Christmas gifts that you have made yourself will be the most appreciated and, if your talent lies in cooking, what better gifts than those from your kitchen? Practically everyone, young and old, can be given an edible gift in an attractive container.

CLOCKWISE FROM TOP Tipsy Prunes; Herb Sachet; Herb Jelly; Christmas Ring; Caramel Shortbread; Marzipan Petits Fours; Florentines; Spiced Nuts, Miniature Pudding; Herb Vinegar.

Miniature puddings

For people living alone, making miniature Christmas puddings in teacups or small bowls. To improve the flavour, prick the bottom of the pudding and spoon over a tablespoon of brandy. Store, wrapped in greaseproof paper and foil.

To present, wrap the puddings in cling film, then tie them into a square of decorative transparent paper and fasten with a pretty ribbon. Present a small pot of rum butter or brandy butter with the pudding.

HERB JELLIES

Use basic apple jelly to make a herb-flavoured jelly to go with hot or cold meats.

INGREDIENTS

1kg (2 lb) cooking apples, cut into chunks, skin retained
1.2 litres (2 pints) cold water
3 tablespoons lemon juice
5 tablespoons fresh or 2 tablespoons dried herbs
500g (1¼ lb) granulated sugar for each 600ml (1 pint) of juice
green vegetable colouring (optional)

METHOD

1 Put the apples in a pan with the water and lemon juice. Add the herbs in a muslin bag. Bring to a boil and cook the apples until soft, mashing occasionally with a wooden spoon.
2 Remove the herbs. Put the pulp into a jellybag to drip overnight. Measure the juice and put it in a pan with the sugar. Heat gently, stirring, until the sugar is dissolved.
3 Test the taste and if necessary prepare another bag of herbs.
4 Tie to a stick or a wooden spoon and support it over the pan. Bring the jelly to the boil and boil until the jelly coats the back of a spoon or has reached setting point. Remove the herbs. Add colouring if desired. Pour the jelly into jars or glasses. Cover and seal with wax topping (see page 83).

CHRISTMAS RING

This Christmas Ring can also be decorated with a little glacé icing drizzled over the top after the fruit and nuts have been added.

INGREDIENTS

225g (8 oz) pack of puff pastry

FOR THE FILLING

100g (4 oz) ground almonds
75g (3 oz) caster sugar
finely grated rind of 1 lemon
salt
1 small egg, beaten
icing sugar

TO DECORATE

apricot jam
glacé cherries, washed, dried and halved
candied peel
flaked almonds lightly toasted

METHOD

1 Make the filling first. Mix the ground almonds, sugar and lemon rind with a pinch of salt. Bind with half the beaten egg to make a stiff mixture.
2 Knead on a surface dusted with icing sugar, then roll into a "rope" about 21 × 2.5cm (9 × 1 inch). Wrap in cling film and chill in the refrigerator for 1 hour.
3 Heat the oven to 220°C, (425°F), Gas Mark 7. Roll out the pastry to make an oblong shape about 33 × 13cm (13 × 5 inches) wide and about 3mm (⅛ inch) thick. Lay the rope of filling along the pastry, then seal the edges with water.
4 Form the pastry into a ring, bringing the ends together and joining the pastry with a little water. Lay the ring on a floured baking sheet, join side down. Brush with the remaining beaten egg. Bake in the oven for about 30 minutes, until the top is golden brown.

While the Christmas Ring is still hot, brush warmed apricot jam over the surface and decorate with glacé cherries, pieces of candied peel and flaked almonds.

SPICED NUTS

A delicious way to dress up plain nuts.

INGREDIENTS
100g (4 oz) caster sugar
1 teaspoon cinnamon
½ teaspoon ground ginger
pinch of ground nutmeg
½ teaspoon ground coriander
1 egg white
50g (2 oz) each of shelled walnuts, blanched almonds, shelled hazelnuts

METHOD

1 Heat the oven to 180°C, (350°F), Gas Mark 4. Mix the sugar and spices together in a bowl. Beat the egg white. Dip each nut in the egg white to coat it, then drop into the spice and sugar mixture, tossing until covered.

2 Place the nuts, spaced so that they do not touch, on a lightly oiled baking sheet. Bake in the oven for about 20 minutes.

3 Remove the tray of nuts from the oven, sprinkle with the remaining sugar and spice mixture and return to the oven for another 5 minutes. Allow the nuts to cool and then pack on layers of greaseproof paper.

TIPSY PRUNES

These improve with keeping so make them for gifts at least 3 or 4 months ahead. They are easy to make and perfect for Christmassy gifts. Makes 2 × 450g (1 lb) jars.

INGREDIENTS
600ml (1 pint) cold tea
450g (1 lb) demerara sugar
450g (1 lb) prunes
300ml (½ pint) port or sherry

METHOD

1 Put the cold tea and sugar together in a pan and heat to boiling, stirring all the time. Simmer for 15 minutes. Add the prunes and cook them until tender (about 40 minutes).

2 Put the prunes into sterilized jars, using a slotted spoon. Pour in sufficient port or sherry to come halfway up the jars. Fill with remaining syrup. Cover and seal the jars.

CARAMEL SHORTBREAD

Shortbread biscuits make a gift on their own, either packed into a brightly coloured card box lined with lace paper doilies, or tied into bags of coloured cellophane, with a large ribbon bow. Makes about 16.

INGREDIENTS
150g (5 oz) unsalted butter
100g (4 oz) sugar
275g (10 oz) plain flour

FOR THE FILLING
25g (1 oz) butter
100g (4 oz) caster sugar
2 tablespoons golden syrup
400g (14 oz) can condensed milk
100g (4 oz) plain chocolate, broken up

METHOD

1 Heat oven 180°C(350°F), Gas Mark 4. Grease a 30×23cm (12×9in) Swiss roll tin.

2 Cream the butter with the sugar, then gradually work in the flour. Press the mixture into the tin.

3 Bake in the oven for 15-20 minutes until golden. Leave to cool.

4 For the filling, place the butter, sugar, syrup and condensed milk in a saucepan and heat gently until the sugar has dissolved, stirring occasionally.

5 Increase the heat and boil for 5 minutes, stirring continuously. Remove from the heat, leave to cook for 1 minute, then pour onto the shortbread base. Leave to set.

6 Place the chocolate in a small bowl over a pan of hot water and stir over gentle heat until melted. Spread over the filling.

7 Mark into squares and leave to cool completely before cutting into pieces and removing from the tin.

CHERRY BRANDY JELLIES

Here are little cherry candies coloured a Christmassy red. Makes about 450g (1 lb).

INGREDIENTS
4 tablespoons powdered gelatine
150ml (¼ pint) water
450g (1 lb) granulated sugar
1½ tablespoons cherry brandy
red food colouring
50g (2 oz) caster sugar

METHOD
1 Dissolve the gelatine in 4 tablespoons of the water. Heat the sugar and remaining water together, stirring continuously, until the sugar has dissolved. Bring to a boil.
2 Add the gelatine mixture to the syrup. Stir in the cherry brandy and the colouring to make a rich red colour.
3 Pour the gelatine mixture into a wetted tin and leave to set for a day.
4 To finish, turn out the jelly onto a sheet of greaseproof paper, sprinkled with caster sugar. Cut shapes with fancy pastry cutters and roll in the sugar to cover them. Place in paper cases.

FRUIT CHEWS
Makes about 450g (1 lb)

INGREDIENTS
50g (2 oz) dried pears
50g (2 oz) dried apricots
50g (2 oz) seedless raisins or sultanas
25g (1 oz) thick honey
25g (1 oz) hazelnuts, ground
15g (½ oz) dried coconut
50g (2 oz) chocolate vermicelli

METHOD
1 Process all the ingredients except the honey together. Work in the honey.
2 Divide the mixture into pieces and roll into log shapes about 1 inch long. Roll each log shapes about 2.5cm (1 inch) long. Roll each log in a mixture of hazelnuts and coconut, or in chocolate vermicelli. To serve, place each chew in a petit four paper case.

TRUFFLES

These popular sweets can be flavoured and shaped many different ways. Makes about 450g (1 lb).

INGREDIENTS
225g (8 oz) cake crumbs
1 tablespoon unsweetened cocoa
2 tablespoons apricot jam, sieved
1 tablespoon rum or brandy essence
75g (3 oz) plain chocolate, melted

TO DECORATE
75g (3 oz) chocolate, melted
chocolate vermicelli
glacé cherries
icing sugar

METHOD
Mix all the ingredients together to make a soft dough. Use as desired to make different truffle shapes. Leave the truffles to dry and then place in paper petit four cases.
Vermicelli truffles Shape balls about the size of a walnut, coat lightly in melted chocolate and roll in vermicelli.
Truffle logs Shape small pieces into log shapes, dust with icing sugar and mark with a fork to make a log bark effect.
Cherry truffles Roll the dough to 6mm (¼ inch) thick, cut into 2.5cm (1 inch) circles and place a half cherry on top. Cover with melted chocolate.

WAX TOPPING

Jellies and preserves for gifts can be packed into glasses, tumblers, large wine glasses, brandy snifters, etc. and topped with a layer of paraffin wax. Buy this fresh from a chemist, melt it in a bowl over hot water and simply pour over the preserve. It seals the food and looks like a white "head" on top of the glass. Cover with cling film and tie a bow of ribbon around the glass. Fresh paraffin wax is re-usable and does not affect the taste of food.

FLORENTINES

For a variation drizzle a little glacé icing over the surface of the Florentines. Plain caster sugar can be used but sugar in which a piece of vanilla pod has been stored makes a delicious flavour. Makes about 12.

INGREDIENTS
50g (2 oz) unsalted butter
50g (2 oz) caster sugar, vanilla flavoured (see above)
1 tablespoon double cream, whipped
25g (1 oz) chopped mixed peel
25g (1 oz) glacé cherries, washed, dried and chopped
25g (1 oz) angelica, chopped
15g (½ oz) flaked almonds
15g (½ oz) plain flour
175g (6 oz) plain chocolate, broken up

METHOD
1 Heat oven 180°C(350°F), Gas Mark 4.
2 Melt the butter in a saucepan slowly. Stir in the sugar and the cream, and slowly bring to the boil. Boil for about 1 minute, then remove from the heat. Cool a little.
3 Stir in the fruit and nuts, then the flour. Drop teaspoons of the mixture onto greased baking sheets 7.5cm (3 inches) apart; Florentines spread in baking.
4 Bake in the oven for 10-12 minutes or until the biscuits look brown at the edges.
5 Remove from the oven, leave for a few seconds to set, then lift from the sheet with a broad spatula. Cool on a wire rack. They may harden while you are trying to lift them from the baking sheet. If this happens, return the sheet to the oven for a few minutes and they will soften again.
6 Melt the chocolate pieces in a bowl over hot water and then spread the chocolate over the back of the Florentines. Mark lines with a fork to decorate.

CLEOPATRA'S SWEETMEATS

Makes about 550g (1¼ lbs).

INGREDIENTS
100g (4 oz) no-soak apricots
50g (2 oz) candied citrus peel, chopped
75g (3 oz) shelled, chopped walnuts
75g (3 oz) seedless raisins, chopped, or whole sultanas
2 tablespoons orange juice

METHOD
1 Process all the ingredients together. Roll into 2.5cm (1 inch) balls and flatten slightly. Leave to dry, then store in paper cases in an airtight jar or tin.
Variation: Roll the balls in dried coconut or sesame seeds before flattening them. Chopped mixed fruit can be used in this recipe but homemade candied peel is better.

STUFFED DATES

Stuffed dates are quick to make and are popular served with coffee after a meal. They can also be put into boxes of homemade sweets. Makes about 24.

INGREDIENTS
175g (6 oz) ready-made marzipan (see below) or 75g (3 oz) ground almonds and 75g (3 oz) caster sugar
1 teaspoon rum
green food colouring
little egg white
1 box dates
icing sugar
granulated sugar, to finish

METHOD
1 If ready-made marzipan is used, put in a bowl and mix with the rum and a drop or two of green food colouring, using a fork. Blend smoothly together.
2 Alternatively, to make the almond paste, put the ground almonds, sugar and rum in a bowl and add sufficient egg white to mix to a stiff paste. Blend in 1-2 drops green food colouring to colour the mixture to a soft apple green.
3 Slit along the top of each date and remove the stone. Sprinkle a pastry board or

working surface with a little sifted icing sugar and roll the almond paste into a long sausage shape. Cut into as many pieces as there are dates. Shape each piece into a plump roll and use to replace the stone in each date.

4 Roll in granulated sugar and place in paper cases to serve.

Keeps up to 4 weeks in an airtight tin.

HOMEMADE MARZIPAN

Marzipan sweets are suitable for the beginner to try. An uncooked marzipan is easy to make but, like bought marzipan, tends to oil and crack if over-handled. The cooked marzipan needs more care in preparation but is easy and pliable to handle. If you want to add a touch of luxury, blend a little rum, brandy or liqueur into the paste.

A pretty box of confectionery makes a welcome gift at Christmas. This selection includes two different types of truffle and stuffed dates.

UNCOOKED MARZIPAN
Makes 225g (8 oz) paste.

INGREDIENTS
100g (4 oz) icing sugar, sifted
100g (4 oz) ground almonds
2 teaspoons lemon juice
1 egg white

METHOD

1 Mix the icing sugar and ground almonds together in a bowl. Add the lemon juice and egg white and mix to a paste. Knead lightly until smooth.

2 Keep tightly covered in a plastic bag until required. Use within 7 days.

COOKED MARZIPAN
Makes about 750g (1½ lb) paste.

INGREDIENTS
225g (8 oz) sugar
6 tablespoons water
175g (6 oz) ground almonds
50g (2 oz) liquid glucose
1 egg white
1 teaspoon lemon juice
225g (8 oz) icing sugar, sifted

METHOD
1 Put the sugar and water into a saucepan and stir over low heat until dissolved, then stop stirring and boil until the soft ball stage of 115°C, (238°F), is reached.
2 Remove from the heat, stir in the ground almonds and glucose. Cool slightly, then add the egg white. Return to a gentle heat and cook, stirring all the time, for 2-3 minutes. Add the lemon juice.
3 Knead the mixture well while it is cooling, either on a board or in an electric mixer using a dough hook, working in sufficient icing sugar to give a firm but pliable consistency. Keep tightly covered in a plastic bag until required. Use within 7 days.

Marzipan fruits.

MARZIPAN FRUITS
With a little practice, you will soon find marzipan fruits easy to mould. If you intend to make a lot, it is well worth sparing the time to make a sago board to make the pitted skins of lemons, oranges and strawberries. To do this, spread a thin layer of glue on to a thin piece of hardboard. Sprinkle well with fine sago and shake off any surplus. Leave to dry. Store it in a plastic bag and it will last a lifetime. Otherwise use a fine grater. Makes 20 fruits.

INGREDIENTS
225g (8 oz) marzipan
yellow, red, green, orange, brown and mauve food colouring
few cloves
small strip of crystallized angelica
2 teaspoons sugar

METHOD
1 To make marzipan fruits, divide the mixture into 3 portions. Colour 1 portion yellow. Divide two-thirds into 4 and colour them red, green, mauve and orange. Remember to keep the marzipan in a plastic bag when not in use, as it will soon dry on the surface, crack and become difficult to handle.
2 To mould, each piece should weigh slightly less than 15g (½ oz); 25g (1 oz) will make 3 pieces.
Lemons (yellow) Form into an egg shape, pinch the ends and roll against a fine grater or sago board.
Plums (mauve) Form into balls. Hold the ball against the back of a small vegetable knife and roll the knife back to make an indentation or crease on 1 side of the plum. Roll each one in sugar. Use a clove or small piece of angelica for a stalk.
Bananas (yellow) Form into a 4-sided bar about 3cm (1¼ inches) long. Point each end and slightly curve the bar until it resembles a banana shape. Using a very fine paint brush and a little brown food colouring, paint soft lines along the square edges.
Strawberries (red) Make a ball, then work 1 end to make a strawberry. Roll against a fine grater. Use angelica for a stalk.

Oranges (orange) Form into a ball. Roll against a sago board or fine grater. Use cloves for the stalk and calyx.

Apples (green) Form into balls. "Blush" with red food colouring and press cloves into each end to simulate the calyx and the stalk.

APPLE CHUTNEY

This makes about 1.8kg (4 lb) of chutney.

INGREDIENTS
1kg (2 lb) cooking apples, peeled, cored and chopped
450ml (¾ pint) vinegar
275g (10 oz) sultanas
450g (1 lb) demerara sugar
75g (3 oz) chopped preserved ginger
2 cloves garlic, crushed
·½ teaspoon ground allspice
½ teaspoon cayenne pepper
½ teaspoon salt

METHOD
1 Place the apples and half the vinegar in a large pan.
2 Bring to a boil and simmer gently, stirring occasionally, until the apples have softened.
3 Add the rest of the vinegar and the remaining ingredients. Stir well. Return to a boil, reduce the heat and simmer gently for about 20 minutes, stirring occasionally, until thick.
4 Spoon while still hot into warm, sterile jars (see the box, Sterilizing Jars). Seal with airtight, non-metallic lids.

LEMON CURD

To make orange curd, substitute 3 oranges for 3 of the lemons. This makes about 800g (1¾ lb).

INGREDIENTS
grated rind and juice of 4 lemons
100g (4 oz) slightly salted butter
350g (12 oz) caster sugar
4 eggs, lightly beaten

METHOD
1 Put the lemon rind and juice into the top of a double boiler. Cut the butter into pieces and add it with the sugar. Strain the eggs into the mixture.
2 Place the top of the double boiler over the bottom containing simmering water. Stir until the sugar has dissolved and the butter has melted.
3 Continue to cook, stirring constantly, until the curd thickens enough to coat the back of a wooden spoon. Do not overcook or the eggs may curdle.
4 Pour into prepared jars. Cover and label. Lemon curd keeps for 1 month, or 3 months if refrigerated.

MINCEMEAT

Homemade mincemeat makes a perfect Christmas gift. Makes about 2.7kg (6 lb).

INGREDIENTS
350g (12 oz) seedless raisins
225g (8 oz) sultanas
225g (8 oz) currants
225g (8 oz) cut mixed peel
350g (12 oz) soft dark brown sugar
450g (1 lb) cooking apples, peeled, cored and finely chopped
225g (8 oz) shredded suet
grated rind and juice of 2 lemons
grated rind and juice of 2 oranges
50g (2 oz) chopped almonds
1 tablespoon ground mixed spice
1 teaspoon cinnamon
1 teaspoon ground nutmeg
75ml (3 fl oz) brandy

METHOD
1 Mix all the ingredients together, except the brandy, in a large ovenproof bowl. Cover with a clean tea towel and allow to stand overnight.
2 Preheat the oven to 110°C, (225°F), Gas Mark ¼. Remove the tea towel, cover with foil and place in the oven for about 3 hours.
3 Allow to cool, then mix in the brandy and put in sterile jars (see the box, Sterilizing Jars).
4 Cover and allow the mincemeat to mature for at least 2 weeks before use.

CHRISTMAS GREENERY AND FLOWERS

❧ DECK THE HALLS WITH BOUGHS OF HOLLY ❧

Evergreens have always been regarded as symbols of life continuing through the long cold days of winter. So they were used as decorations in pagan festivals, and the Romans, for whom evergreens signified good fortune, would deck their homes with holly and ivy and give sprigs of them to friends as good luck tokens during the midwinter feast of Saturnalia. With the arrival of Christianity in the West, St Augustine was advised by Pope Gregory to encourage such of the local customs as were capable of Christian interpretation. It was easy for the

Christian church to endow holly with the symbolism of Christ's crown of thorns. Ivy was a bit more difficult for them to adopt. It was the badge of Bacchus, the Roman god of wine. Mistletoe, however, was completely beyond the pale, because it played a particularly significant role in Druid rites. The Arch Druid was supposed to have cut the mistletoe with a golden sickle, and it was caught as it fell from the tree by virgins holding out a

white cloth. There followed the sacrifice of white oxen, thought to have replaced human sacrifice; the mistletoe was then divided up among the people, who took it home to hang over their doors to protect against witchcraft, and to ensure fertility. So at Christmas we may sing of the holly and the ivy, but never of the mistletoe, and to this day it is never used in church decorations.

But for decorating their houses inside and out, at Christmas time, the late Victorians used every kind of greenery they could lay their hands on. Gathering sufficient foliage was quite a task, and there would often be a family expedition to the woods. Enterprising countrymen would load up carts with evergreen branches, which they would then sell on the city streets. Holly, ivy, rosemary, pine, bay, laurel, box, yew were all pressed into service, and used with the same abandon with which today we use paper chains or streamers.

Such an abundance of evergreens could

produce a rather sombre effect, so coloured glass balls or Chinese lanterns might be introduced among the greenery. And *The Lady* advised, "the general effect is heightened and the decoration becomes more elaborate and more elegant" by arrangements of fresh flowers, such as chrysanthemums, Christmas roses, stephanotis, primulas or camellias.

Today, we add many other flowers to our Christmas greenery. There is, of course, *the* Christmas flower, poinsettia (whose red, white, pink or marbled "flowers" are not flowers at all, but coloured bracts that sit beneath the inconspicuous tiny green flowers), as well as carnations, lilies, and every kind of dried flower imaginable.

A gift of evergreens delivered to the door deserved some reward.

MISTLETOE FOR GOOD FORTUNE

Mistletoe may have had slightly sinister Druidic associations, but no Christmas was thought complete without it, and the maiden who escaped being kissed beneath it at Christmas time, it was said, had no hope of marrying within the year. It was therefore suspended in the most unavoidable place, usually from the central chandelier in the hall, or as Dickens describes in *The Pickwick Papers* from the kitchen ceiling:

. . . old Wardle had just suspended with his own hands a huge branch of mistletoe, and this same branch of mistletoe instantaneously gave rise to a scene of general and most delightful struggling and confusion . . . Mr. Winkle kissed the young lady with the black eyes, and Mr. Snodgrass kissed Emily; and Mr. Weller, not being particular about the form of being under the mistletoe, kissed Emma and the other female servants, just as he caught them.

In an age hide-bound by propriety, the opportunity afforded by mistletoe, to kiss and embrace people out of wedlock and out of one's own social class was not to be missed, and then as now mistletoe was used as an excuse to plant kisses where they were least expected.

Mr Pickwick steals a kiss at a Christmas party.

HOLLY, THE PRETTIEST CHRISTMAS GREEN

The traditional use of holly goes back to Roman times, where it was used as a decoration to celebrate the renewal of life at New Year. It was a particularly potent symbol because it bore fruit when much else lay dormant beneath a blanket of snow.

Holly in arrangements

Holly is a versatile plant during the festive season: it can be used in table arrangements, to make door wreaths, and sprigs and boughs of it are often dotted about the house.

Traditionally combined with red flowers – carnations are the popular choice – holly is an effective foil to rich, creamy flowers. Use cream spray carnations, lilies and creamy rosebuds, if they are available. Cream or greenish white chrysanthemums, too, are a good colour to mix with the shiny green of holly leaves.

For a quite different effect, mix green and variegated holly with other variegated evergreen foliage. Silvery foliage, too, looks good with holly. Use fronds of silvery gray ballota, or perhaps a few sprays of grey-leaved sage.

If you can bring yourself to cut a stem of poinsettia from a pot plant, it will make an exotic focus for an arrangement of plain and variegated hollies.

Caring for holly

Use a pair of sharp pruners to cut holly from your own garden. Condition as for woody-stemmed evergreens, described elsewhere in this chapter.

Holly will last through the Christmas period if it is kept moist, so check that there is sufficient water in your vases, and spray mist the leaves from time to time.

Looking at holly

English holly or *Ilex aquifolium* is used as hedging in gardens and grows wild in hedge-rows where it can reach 7.5 metres (25 feet) despite being fairly slow-growing.

The dark green shiny leaves have wavy edges that are pointed and can be sharp so wear gloves when you work with prickly varieties.

Holly flowers, borne in spring, are very small. Female trees bear bright red berries, provided there is a male tree nearby. Some varieties carry both male and female flowers on the same tree. The berries are poisonous, so make sure that none drop from your designs or are within the range of children or pets.

GROWING YOUR OWN

- Holly grows in all soils, but variegated forms need sunlight for better leaf colour.
- You need a male plant to pollinate the female and produce berries, but some varieties of holly 'J.C. van Tol' and 'Pyramidalis', can pollinate themselves.
- Plants only fruit after about six years in the ground, so you may have to wait a few Christmasses for your berries.
- Plant young trees in spring or autumn. They can even be planted in winter, providing the soil is not frozen or too wet.
- If a variegated form reverts to green, cut out all green shoots.

Holly bushes can grow as high as 7.5 metres (25 feet) but they can be clipped, using a pair of garden shears, to make into a hedge or into a more manageable bush.

If you have the space in your garden to plant several hollies, choose a plain green one and a variegated species. A good combination would be *Ilex aquifolium* 'Golden van Tol' (a female tree with creamy yellow leaf edges) and a male common holly.

Use variegated holly boughs to bring a burst of brightness to dark hallways and dull corners in the house. Mix them with the foliage of other variegated evergreens.

Ilex aquifolium 'aureo-marginata'.

BUYING GUIDE

Season: Holly berries in winter. Branches of berried holly are sold in markets during the weeks preceding Christmas. Buy close to the time you want to arrange.

At the market or florist: Buy from a source where holly has been standing in water or where fresh holly is delivered daily, to ensure it has not dried out too much.

Vase life: Long, but you should mist the leaves regularly to prevent them drying out. Keep away from sources of heat.

Stem height: Long.

Tip: Keep berries out of reach of children and pets. Berries are poisonous and eating them can be fatal. When you buy holly check that leaves are shiny and the berries smooth and bright. If quantities of berries fall from the branch it is too dry to use.

OTHER EVERGREENS

Greenery – ivy, laurel, Lawson cypress and fir – has been a traditional decoration for the festive season for thousands of years. In the dead of winter it brings the fragrance of the forests and the sense of being in touch with nature that we can all enjoy, no matter how urban our surroundings. Even with a minimal amount of arrangement, it gives an unmistakable atmosphere of wassail and carols, feasts, good cheer and gift-wrapped surprises.

If you have greenery in your garden the children will enjoy helping to gather it. Supply them with big baskets to carry it in and thick gloves to guard against any prickles.

Greenery is also a symbol of success and eternal life, so make a door ring, hang some garlands, and dress the tree for a happy and prosperous New Year!

Evergreen foliage, whether shiny like ivy, mat like fir and Lawson cypress, or brightly variegated like spotted laurel, can provide a framework for flower arrangements throughout the year. But it is particularly useful in winter, once the glowing shades of autumn leaves have faded. It makes a dramatic filler, in with fresh or dried flowers. And because each type of foliage is quite a different shade of green, a display of only foliage – but several types of it – can make very colourful green arrangements all on its own.

Evergreens are so varied and versatile that you can let your imagination run riot in the ways you use them. Graduate from the traditional trick of tucking a sprig of green foliage behind the picture and mirror frames, to working on a larger scale, outlining door and window frames and pieces of furniture, too.

Time may be the deciding factor in exactly how you do this. The neatest way is to form short sprays of foliage into bunches and then bind them to a piece of cord or rope. The quickest way – which works well for lightweight stems such as ivy and mistletoe – is to press them to the surface, using sticky fixing pads or blue tacky clay to hold them in place. Outline the edge of bookshelves, room dividers or other open shelving in a similar

Some varieties of aucuba such as A. japonica
*'Crotonifolia', can also produce a good crop of berries:
a priceless bonus for your arrangements.*

way. A snaky trail of ivy will lend even the most workmanlike of shelves the Christmas spirit.

For a pretty hanging decoration with a natural moisture source, cut ivy or other stems of evergreen or flowers such as spray chrysanthemums to an even length and stick them all around a large potato. The potato shrinks, the leaves or flowers flourish, and the design looks delightful in a hall or over a stairway.

Think of evergreen trails and ribbons, hoops and spheres as you think of the Christmas tree – a vehicle for small decorations – and you can give your foliage designs a new and sparkling personality. Hang the stems and branches with cones or Christmas balls, clusters of nuts or artificial berries, bonbons and wrapped sweets, mini dried-flower posies or showy dried flowerheads, all chosen to be in step with your colour theme.

As a general rule, the simpler the better is the safest guideline for floor designs – and talking of safety, do be sure to use sturdy containers. A large vase of evergreens – with or without added ingredients – can be a decorative boon in a room corner, filling an awkward gap when the furniture has been rearranged for a large gathering.

A basket of cones highlighted by a few twinkling glass balls; a couple of trails of ivy tucked in among the logs in a basket; a wooden tub filled with an armful of evergreens just as they are cut; a pot of poinsettias filling an unused fireplace; a verdant pot plant given festive pretend blooms in the colour and shape of silk poinsettias, poppies or peonies. Designs do not have to be complicated or time-consuming to be effective.

CONDITIONING FLOWERS AND FOLIAGE

If you will be putting cut flowers in vases or making arrangements with them, take a tip from professional florists that will make your arrangements last longer. Buy your flowers a day before you want to arrange them; this will give you sufficient time to condition them by standing them in a deep vase or pail of lukewarm water overnight or for at least 5

GREENERY TIPS

When one thinks of holiday greenery, holly immediately comes to mind, as does the fir of Christmas trees and wreaths. But there are other greens that provide lovely contrast in colour, texture and shape and work well in all sorts of winter arrangements.

Two of these are spotted laurel, particularly the glossy and brightly variegated variety *Aucuba japonica* 'Variegata' (also known as 'Maculata'), and Lawson cypress, *Chamaecyparis lawsoniana*. Spotted laurel's dazzling green and yellow leaves brighten up all-green displays, and Lawson cypress, with its mat, almost fernlike leaves, will soften a vase or wreath of bolder foliage, and provide a gentle background and filler for fresh flowers readily available in winter, like chrysanthemums.

Spotted laurel has smooth, yellow-spotted leaves. Bright red berries follow clusters of small greenish, starlike flowers, provided male and female forms are growing together. The berries may last through to spring in the garden but will need special conditioning to stop them from shrivelling up indoors (see the section on conditioning, elsewhere in this chapter).

Lawson cypress is available in shades from dark green to greenish gold. The golden varieties develop their colour best when growing in sunny places. The foliage is feathery and flat, like a pressed spray, and it has a fresh herby smell when crushed.

Season: Both these evergreens have foliage for cutting all through the year.

At the florist: You may find them at your florist's, but your best source is a home garden. Both evergreens have abundant foliage so there's no need to worry about spoiling a specimen when cutting for arrangements. Just remember to take stems from all over the plant.

Vase life: Both will last for up to 2 weeks, if conditioned properly.

Stem height: Cut medium to short stems depending on vase size.

Tip: For a glossy look give leaves of aucuba a wipe with a houseplant leaf-shine.

LAWSON CYPRESS

- Will grow well in most garden soils and in sun or shade. Golden varieties develop their colour best in sunny positions.
- Plant young trees in autumn if you have light, well-drained soil, but in spring if your garden is heavy clay.
- Specimen trees need no pruning. If the main stem becomes forked, cut one stem off to leave a main shoot. Cut hedges back when they have reached the required height.
- Keep the shape of your trees by taking stems from different parts of the tree.

AUCUBA JAPONICA 'VARIEGATA'

- Grows well in both shade or sun, but its variegation will be brighter in a sunny position.
- Can be grown in a tub, but will need fertilizer and lots of water during the summer.
- No need to prune, but if stems get leggy you can cut them back in late spring.
- When cutting for flower arranging, keep your plant in good shape by taking stems from different parts of the plant.
- Buy plants from good garden centres or grow from cuttings taken in spring.

hours in a cool, dark place. This conditioning allows the flowers to soak up as much water as they can and they will stay fresher longer once in arrangements, especially those set in florist's foam.

Scrape off the bottom 5cm (2 inches) of bark from heavy, woody cuttings from trees and shrubs and then split the cutting up about 5cm (2 inches) from the bottom. After soaking (see below) cut off the split part of the cutting at a slant. Other, more delicate greenery like cuttings of ferns and ivies do not need to have their stems split at the ends. Rather, submerge all of them – stems and leaves – in a pail of cold water for at least 5 minutes before arranging.

Split the stem ends and take off some of the leaves of cuttings from flowers that have woody stems like roses, chrysanthemums and flowering shrubs before conditioning them in water. Cut off, under water, if possible, the white portions of the lower stems of bulbous flowers like tulips, iris and narcissi. And flowers that bleed a sticky "milk" (which is actually a latex) like poppies may have their stem ends burned by briefly holding them over a flame. This will seal the ends.

Making arrangements last

Make sure that your vase is perfectly clean so that you are sure there is no bacteria left over from the last flowers in it. Then fill it up about halfway with water and add a few drops of household bleach (no more). The bleach acts as an antibacterial agent, keeping flowers fresher longer. Never add sugar to the water, thinking that you are providing food for the flowers. Sugar will encourage the growth of bacteria. Instead, use a commercial floral preservative that usually comes in little packets. A charcoal tablet will also help to keep the water pure.

Always cut the bottom stems off flowers and foliage that you buy. And remove all the bottom leaves so that none are under the water when the arrangement is complete. Do not leave cut flowers sitting out before you arrange them.

Keep the arrangement away from direct heat and draughts, and if it is in a heated room, mist the foliage occasionally with warm water.

For some people there will never be anything to replace the beauty – and at this time of year, the luxury – of fresh flowers for the party season. Sometimes the most expensive buys – lilies and gerberas, for example – can prove to be the most economical in both money and time-saving terms. If properly conditioned and arranged and kept out of direct heat, both types of flowers can last for the 12 days of Christmas. Evergreens last even longer.

The pale pastels of the tabletop arrangement mix with the greenery to achieve a pretty, fresh look for the table while the mistletoe and berries on the wreath add a Christmassy feel.

TIMING THE BLOOMS

Unfortunately there is no magic formula for getting flowers to open at exactly the right time. For special occasions, like a formal holiday dinner party, it's best to order from your florist, but for everyday use, there are a few tricks you can use to help time the opening of flowers you buy and arrange.

To get flowers to open faster, put them in a warm room (out of direct sunlight) or stand them under an electric light such as a spotlight or table lamp. The warmth from the light helps them to open, but don't put them too close as intense heat is harmful. Or try standing the flowers in warm water instead of lukewarm as you condition them. For faster results, try a combination of all 3 methods.

If it's really essential that flowers open in a hurry, shut them in a confined space with lots of ripening fruit; the ethylene gas given off by the fruit "ripens" the flowers as well. But be warned, if you artificially advance flowers, you'll also be shortening their vase life.

To slow down flower opening, keep them in a cool 8-10°C (45-50°F), dark room in water with barely the chill taken off (don't use completely cold water). In an emergency, when flowers need to look good for a short time only, wrap the stems in damp tissues or cotton wool, slip them into a large plastic bag and put them in the vegetable compartment of the refrigerator.

FLOWERS FOR THE TABLE

For most families, Christmas dinner is the meal of the year. With such a high profile, the table setting deserves to be planned with as much attention to detail as is given to the meal itself.

To make sure that the dinner table not only looks as pretty as you can make it, but that it will actually "work", stage a dress rehearsal. Set out the plates and side plates, the carving dish and vegetable dishes, the sauce boats and butter dishes, and the glasses, and then take stock.

First make sure there is enough room for your guests to sit comfortably. Then look at the table setting. If the arrangement itself looks too cramped for comfort, consider carving and serving from a sideboard or a table brought in for the occasion.

Assess how much space there is for table flower decorations, and then decide how to make the most eye-catching use of it. Perhaps there is space in the centre of the table for a hoop of evergreens and candles or a bowl of nuts decorated with trails of holly and ivy.

There may be limited space, but enough for one, 2 or 3 slender candlesticks. In this case, turn them to decorative advantage, and trim the candlesticks with greenery or dried or fresh flowers. Remember that tall designs – candles and flowers arranged in a dish secured to the top of a long candlestick or tall vase, or a dried flower tree in a small container – save precious table space because you can push plates and dishes beneath them.

A long thin "ribbon" of greenery, small cones and Christmas balls, with or without candles, in the centre of a narrow table can be particularly effective as well as practical. Cut thin strips of foam and put them in the longest, narrowest containers you can find, such as corn-on-the-cob dishes or wooden date boxes lined with foil (to save moisture seeping onto the table's surface).

More space-saving still are trails of ivy and long sprigs of holly – the more the merrier – along the centre of the table or wherever there is a tiny space. Add a few Christmas balls – the hanging loops will prevent them from rolling off – or cut-out gold or silver paper stars for a dash of glitter.

Decorative place settings

As an alternative, or a pretty addition, consider taking the decorative action to each place setting – certainly a more personal touch than any central design. A tiny posy of holly, mistletoe and a mini-Christmas ball tied with ribbons and standing in a narrow glass or an egg cup or a tussie mussie – a lovely old-fashioned word for nosegay – of a few leaves and flowers surrounded by a paper doily. These designs leave the centre of the table completely clear for your dishes as space is nearly always at a premium.

If there is really no space on the table at all, the food itself may be the only place left for a deft touch of floral art. Stand the vegetable dishes on plates and edge them with rings of holly or tinsel: turn out the Christmas pudding (or put the cake or biscuits) onto a large plate or a pedestal cake stand, and surround it by a circle of holly.

A triangle of red spray carnations, roses and hawthorn berries, white spray chrysanthemums and chincherinchee, is high on impact but economical with table space. The crystal candlestick is fitted with a candle cup holder and foam.

Present small ramekin-desserts such as chocolate mousse on plates lined with leaves or ringed with dried flowers and, for good measure, decorate the top of the dish with a single flower and leaf.

If you hand around after-dinner coffee and mints on a tray, add a very small floral decoration, just a couple of blooms such as freesias in a small glass, or a trail of leaves around one edge of the tray. Avoid anything too straggly though in case it gets caught in the furniture as you pass. Whatever you use, make sure it is attached to the tray securely.

Buffet parties

Many of the same considerations of space apply to a table set for a buffet party – and many of the decorative solutions can be applied, too. A tall, central flower arrangement that can be easily seen from the other side of the room beckons guests to the buffet table and will remain as a decoration when the meal has finished.

Be sure to use a sturdy and steady container, for even in the politest of circles, people reaching across a table can spell disaster to any container that is delicate and vulnerable. If you are in any doubt, secure the base of the container by pressing a few dabs of blue tacky clay and then pressing them firmly to the table surface. Remember, too, that you have done this when it comes to taking the dish away for refilling.

Keep lit candles and any candle arrangements well away from the edge of a table, or any position where guests will have to reach over them.

Putting elaborate flower decorations on food isn't a particularly good idea at a help-yourself buffet. The dishes can soon look bedraggled and a spray of yellow statice floating in a sea of blackcurrant mousse can be unappetizing. It is best to confine the floral garnishes to the table top. A few dried flowerheads scattered on the cloth look remarkably pretty – and help to hide the inevitable crumbs and spills.

This dresser, bedecked with trails and sprays of ivy and shimmering with Christmas lights and balls, makes an ideal "away-from-it-all" serving table.

Fresh or dried flowers?

With so many occasions to plan for in such a short space of time, dried flower arrangements have the built-in advantage that they can be made-up and ready and waiting for any occasion. Choose colours that harmonize with your room, or neutral shades that blend with more than one of your furnishing plans. A dried flower arrangement can be a portable feast for the eyes, moved from dining room to hall to living room as the occasion demands.

Pretty-up existing dried flower arrangements by adding a few special blooms – a trio of dried peonies, perhaps, in a pink and blue design, or splash of white flowers to one that looks a little too subtle. Give a design a party face by tying a ribbon around the container and finishing it with a flourish, or tie several bows and fix them to the rim of the container. The basket of gypsophila with its white and gold ribbon trim, shows how effective this can be.

Bring pot plants into the decorative act for long-lasting fresh blooms. Make a pot-et-feuilles design (an adaptation of pot-et-fleur, using foliage rather than fresh cut flowers) by burying a pot of poinsettia, cyclamen or begonia among evergreens, and it will become the star of the occasion.

A festive basket

Elegant and impressive, a weathered country basket brimming with wine-red dried roses makes an eyecatching feature at any time of year, but at Christmas it looks particularly appealing, as the rich red of the roses and green of the foliage will echo the colours of other festive decorations in your home.

Unlike many other Christmas decorations, however, you won't have to dismantle this one or pack it away after Twelfth Night. You can display your rose-filled basket proudly and be sure that it will carry the festive spirit well into the new year.

A gift with meaning

Red roses are traditionally given as a token of love and affection – so as well as treating yourself to a basket, it's all the more rewarding to make a second basket and give it as a thoughtful gift to a favourite friend. And there's no need to stick to red roses; if you (or the friend for whom the basket is intended) have a favorite colour, roses in this shade can be ordered from the florist. As well as the deep red variety used here, dried roses are available in scarlet, salmon pink, deep pink, pale pink, apricot, yellow, cream and white.

Choosing the materials

The roses for this display could be those that you pick from your own garden and dry yourself, or bought fresh roses that you also dry at home. Though ready-dried roses from a florist's are expensive, they cost little more than fresh ones.

To keep costs down, buy dried short-stemmed "Sweetheart" roses or miniature roses, rather than the long-stemmed types. Though the flowerheads are slightly smaller, it won't matter for this kind of display, and the stems have to be cut short anyway. The dried sphagnum moss used here is the best choice for foliage. White statice is always available at florist's, but for a more unusual touch you could use sprigs of dried grasses.

Choosing a basket

All sorts of baskets, but weathered-looking ones in particular, are ideally suited to dried flower arrangements – the textures and muted colours complement each other so well.

The basket in this display is made of woven wooden twigs, but you could use a woven wicker or straw basket instead. Many shops now sell handsome pretrimmed baskets with lavender, artemisia or other dried materials woven by hand into the rim and even over the handle. This sort of basket is more expensive than a plain type, but there are two advantages to using one – smaller amounts of dried materials are required and less time is needed to complete the project. You may want to use a larger or smaller basket than that in this display, but remember to adjust the amounts of ingredients accordingly.

Dried flowers have a great deal going for them throughout the party season. You can arrange the grasses, larkspur, seedheads and everlastings some time in advance and they will last.

CREATING YOUR SINGLE-COLOUR FLOWER BASKET

MATERIALS

dried red roses (22 are used
   here)
statice
sphagnum moss
a round wicker basket
a rectangular block of
   florist's fresh foam
a prong
florist's fixative
transparent glue
florist's scissors

BASKET ON A BUDGET

By using different materials you can create an
equally stunning basket on a tighter budget. Instead
of roses use bunches of dried helichrysum in a deep
wine red or even a pale peach colour. You will need
to wire the flowerheads before arranging, however,
as the natural stems are too weak to support the
flowers. Remember, too, to buy dried or glycerined
foliage to help hide the wire stems, as dried

helichrysum has no leaves of its own. Unlike
bunches of roses, bunches of helichrysums usually
contain flowers in mixed sizes and unopened buds;
the smaller flowers and buds would be ideal for
gluing to the rim and over the handle. Or, for an
unusual effect, substitute large, wired up echinops
heads for the roses – again, remember to have
plenty of foliage on hand.

1 Fix the prong to the base of the basket with fixative and press on the foam block. Break the statice into florets and tease the moss into tufts. Make tiny bunches of moss and statice. Dot glue over the handle and press the bunches on firmly, placing them closely together.

2 Glue more bunches around the basket rim in the same way. Next, cut off 4 rose heads, leaving 15cm (½ inch) of stem attached. Dot a little glue on each stem then press the roses firmly onto the moss to form a group in the centre of the basket handle.

3 Cut the stems off several more roses (keep aside about one-third of the flowerheads for the rim and handle and use the remainder in the rest of the arrangement). Glue the flowers individually onto the handle and rim, pressing them into the moss and statice bunches.

4 Begin filling the basket. Set the height of the central 5 roses first. Here, the stems are cut to 4 inches below the flowerhead. Remove the bottom leaves and set aside for later use. Insert the roses, close together, in the centre of the foam, with the central rose the highest.

5 Make a circle of roses around the outside edge of the basket. For this size basket 15 roses are used. Cut these stems to 7.5cm (3 inches) below the flowerhead. Save the bottom leaves, as before, and insert the flowers, spaced evenly apart, into the foam block.

6 Fill in the space between the central roses and outer ring, making a dome shape. Use the curve of the handle as your guide, and keep turning the basket as you proceed. Cut these stems midway between the lengths of the other roses. Lastly, fill in any gaps with the spare leaves.

A FORMAL FLORAL DISPLAY

For a Christmas buffet table, hall table or sideboard, here is the perfect, front-facing display. The conifer sprays and holly give it that special festive touch. Although the display looks expensive (and it would be if you bought it), relatively few flowers are used, so it's surprisingly economical to make yourself.

All the flowers used in this display are available during the Christmas season, and if bought fresh and properly conditioned, should remain attractive for at least a week. When they start to fade, carefully remove them and replace them with fresh flowers, so you get more for your efforts.

Choosing the flowers

Pink lilies provide the focal point for this composition, but you could use creamy white or pure white ones instead. And although they are fairly expensive, only 3 stems are needed. Choose stems with a mixture of open flowers and buds, but make sure that the buds are showing a little colour.

Alstroemeria, or Peruvian lily, is available all year round – in spite of its deceptively summery appearance! Again, pink is used here, but alstroemeria also comes in yellow, purple, scarlet and creamy white tones, often attractively streaked, splashed or striped with second colors. Alstroemeria is often sold by the stem, so you can choose, if you prefer, flowers in colours that best fit in with your decor. As before, go for a mixture of buds and open flowers.

Choosing sedums

It is unlikely that you will find sedums growing in the garden at this time of year, but your florist should be able to order them if given plenty of advance warning. There are many colourful rockery sedums, but larger herbaceous perennial types, such as those used here, are especially valuable in arrangements. The tightly packed, flat flowerheads start as green buds (charming with summer roses), then open into starry pink flowers, ideal with autumnal asters; and finally mature to rich pink or red – perfect for winter displays.

Sedum flower stems often take root in water, so check the stems when taking the display apart and plant (in the garden) any that have rooted. Sedums are happy in sun or light shade, and any well-drained soil. Grow them either in containers or the open ground.

Even the tiniest corner flowerstalls stock a good selection of carnations, and at Christmas, red carnations are everywhere. Graceful spray carnations are used here as they are more suited to this kind of display than the larger, single-flower varieties. And though their bright red emphasizes the Christmas theme, pink, pale yellow or white carnations would be just as effective. (If you choose another colour than red, change the candle colour accordingly.) Spray carnations are sold in bunches, rather than singly, but the extra sprays are sure to come in handy over the Christmas period. Always cut carnation stems between the swollen joints, or nodes, otherwise, they won't absorb water properly.

Chincherinchees are imported from South Africa, especially at Christmas, and last for weeks in water. It is said that their unusual name comes from the sound the wind makes as it blows through their stems. Choose bunches where the lowest flowers are open, and a third of the rest are showing colour.

Spraying cones and foliage

The wired-up pine cones and lichen-covered larch branches in the display are sprayed gold with florist's spray paint designed specifically for dried and artificial flowers. Two types of foliage are needed for this arrangement. As well as fir pine, you could use sprigs of dwarf conifers or conifer hedging such as Leyland cypress or *macrocarpa* – or any other foliage that you like the look of.

This handsome, front-facing display combines the delicacy of lilies, the elegance of tall candles and the cheerfulness of gold-tinted larch branches, pine cones and holly sprigs. The striking combination of pure white, rich red and a whole spectrum of pinks is an exciting variation on the more traditional Christmas colour scheme of red and white. It would make an ideal centrepiece for a buffet table, or an eyecatching focal point on an entrance hall table.

A FORMAL FESTIVE DISPLAY

MATERIALS

1 3 dusty pink lilies
2 5 alstroemeria
3 10 chincherinchee stems
4 3 sedum stems
5 3 red carnations sprays
6 dried larch stem with cones
7 2 holly sprigs
8 3-4 fir pine sprays
9 3-4 sprays of conifer foliage
10 5-6 cones
11 glass cakestand
12 florist's foam block
13 stub wires
14 red ribbon
15 florist's gold spray
16 prong
17 florist's adhesive tape
18 wire cutters
19 4 thin red candles
20 florist's adhesive clay

DISPLAY CARE

● The unopened lily and alstroemeria buds should open after a few days. At this stage, remove or deadhead any faded, older flowerheads to give the young blooms more space. It is also important to do this because the dying blooms give off a gas that is harmful to the development of nearby flower buds, and can even prevent them from opening properly.

● The foliage of lily and alstroemeria turns yellow long before the flowers fade. To keep your display looking its best, inspect it regularly and carefully snip off any yellowing leaves. If you use cut-flower food in liquid form only add a drop; too much makes the leaves turn yellow. Never add sugar to water as it encourages the growth of bacteria.

1 Soak the foam block then, using a prong and florist's adhesive clay, fix it to the cakestand. Shape the block into 2 roughly horizontal steps, cutting a corner out of the upper step. Cut medium-strength stub wire into 12 pieces, each 7.5cm (3 inches) long. Tape 3 wires to the base of each candle, to form prongs. Firmly insert 2 candles on each level, in staggered rows.

2 Spray the pine cone, larch branches and holly gold (optional). When dry, break the larch into 15-30cm (6-12 inch) lengths. Starting on your lefthand side, insert a long piece, slightly angled downward, into the lower-level foam. Repeat on your righthand side, but angle it slightly upward. Place a third, steeply angled branch at the rear, on the right.

3 Divide the fir foliage into 7.5-15cm (3-6 inch) lengths, and the conifer foliage into 10-21cm (4-8 inch) lengths. Insert the fir sprigs horizontally into the front and sides of the block, and angled upward in the back. Insert the floppier, darker conifer foliage underneath the fir. Concentrate the large conifer sprigs on your lefthand side, to create a waterfall of greenery.

4 Remove the lily stamens and shorten the stems to 15cm (6 inch) lengths. Insert a stem facing front, between the candles, to build up the centre and set the height of the display. Shorten and insert the other stems clustered among the candles, placing 1 stem at the back. Divide the sedum heads into clusters. Insert 1 tight mass in front, 1 diagonally at the back.

5 Cut the chincherinchee stems to 5-21cm (2-8 inch) lengths. Inserting the longest stem first, create a tight cluster on your lefthand side, carrying through the diagonal line of the larch. Cut the alstroemeria stems to 7.5-15cm (3-6 inch) lengths. Insert them downward, on the rear opposite side, to balance the chincherinchees.

6 Shorten the carnation stems to 5-18cm (2-7 inch) lengths. Insert them in the centre front of the display. Run a staggered row of wired cones (see the box on wiring cones), alternating small and large, along the front, between the carnations and alstroemeria. Make 4 bows with the red ribbon, and insert them near the candle bases. Insert the holly off centre, one in front and one at the back.

FRAGRANT POT POURRI

Everyone likes their home to smell fresh and fragrant, and there is no better way to achieve this than by placing a bowl or two of fragrant pot pourri (pronounced po-poo-ree), around the house – the living room, bathroom and bedroom are the most popular locations. The range of scents that you can buy is enormous and you are sure to find one or even several that you particularly like. And now that retailers are finding out just how popular pot pourri has become, they are regularly introducing ever-more-delicious fragrances.

Origins of pot pourri

For many centuries, however, pot pourri was used for practical and medicinal purposes. In Tudor and Elizabethan times, it helped to mask unpleasant household odours, and kept linens and clothes sweet smelling. At one time, it was thought to keep illness and plagues away. Floors were strewn with dried flowers and herbs, bags of pot pourri were tied to furniture, and people carried pot pourri to ward off disease.

Today, pot pourri is decoratively displayed in bowls, glass jars or special perforated pot pourri pots. Fragrances range from delicate to intense, and from single scents – lavender for example – to richly complex ones. As well as the popular mixed-colour pot pourris, in mainly pastel hues, there are single colour pot pourris ranging from palest beige to lavender and deep rose red, to complement or tone with any colour scheme.

What is pot pourri?

Not often seen today, moist pot pourri is the original type. It is made by layering partially dried petals with salt, storing them under pressure for several weeks and adding spices, fixatives and essential oils. The name pot pourri comes from the French for "rotten pot" and refers to the fermented ingredients that make up moist pot pourri.

Flower petals are the main ingredient of pot pourri and it usually also contains fixatives and essential oils. Leaves, berries, cones, spices and even fruit may be added. There are dozens of pot pourri recipes.

Scented petals

Rose petals form the basis of most pot pourris, as they retain their fragrance and dry easily. Other scented favourites include lavender, jasmine, honeysuckle, lily-of-the-valley, sweet violet, lilac and orange blossom. Some flowers, such as cornflower and marigold, have no fragrance but provide bulk and colour.

Leaves, spices and cones

Scented-leaf geraniums and lemon verbena are popular ingredients in pot pourri, and rosemary, bay, myrtle, sweet marjoram, peppermint, lemon thyme, lemon balm or basil leaves are sometimes used. The main pot pourri spices are all-spice, nutmeg, cloves and cinnamon, and for oriental recipes, cardamom, coriander, ginger root and anise. Various conifer cones, twigs and shredded bark add an unusual texture and scent to woodland mixes and country assortments and are particularly appropriate for Christmas mixes.

Fixing the scent

Fixatives are used to absorb and hold or "fix" the fragrance of the essential plant oils, which would otherwise quickly fade. Fixatives often have a scent of their own, adding to the general richness of pot pourri. In the past, animal fixatives, ambergris from whales, musk from deer and civet from wildcats, were used. Today, vegetable fixatives are more common, such as orris from *Iris florentina* root and gum benzoin.

Concentrated perfume – essential oils

Essential oils contain concentrated natural fragrances, and reinforce delicate scents or add fragrance to flowers that have none. Many shops sell them but they must be used with care, a drop at a time, as they can be overpowering.

Making pot pourri last

Good pot pourri can last for years, but it benefits from being stored and used with care. When the scent starts to fade, add a reviver essence or essential oil.

A selection of pot pourri (clockwise from top left)

SWEET ROSE
Richly coloured and sweetly scented mix of fruit and flowers.

LAVENDER
Just lavender flowers, to give the simple, fresh fragrance of summer.

EDWARDIAN
A fresh forest fragrance with pine cones, mountain ash berries and camomile.

BRIAR ROSE
Contains pink rose-buds and petals with a delicate, traditional perfume.

COUNTRY SPICE
Contains rosemary and coriander. A very spicy herbal assortment.

CITRUS
A sharp, citrus aroma from a mix of orange peel and lemon verbena.

STRAWBERRY
A summer offering of nettle and rose, with a heady strawberry scent.

WOODS AND BALSAM
A clean-smelling assortment of sandalwood, cedar and balsam.

ORIENTAL
A dry sweet-scented mixture of eastern spices.

FRESH YELLOW
A bulky selection of flowerheads with a light, spring fragrance.

FESTIVE FARE

 FOOD FIT FOR THE HOLIDAYS

All cooks know the pleasure food gives, and that is why Christmas dinner and other holiday meals are such important parts of the season. All too often, though, the joys that come from such feastings are savoured only by the guests, not by the person who made it all possible – the cook. Preparing meals worthy of the occasion is a lot of work! The stress effect of planning menus, shopping and then cooking can dampen holiday spirits and dull the keenest of appetites.

The best host or hostess is someone who is having as good a time as the guests. This means feeling relaxed and having time to enjoy the company of the people you've gathered together. Remember those priorities when you gear up for Christmas meals and let them guide you in your plans. Consider the menu carefully. Unless you're a super cook, don't attempt to make every dish a star attraction. Have one or two show stoppers if you like, and make the rest the supporting cast. Common sense will tell you to balance rich dishes with lighter ones, simple ones with those that are more complex.

Organize your menu so that at least half of the dishes can be made before the day you'll be serving them. And practise new dishes on your family before you serve them to guests, unless you thrive on risk-taking and are not put off by the possibility of last-minute disasters.

Then make yourself a promise: This year you really, *really* will plan ahead. Start early. Make lists and maybe even a time plan, keeping in mind other projects and social commitments. Get as much of the shopping out of the way as early as you can. Cook and freeze, and cook and pack away in the larder if possible. Keep reminding yourself that a relaxed cook is a happy cook, and a more gracious host or hostess. Remember, above all, that this is your holiday time too.

PLANNING AHEAD
As soon as your Christmas entertaining plans have been finalized and a menu roughed out, draw up a shopping list, dividing it into larder and freezer items that can be bought well in advance when the stores are not so crowded, and perishable items that need to be bought nearer the time.

Perishable foods
Storage can be a problem for these, as refrigerator space always seems to be quite inadequate at Christmas. However, many perishable foods, especially vegetables, can be successfully stored, provided they are carefully wrapped and protected, in a cold, dry place away from centrally heated rooms.

A Christmas dinner to remember!

The Storecupboard

You may keep many of these foods on hand regularly, but it's not a bad idea to check your shelves before December comes and stock up on some extras. No need to have to add these good-keeping items to last-minute shopping trips.

Dried beans and peas: a good supply of these is invaluable for soups and casseroles, which make excellent family fare between the festive meals. Include some of the quicker-cooking ones, like split peas.

Canned beans and peas: a selection of red kidney beans, haricot beans, butter beans, chick peas, etc. is very useful for salads and dips.

Dried pasta: make sure you have spaghetti in stock and one or two interesting shapes like bows or shells: a steaming bowl of pasta can make a change from rich food.

Canned chestnut purée: excellent for stuffings. The sweetened variety makes a wonderful instant dessert, whipped up with cream, or a filling for Christmas log cake.

Olives: canned or bottled olives – include some stuffed ones, and the small black Greek olives, which have a specially good flavour – are an extremely useful larder item, for serving with Christmas drinks, or garnishing.

Nuts: assorted salted nuts, in cans or bags, are always popular as cocktail nibbles. Unsalted nuts, particularly blanched almonds, Brazils, hazelnuts and walnuts, are useful for salads, and for decorating desserts. A bowl of mixed nuts in their shells – make sure you've got a nutcracker! – looks very attractive on the Christmas table. Don't forget ground almonds for almond paste.

Biscuits: you will need plenty of these, for serving with cheese, or as a base for canapés.

Mincemeat: you may be making your own, but a jar or two is always handy for emergency mince pies.

Dried and preserved fruit: you will need a good supply of these for puddings and cakes.

Cranberry sauce: even if you are making your own, it's a good idea to have some canned cranberry sauce on hand; it's a nice accompaniment to cold sliced turkey and many hot dishes made from leftover turkey.

Drinks: lay in Christmas wines and spirits, mineral water, mixers and fruit juice.

Freezer foods

Depending on the capacity of your freezer, all the following foods could be usefully bought in advance and frozen until Christmas:

FREEZER LIFE

Turkey	6 months
Goose	4 months
Duck	6 months
Beef roast	8 months
Smoked ham	6 weeks
Bacon	6-8 weeks
Smoked salmon	6 months
Vegetables such as Brussels sprouts, peas, broccoli spears	12 months
Cranberries and other berries	12 months
Butter (unsalted)	6 months
Butter (salted)	3 months
Cream	3 months
Pastry (unbaked)	3 months
Bread (baked)	6 months

Freezer Christmas cooking

Make optimum use of your freezer, not only to store ready-frozen ingredients but also to stock up on many of the dishes, either fully or partially cooked, that you'll be serving over Christmas. Any of the following make invaluable additions to the freezer, from the beginning of November:

Soups, stocks and sauces
Casseroles
Vegetable purées
Chopped herbs
Breadcrumbs and stuffings
Mincemeat
Pastry shells (baked or unbaked)
Mince pies (baked or unbaked)
Sponge cake for trifle
Ice cream and sorbet

The months before christmas

Cooking for Christmas can usefully begin as far as 3 months in advance.

October: Make Christmas pudding and fruit cake.

November: Start cooking for the freezer.

December: Begin making Christmas biscuits. About 1 week before Christmas, make stuffings, mayonnaise and salad dressings and store well covered in the refrigerator.

Start thawing a large frozen turkey the day before Christmas Eve in a cool place – but not in the refrigerator.

Few people nowadays buy a really huge turkey at Christmas. It is a good idea to buy a relatively small bird and eat off it twice, once hot and once cold, using the remains to make a good soup.

A complete recipe for roasting a turkey can be found later, as part of the traditional Christmas Day menu. Here you will find some useful facts, figures and tips to help you make the most of your turkey.

BUYING AND PREPARING THE BIRD

Turkey is the most popular choice of Christmas poultry because unlike goose and duck, which are at their best hot, turkey is equally good hot or cold, and can feed a crowd.

Here is a rough guide to help you work out the correct size turkey to buy:

OVEN-READY WEIGHT	SERVINGS
6-8 lb	6-10
10-13lb	12-20
14-20lb	20-30

A 10-lb bird will yield about 5 lb 8 oz meat. It would serve 8 people as a hot meal, with enough for seconds, plus another 4-6 servings as cold cuts.

Whatever the weight of turkey you decide, on, do make sure that it will fit inside your oven! If you are planning to feed a great many people over Christmas, you might find it easier to buy 2 smaller birds and cook one in advance to keep for a later buffet, for example.

AT ROOM TEMPERATURE

OVEN-READY WEIGHT	THAWING TIME
2.7-3.6kg (6-8 lb)	16 hours
4.5kg (10 lb)	18 hours
6.8kg (15 lb)	24 hours
9kg (20 lb)	30 hours

Fresh or frozen?
The big advantage of a frozen bird is that it can be kept in the freezer, leaving you free of that nagging worry that you may not get to the stores before stocks run out! You may like to buy one of the self-basting, "butter-ball" birds, which yield specially moist, succulent meat. Frozen turkey needs very careful thawing (see below) and once thawed must on no account be refrozen.

Many people prefer to buy a fresh turkey, in which case it is highly advisable to order it in advance, and of course you must make sure that you have room to store it in the refrigerator or other place at a temperature of no more than 4°C (40°F).

Thawing frozen turkey
It is most important that turkey should be thoroughly thawed in its bag, and the liquid drained off as it is exuded. Take a small turkey out of the freezer early on Christmas Eve, or on December 23 if it is a large bird, over 6.8kg (15 lb). *Do not thaw in the refrigerator.*

Thawing in the microwave
The freezer bag must be pierced and the metal tag removed before placing the turkey in the microwave. Allow 10-12 minutes per 450g (1 lb) on LOW, then drain off any liquid and stand the bird, still in its bag, in cold water for 2-3 hours.

Stuffing a turkey
Allow about 50g (2 oz) stuffing per 450g (1 lb) of turkey (oven-ready weight). Stuff the bird at the neck end only just before cooking. Do not pack the stuffing too tightly, and do not stuff the vent end, or the bird will not cook properly in the calculated time (see page 115). Any leftover stuffing can be baked in a separate casserole dish or shaped into small balls and cooked separately, either in the oven with the turkey or shallow fried.

There are many delicious traditional stuffings but its nice to try something new, too. The Christmas Day menu, later, includes two stuffings, a favourite, Pecan Stuffing, and a new Sweetcorn and Honey Stuffing. After stuffing, the turkey is ready to roast.

CHRISTMAS FEAST COUNTDOWN

Christmas Day is so full of excitement, with the opening of presents and the arrival of guests, that planning and cooking before Christmas Day will ensure that a lot of the food needs only heating through to make a feast to remember.

Christmas Eve: Prepare Watercress Creams, Chocolate Truffles.

Thaw Stuffings, Cranberry Sauce, Baby Onions and Chestnuts, Strawberry Mousse Cake.

Peel potatoes, parsnips, sprouts and carrots. Keep the potatoes in cold water to prevent browning and wrap the other vegetables in plastic bags and chill.

Christmas Day: 9:00 am Heat the oven to 160°C, (325°F), Gas Mark 3: Stuff and prepare the 5.4kg (12 lb) turkey, wrap in foil and put in the oven.

11:00 am Begin steaming the Christmas pudding. Baste the turkey.

12:00 am Put the potatoes and parsnips to roast on top shelf of the oven. Decorate the Strawberry Mousse Cake.

12:15 pm Arrange Watercress Creams on serving plates. Garnish, cover with cling film and chill.

12:30 pm Baste the turkey. Remove the foil and raise the oven to 200°C, (400°F), Gas Mark 6. Prepare the garnishes.

12:45 pm Put the Cocktail Sausages and Bacon Rolls in the oven.

1:00 pm Test the turkey and remove to a serving dish if ready. Cover with foil to keep warm. Heat the Casseroled Onions and Chestnuts, and the Cranberry Sauce.

Make gravy, pour into a gravy boat and keep warm. If you are having red wine with the turkey, open the bottle to allow the wine to breathe.

1:15 pm Cook the Buttered Sprouts with Almonds and the Orange-Glazed Carrots. Place the vegetables in serving dishes and keep warm. Make Brandy Sabayon Sauce and keep warm. Carve the turkey.

1:30 pm Serve the first course.

MENU

Watercress Creams

Roast Turkey with Two stuffings
Wine Gravy
Cranberry Sauce
Cocktail Sausages with Bacon Rolls
Roast Potatoes
Roast Parsnips
Buttered Brussels Sprouts with Almonds
Casseroled Baby Onions and Chestnuts
Orange-Glazed Carrots

Christmas Pudding with Brandy Sabayon Sauce
Strawberry Mousse Cake

CHRISTMAS DAY DINNER
This elegant dinner is as special as the occasion. Several of the dishes can be made ahead and frozen, namely the stuffings, Cranberry Sauce, Baby Onions and Chestnuts and the Strawberry Mousse Cake. See the box, Christmas Feast Countdown, for a suggested schedule for pacing yourself through food preparation and cooking.

CLOCKWISE FROM TOP Roast Potatoes, Roast Parsnips and Orange-Glazed Carrots; Rich and Boozy Christmas Pudding; Brandy Sabayon Sauce; Watercress Creams; Roast Turkey with Wine Gravy, Pecan Stuffing, Sweetcorn and Honey Stuffing, Cocktail Sausages in Bacon Rolls, Buttered Brussels Sprouts and Cranberry Sauce; Casseroled Baby Onions and Chestnuts.

WATERCRESS CREAMS

You might like to pour the purée into individual ramekins to set instead of letting it set in 1 large bowl and then scooping it out to serve. Also, try serving garnished with twists or slices of lime instead of lemon. Serves 6-8.

INGREDIENTS
450ml (¾ pint) strongly flavoured chicken or vegetable stock
4 bunches watercress, trimmed
20g (¾ oz) powdered gelatine
3 tablespoons water (or stock)
freshly ground black pepper
finely grated rind of ½ lemon
1 teaspoon lemon juice
150ml (¼ pint) sour cream or yogurt
100g (4 oz) curd, cottage or cream cheese

TO GARNISH
watercress sprigs
lemon twists
Melba toast

METHOD
1 Bring the stock to a boil, add the watercress and simmer gently for 4 minutes.
2 Blend the watercress and stock together in a blender or food processor until smooth.
3 Sprinkle the gelatine over the water in a bowl, set it over a pan of hot water and stir until the gelatine is completely dissolved.
4 Allow the gelatine to cool, then blend into the watercress purée with the pepper, lemon rind and juice. Finally, add the sour cream or yogurt and cheese. Check the seasoning and adjust if necessary.
5 Pour the purée into a bowl and allow to set in the refrigerator for 1 hour. Serve the watercress cream in scoops on plates, garnished with sprigs of watercress and lemon twists. Serve with Melba toast.

ROAST TURKEY
Serves 8-12.

INGREDIENTS
5.4 kg (12 lb) turkey
50g (2 oz) dripping or butter, melted
salt
freshly ground black pepper

METHOD
1 Heat oven 160°C, 325°F, Gas Mark 3.
2 Wash the turkey and pat dry with kitchen paper.
3 Spoon the stuffings into the neck and body cavity of the turkey. Sew up both openings with trussing string, or secure with skewers. Weigh the stuffed bird and calculate the cooking time at 15 minutes per 450g (1 lb), plus 15 minutes.
4 Brush with dripping and season. Place on a rack in a roasting tin and cover with foil. Roast for the calculated time; baste and turn occasionally. Remove the foil for the last 15 minutes. To test, pierce a thigh with a skewer; it is done when the juices run clear.

Remove from the oven and transfer to a heated serving plate. Remove the string or skewers and keep the turkey warm by covering it with a piece of foil.

SWEETCORN AND HONEY STUFFING
This recipe makes enough to stuff 1 cavity of a 5.4kg (12 lb) bird.

INGREDIENTS
200g (7 oz) can sweetcorn, drained
grated rind and juice of 1 lemon
2 tablespoons clear honey
1 dessert apple, grated
100g (4 oz) fresh brown breadcrumbs
1 egg yolk
salt
freshly ground black pepper

METHOD
Combine all the ingredients in a bowl and season to taste. The mixture should be moist and stick together without being sloppy.

PECAN STUFFING

This recipe makes enough to stuff 1 cavity of a 5.4kg (12 lb) bird.

INGREDIENTS
heart and liver from the turkey
50g (2 oz) fresh breadcrumbs
50g (2 oz) shelled pecan nuts, finely chopped
1 egg, hardboiled and chopped
pinch each of nutmeg, ground mace, dried thyme
1 tablespoon chopped fresh parsley
pinch of celery salt
40g (1½ oz) butter
50g (2 oz) mushrooms, wiped and chopped
1 small onion, peeled and chopped
2 tablespoons sherry
freshly ground black pepper

METHOD
1 Put the meat in a pan, cover with water and cook for 10 minutes. Drain, chop finely, and cool.
2 Put the meat in a bowl and add the breadcrumbs, nuts, egg, spices, herbs and celery salt.
3 Melt the butter in a pan, sauté the mushrooms and onion until soft. Stir into the meat, add sherry and season.

ROAST POTATOES

These delicious potatoes are brown and a bit crispy on the outside and tender in the middle. Serves 8.

INGREDIENTS
12 medium potatoes
salted water
cooking fat, or a combination of butter and vegetable oil
salt
freshly ground black pepper

METHOD
1 Peel potatoes and cut them to approximately similar sizes.
2 Parboil in salted water, drain, then put into a small roasting pan.

3 Dot with pieces of cooking fat or a combination of butter and vegetable oil, season and place in the oven with the turkey, until browned.

ROAST PARSNIPS

A simple dish that can be roasted with the turkey. Serves 8.

INGREDIENTS
1kg (2 lb) parsnips (about 8 medium-sized)
salted water
dripping or butter (melted)
salt
freshly ground black pepper
chopped parsley to garnish

METHOD
1 Peel, quarter and slice the parsnips, then cook in boiling, salted water for 5 minutes.
2 Drain and place in a small roasting pan. Pour over dripping or butter, season, and roast for approximately ¾ hour. Garnish with chopped parsley.

BUTTERED BRUSSELS SPROUTS WITH ALMONDS

Simple Brussels sprouts dressed up with almonds. Serves 8.

INGREDIENTS
50g (2 oz) butter
50g (2 oz) flaked almonds
1kg (2 lb) Brussels sprouts, trimmed

METHOD
1 Melt the butter in a small pan until foaming. Add the almonds and sauté until golden but do not allow the butter to burn.
2 Cook the Brussels sprouts in boiling water until just tender. Drain. Return to a clean pan with the butter and almonds and toss to coat. Serve immediately.

CASSEROLED BABY ONIONS AND CHESTNUTS

Roasted chestnuts blend beautifully with tiny onions in this sidedish. Serves 6.

INGREDIENTS
450g (1 lb) chestnuts
50g (2 oz) butter
450g (1 lb) pearl onions
300ml (½ pint) chicken stock
1 teaspoon sugar
freshly ground black pepper

METHOD
1   Heat oven 180°C, 350°F, Gas Mark 4.
2   Make a slit in the skin of each chestnut and boil them for 5 minutes. Peel the chestnuts while warm, removing the outer and inner skins. Set aside.
3   Melt the butter in a small flameproof casserole dish. Add the onions and cook for 3 minutes without browning. Pour in the stock, cover and bake in the oven for 30 minutes until tender.
4   Add the chestnuts, sugar and pepper and simmer, uncovered, until the liquid is reduced to a glaze. Serve hot.

ORANGE-GLAZED CARROTS

Be careful not to cook these in too much water or else the carrots will be mushy and lose their bright colour. Serves 8.

INGREDIENTS
1kg (2 lb) young carrots
50g (2 oz) butter
salt
freshly ground black pepper
pinch of sugar
300ml (½ pint) orange juice
butter, to garnish
chopped parsley, to garnish

METHOD
1   Peel or scrape carrots and quarter them lengthwise.
2   Melt a little butter in a pan, add the carrots and season. Add a pinch of sugar and just enough water to cover.
3   Cook slowly, uncovered. As the water evaporates, add the orange juice. Cook until the carrots are tender and the liquid has evaporated, leaving a slight glaze.
4   Serve with a pat of butter, and sprinkle with chopped parsley.

RICH AND BOOZY CHRISTMAS PUDDING

This makes a large pudding that will serve 8.

INGREDIENTS
175g (6 oz) currants
175g (6 oz) raisins
100g (4 oz) sultanas
juice and grated rind of ½ orange
grated rind of ½ lemon
175g (6 oz) fresh brown breadcrumbs
50g (2 oz) blanched almonds, chopped
½ teaspoon freshly grated nutmeg
½ teaspoon cinnamon
50g (2 oz) soft dark brown sugar
2 eggs, beaten
2 tablespoons brandy
2 tablespoons port
2 tablespoons rum
100g (4 oz) unsalted butter, melted and cooled
holly sprig, to decorate

METHOD
1   Mix together the dried fruit, orange and lemon rind, breadcrumbs, nuts, spices, and sugar. Whisk together the orange juice, eggs, spirits and melted butter. Stir the 2 mixtures together and mix well.
2   Turn into a 1.2 litre (2 pint) buttered pudding basin. Leave to stand for 1 hour.
3   Cover the basin with double, greased greaseproof paper, pleating the edges to allow for expansion. Then cover with foil, pleating the edges to secure. Tie securely with string. Steam the pudding for 7 hours, adding boiling water to the steamer or saucepan as necessary. If you are using a pressure cooker, place the bowl on a trivet and add 2 litres (3½ pints) of boiling water. Fit the lid and steam without pressure for 30 minutes. Bring to high pressure and cook for

3 hours. Reduce the pressure slowly. When cooked, allow to cool completely. Replace the paper and foil with fresh wrappings. Store in a cool, dry place, or freeze. Use within 1 year.

To reheat, steam for 2½ hours, cook at high pressure for 30 minutes in a pressure cooker and reduce the pressure slowly, or microwave for 4-6 minutes and allow to stand for 5 minutes. Remove the papers and turn out onto a hot serving dish. Decorate with a sprig of holly to serve.

BRANDY SABAYON SAUCE

Serve warm with Christmas pudding.

INGREDIENTS
4 egg yolks
4 tablespoons caster sugar
4 tablespoons brandy
juice and grated rind of ½ lemon
6 tablespoons orange juice
shredded peel, to garnish

METHOD
1   Whisk the egg yolks and sugar together in the top of a double boiler over hot water until light and frothy. Whisking continuously, gradually pour in the brandy, lemon juice and rind, and the orange juice. Continue whisking over the hot water until the sauce is thick and fluffy.
2   Garnish with shredded orange peel.

STRAWBERRY MOUSSE CAKE

This cake may be made ahead of time and frozen for up to 1 month. Thaw in the refrigerator overnight. Serves 6-8.

INGREDIENTS
2 eggs
50g (2 oz) caster sugar
50g (2 oz) plain flour
few drops of almond essence
2 teaspoons boiling water
2 tablespoons orange juice
2 tablespoons marsala or sweet sherry

FOR THE MOUSSE
50g (2 oz) cottage cheese, sieved
50g (2 oz) cream cheese, softened
50g (2 oz) caster sugar
1 egg, separated
juice and finely grated rind of ½ lemon
175g (6 oz) frozen strawberries
1 tablespoon gelatine
3 tablespoons water
150ml (¼ pint) whipping cream, whipped
sliced strawberries to decorate

METHOD
1   Preheat the oven to 220°C, 425°F, Gas Mark 7. Whisk the eggs and sugar together in a bowl over a pan of hot water until very thick and light.
2   Sift the flour 3 times and sprinkle over the surface of the egg mixture. Gently fold in the almond essence and boiling water. Pour into a greased, lined Swiss roll tin. Bake in the oven for 8-10 minutes or until golden and risen. Turn out onto a wire rack to cool.
3   Line the base and ends of a 1kg (2 lb) loaf tin with greaseproof paper. Trim one half of the cooked sponge to fit the base of the loaf tin. Blend the orange juice and marsala and sprinkle half of it over the sponge in the tin.
4   For the mousse, beat together the cheeses, sugar and egg yolk. Stir in the lemon rind and juice. Press the strawberries through a sieve onto the cheese mixture, stir well.
5   Sprinkle the gelatine over the water in a small bowl and stir well until completely dissolved over a pan of hot water. Cool thoroughly and blend into the mousse. Beat the egg white until stiff. Reserving 4-5 tablespoons of the whipped cream, fold the remaining cream into the mousse. Finally, fold in the beaten egg white.
6   Pour the mousse over the sponge in the tin. Chill until it begins to set. Trim the remaining piece of sponge to fit on top of the mousse in the loaf tin. Sprinkle with the remaining orange juice and marsala and place the cake on top of the mousse, pressing down. Chill, and allow to set firm.

To serve: run a knife around the mousse and turn out onto a serving plate. Remove the paper and pipe the reserved cream down the centre. Decorate with slices of strawberry.

ALTERNATIVE CHRISTMAS DINNER

While there are not as many dishes in this Christmas dinner menu, the pheasants roasted with chestnuts and served with stuffing balls make it very special indeed, as do the lovely desserts.

GREEN SOUP

A rich, smooth soup that makes the most of winter vegetables. Serves 10.

INGREDIENTS
75g (3 oz) butter or margarine
3 large leeks, about 750g (1½ lb) trimmed and sliced
450g (1 lb) Brussels sprouts, trimmed and shredded
2 litres (3½ pints) chicken stock
2 tablespoons lemon juice
2 teaspoons Worcestershire sauce
pinch of ground mace
salt, freshly ground black pepper
450ml (¾ pint) milk or ½ milk and ½ cream
fried onion rings, to garnish
toasted slices of French bread, to garnish

METHOD
1 Melt the butter in a saucepan, add the leeks and sauté over a gentle heat for 5 minutes, stirring occasionally.
2 Add the Brussels sprouts, stir well, then add the stock, lemon juice, Worcestershire sauce, mace and salt and pepper and bring to the boil.
3 Cover the pan and simmer for 20-25 minutes or until the vegetables are very tender. Cool slightly, then purée in a food processor or blender, or pass through a sieve.
4 Return the soup to the rinsed-out pan the milk. Return to the boil, taste and adjust the seasoning. Serve the soup in warmed individual bowls, garnished with fried onion rings and accompanied by toasted slices of French bread.

MENU
Green Soup

Pheasants in Red Wine with Chestnuts
Scalloped Potatoes
Tangy Red Cabbage

Shortbread Meringue Gateau
Choc au Rhum Mousse

PHEASANTS IN RED WINE WITH CHESTNUTS

Bring the roasted pheasants to the table whole, as pictured, and carve them at the table. Serves 10.

INGREDIENTS
4 oven-ready young pheasants
salt
freshly ground black pepper
3 tablespoons oil
2 large onions, peeled and sliced
2 tablespoons plain flour
450ml (¾ pint) red wine
450ml (¾ pint) beef stock
1 tablespoon black treacle
3-4 tablespoons brandy (optional)
1 bay leaf
440g (15½ oz) canned whole peeled chestnuts, drained

STUFFING BALLS
2 onions, peeled and very finely chopped
175g (6 oz) celery, very finely chopped
50g (2 oz) butter or margarine
2 tablespoons chopped fresh parsley
2 teaspoons dried thyme
350g (12 oz) fresh white breadcrumbs
2 eggs, beaten
a little lemon juice (optional)
parsley sprigs, to garnish

METHOD
1 Wipe the pheasants inside and out and season well with salt and pepper. Heat the oil

LEFT TO RIGHT: Pheasants in Red Wine with Chestnuts, Tangy Red Cabbage, Scalloped Potatoes

in a large frying pan, add the pheasants one at a time and fry, turning, to brown all over. Transfer to a large roasting tin.

2   Add the onions to the pan and sauté over a gentle heat for about 7 minutes until lightly browned. Sprinkle in the flour and cook for 1-2 minutes. Gradually stir in the wine and stock and bring to a boil. Stir in the treacle and brandy if using, season well with salt and pepper and add the bay leaf. Simmer for 2 minutes.

3   Preheat oven 180°C, 350°F, Gas Mark 4.

4   Add the chestnuts and pour the contents of the pan over the pheasants. Cover with foil and cook in a preheated oven for about 1¼ hours or until tender and cooked thoroughly.

5   Meanwhile make the stuffing balls: melt the butter in a frying pan, add the onion and celery and sauté over a gentle heat until soft. Turn into a bowl, season well with salt and pepper and add the herbs. Add the bread-crumbs and stir in the eggs to bind, with a little lemon juice if using. Form the mixture into 20 balls.

6   Arrange the stuffing balls in a greased tin and cook above the pheasants for the last 30 minutes of cooking time.

7   Transfer the pheasants to a large warmed serving dish. Garnish with the stuffing balls and parsley sprigs. Discard the bay leaf from the tin and pour the juices with the onions and chestnuts into heated sauce boats. Pass separately with the carved pheasants.

SCALLOPED POTATOES

These potatoes can be cooked in the morning and then heated up and grilled before serving, if you wish. Serves 10.

INGREDIENTS

1.75kg (4 lb) potatoes, peeled and thinly sliced
3 onions, peeled and thinly sliced
salt, freshly ground black pepper
300ml (½ pint) beef stock
250g (1 oz) butter, melted
2 tablespoons fresh chopped parsley

METHOD

1   Preheat oven 180°C, 350°F, Gas Mark 4.

2   Make layers of the potatoes and onions in a well-greased ovenproof dish and season with salt and pepper.

3   Bring the stock to a boil and pour over the potatoes, then brush liberally with the melted butter.

4   Cover with foil and cook in a preheated oven for 1½ hours. Remove the foil and cook for another 30 minutes or until cooked through and lightly browned.

5   Place under a moderate grill until the potatoes are well browned and crispy on top. Sprinkle with parsley and serve hot.

TANGY RED CABBAGE

The cabbage may be transferred to a casserole at step 2 and cooked in a 180°C, 350°F, Gas Mark 4 oven for 1 hour. Serves 10.

INGREDIENTS

2 tablespoons vegetable oil
1 large onion, peeled and thinly sliced
1.5kg (3 lb) red cabbage, finely shredded
(about 12 cups)
1 large cooking apple, peeled, cored and chopped
4 tablespoons red wine vinegar
3-4 tablespoons water
3 tablespoons soft light brown sugar
salt, freshly ground black pepper

METHOD

1 Heat the oil in a large saucepan, add the onion and sauté over a gentle heat for about 5 minutes until soft and lightly coloured.
2 Add the cabbage, apple, vinegar and water to the pan. Stir well to mix and cook gently, stirring frequently, until beginning to soften. Add the sugar and season with salt and pepper. Mix well. Cover and simmer for 30 minutes, stirring from time to time.
3 Add 2-3 tablespoons water if the pan shows signs of drying out and cook for another 30 minutes. Check the seasoning and transfer to a warmed serving dish.

SHORTBREAD MERINGUE GÂTEAU

Everything can be prepared in advance for this dessert, but it should not be assembled more than 2 hours before serving. Serves 8-10.

INGREDIENTS

MERINGUE

2 egg whites
50g (2 oz) caster sugar
50g (2 oz) soft light brown sugar

SHORTBREAD

125g (5 oz) plain flour
25g (1 oz) custard powder
100g (4 oz) butter
50g (2 oz) demerara sugar

CRÈME PATISSIÈRE

2 egg yolks
50g (2 oz) caster sugar
20g (¾ oz) plain flour
15g (½ oz) cornflour
300ml (½ pint) milk
a few drops of vanilla essence
10g (¼ oz) butter

FILLING

450 g (1 lb) fresh apricots or 2 × 425g (15 oz) cans apricot halves, drained
300ml (½ pint) double or whipping cream
angelica

METHOD

1 Make the meringue: whisk the egg whites until very stiff, sift the sugars together twice, then whisk into the egg whites, a little at a time, making sure the meringue is stiff again before the next addition.
2 Preheat oven 110°C, 225°F, Gas Mark ¼.
3 Draw a 22-23cm (8½-9-inch) circle on a piece of non-stick silicone paper and place on a baking sheet. Spread or pipe the meringue to cover the circle. Bake in a preheated oven for about 2 hours or until crisp and dry. Remove from the oven and leave to cool.
4 Raise oven to 180°C, 350°F, Gas Mark 4.
5 Make the shortbread: sift the flour with the custard powder into a bowl, add the butter and sugar and work together with the hands to make a smooth dough. Roll out a quarter of the dough on a lightly floured board or work surface and cut into 10 × 4cm (1½ inch) circles, using a fluted cutter. Place on a baking sheet lined with non-stick silicone paper and prick all over with a fork.
6 Press the remaining dough into the base of a lightly greased 23-24cm (9-9½ inch) fluted loose-based flan tin. Prick all over.
7 Bake the shortbread circles and base in a preheated oven, with the circles on the lower shelf, allowing 15-20 minutes for the circles and 30-35 minutes for the base. Remove from the oven and leave to firm up, then transfer to a wire rack and leave until cold.
8 Make the crème patissière: whisk the egg yolks with the sugar in a bowl, then beat in the flour, cornflour and a little of the milk until smooth. Heat the remaining milk in a sauce-

pan, pour onto the egg mixture and return to the pan. Cook gently, stirring continuously, until the mixture comes to a boil and thickens. Remove from the heat and beat in the vanilla essence and the butter. Cover and allow to cool.

9   If using fresh apricots, halve and remove the stones and put on a plate. Dredge lightly with caster sugar and leave to stand for 30 minutes or so.

10   To assemble: whip the cream until stiff and fold half into the crème patissière. Reserve 10 of the best apricot halves and slice the remainder, then fold into the cream mixture. Place the shortbread base on a serving plate and top with about two-thirds of the apricot cream. Cover with the meringue disk and spread the remaining apricot mixture in the centre.

11   Put the remaining whipped cream into a piping bag fitted with a vegetable star nozzle and pipe 10 large and 10 smaller whorls of cream evenly around the edge of the meringue. Top the small whorls with apricot halves and the larger ones with shortbread circles. Decorate with pieces of angelica.

CHOCOLATE AU RHUM MOUSSE

This rich chocolate mousse provides a striking visual contrast to the meringue gâteau. Serves 8-10.

INGREDIENTS
350g (12 oz) plain dark chocolate, broken into pieces
2 tablespoons rum
3 tablespoons water
175g (6 oz) butter
175g (6 oz) caster sugar
6 eggs, separated
150ml (¼ pint) whipping cream
ratafia biscuits or pieces of stem ginger, to decorate

METHOD

1   Put the chocolate in a double boiler with gently simmering water in the bottom. Add the rum and water and heat gently until the chocolate melts, stirring until quite smooth. Allow to cool slightly.

2   Cream the butter and sugar together in a large bowl until very light and fluffy, then beat in the egg yolks one at a time.

3   Add the melted chocolate mixture and beat until light and fluffy.

4   Whisk the egg whites until stiff but not too dry and fold evenly through the chocolate mixture, using a large metal spoon.

5   Pour into a serving dish or 8-10 glasses and chill in the refrigerator overnight until set.

6   Decorate with whirls of whipped cream and ratafia biscuits or pieces of stem ginger.

LEFT Choc au Rhum Mousse; RIGHT Shortbread Meringue Gâteau.

TURKEY LEFTOVERS

Turkey is the ideal food for feasting because it feeds lots of people and makes for great leftovers. Here are some new recipes to add to your post-Christmas menus.

TURKEY SOUP

For a thicker, smoother soup, strain, blend or purée it in a food processor. The stock may be cooled and frozen for up to 2 months, or the complete soup may be frozen for up to 2 months. Serves 10-12.

INGREDIENTS
1 turkey carcass
1 onion, peeled and quartered; 2 onions, peeled and finely chopped
4 carrots, scraped and halved
1 bay leaf
2.25 litres (4 pints) water
2 leeks, trimmed and finely chopped
225g (8 oz) parsnips, peeled and finely chopped
2 celery sticks, finely chopped
1 tablespoon Worcestershire sauce
25g (1 oz) long-grain rice
salt, freshly ground black pepper
50g (2 oz) plain flour
50g (2 oz) butter or margarine
150ml (1/4 pint) single cream (optional)

METHOD
1 Break up the carcass and put it into a large saucepan with the onion quarters, carrots, bay leaf and water. Bring to a boil, remove any scum from the surface, cover and simmer for 1½ hours.
2 Strain off the stock. Reserve 2-2.5 litres (3¼-4 pints). Strip off any turkey trimmings and chop finely with the cooked carrots.
3 Place the carrots and turkey trimmings in a clean saucepan with the reserved stock, all the remaining vegetables, the Worcestershire sauce, rice and salt and pepper to taste. Bring to a boil, then lower the heat and simmer gently for 30 minutes, stirring occasionally.
4 Cream the flour and fat together and gradually whisk into the soup, whisking well between each addition. Return to a boil for 5 minutes. Stir in the cream, if using, and serve.

QUICK TURKEY HOLLANDAISE

A delicious main-dish casserole that can easily be doubled or tripled to feed a crowd. Serves 4.

INGREDIENTS
225g (8 oz) frozen broccoli spears
salt
8 slices cooked turkey meat, about 350g (12 oz)
1 × 300g (10 oz) can chicken soup
2 tablespoons lemon juice
2-3 tablespoons dry white wine
4 tablespoons thick mayonnaise
freshly ground black pepper
25-40g (1-1½ oz) fresh white breadcrumbs
25-40g (1-1½ oz) Cheddar cheese, grated

METHOD
1 Preheat oven 220°C, 425°F, Gas Mark 7.
2 Cook the broccoli in a saucepan of boiling salted water for 2-3 minutes, then drain and arrange in a greased shallow ovenproof dish.
3 Arrange the turkey slices over the broccoli.
4 Combine the chicken soup, lemon juice, wine and mayonnaise and season well with salt and pepper. Pour this mixture evenly over the turkey.
5 Mix the breadcrumbs with the cheese and sprinkle evenly over the surface of the dish.
6 Cook towards the top of a preheated oven for 25-30 minutes until bubbling and golden brown. Serve at once.

TURKEY AND SPINACH PANCAKES

The pancakes may be made 2-3 days in advance, making this dish ideal for the busy Christmas season. The filling may be made 24 hours in advance. Serves 4.

PANCAKE BUTTER
100g (4 oz) plain flour
pinch of salt
2 eggs
275ml (scant ½ pint) milk
lard or cooking oil, for frying

FILLING

50g (2 oz) butter or margarine
1 onion, peeled and chopped
2 tablespoons plain flour
300ml (1/2 pint) milk or chicken stock
salt
freshly ground black pepper
1/4 teaspoon ground nutmeg
225g (8 oz) frozen chopped spinach, cooked and drained
300g (10 oz) cooked turkey meat, chopped
40g (1 1/2 oz) shelled walnuts, chopped (optional)

SAUCE

40g (1 1/2 oz) butter or margarine
40g (1 1/2 oz) plain flour
300ml (1/2 pint) apple cider
150ml (1/4 pint) milk
1 teaspoon prepared English mustard
40g (1 1/2 oz) Cheddar cheese, grated

METHOD

1 Make the pancakes: sift the flour with the salt into a mixing bowl. Make a well in the centre, add the eggs and gradually add the milk, drawing the flour into the liquid with a wooden spoon and beat until smooth.

2 Grease a small frying pan with lard or oil, drain off the excess and use the batter to make 8 pancakes in the usual way. Stack with greaseproof paper between each one.

3 Make the filling: melt the butter in a saucepan, add the onion and sauté over gentle heat for 5 minutes until soft. Stir in the flour, cook for 1 minute, then remove from the heat and gradually stir in the milk. Bring to the boil, then lower the heat and simmer for 1-2 minutes, stirring frequently. Season well with salt, pepper and nutmeg.

4 Add the spinach to the sauce with the turkey meat and walnuts, if using.

5 Divide the mixture between the pancakes, roll up and place seam side down in a greased ovenproof dish.

6 Preheat oven 220°C, 425°F, Gas Mark 6.

7 Make the sauce: melt the butter in a saucepan, stir in the flour and cook for 1 minute. Remove from the heat and gradually stir in the cider and milk. Bring to the boil, then lower the heat and simmer for 1 minute, stirring continuously. Season well and stir in the mustard.

8 Pour the sauce over the pancakes and sprinkle with the cheese. Bake in a preheated oven for 15-20 minutes or until well browned. Serve at once.

RAISED TURKEY PIE

Serve cut into slices with a selection of salads for lunch or a light supper. Serves 8.

INGREDIENTS

225g (8 oz) veal or lean pork, ground
225g (8 oz) cooked ham, ground
1 small onion, peeled
½ teaspoon ground coriander seeds
salt, freshly ground black pepper
450g (1 lb) plain flour
100g (4 oz) lard
150ml (¼ pint) water
4 tablespoons milk
350g (12 oz) cooked turkey meat, finely chopped
beaten eggs, to glaze
2 teaspoons powdered gelatine
150ml (¼ pint) hot chicken stock
150ml (¼ pint) cider

METHOD

1 Combine the veal, ham, onion and coriander in a bowl and season well with salt and pepper.

2 Make the pastry: sift the flour with 1 teaspoon salt into a mixing bowl. Put the lard with the water and milk in a saucepan, stir until the lard is melted and then bring to a boil. Add all at once to the flour and work to form a pliable dough. Knead lightly.

3 Preheat oven 200°C, 400°F, Gas Mark 6.

4 Roll out three-quarters of the pastry and use to line a greased raised pie mould, 18-20cm (7-8 inch) round or square loose-based cake tin or a 1kg (2 lb) loaf tin.

5 Put half the ground veal mixture in the base of the pie mould, cover with chopped turkey and then with the remaining ground veal mixture.

6 Roll out the remaining pastry for a lid, damp the pastry edges, cover with the lid and press well together. Trim the edges and crimp and make a hole in the centre. Brush all over with beaten egg.

7 Roll out the pastry trimmings and cut out leaves. Use to decorate around the central hole and brush the leaves with beaten egg.

8 Bake in a preheated oven for 30 minutes. Reduce the oven temperature to 160°C, 325°F, Gas Mark 3 and bake for another 1¼-1½ hours. (Cover the pie with greaseproof paper when sufficiently browned.)

9 Dissolve the gelatine in the stock, season well with salt and pepper and add the cider. As the pie cools pour the stock into the pie through a funnel inserted in the central hole, tilting the pie to ensure that the stock is evenly distributed inside the pie.

10 Cool, then chill overnight until firm, before removing from the mould.

BACK: Raised Turkey Pie
FRONT: Turkey and Spinach Pancakes

MENU

Beansprout Salad

•

Smoked Mackerel and Olive Pâté
Chinese Lettuce Salad
Lasagne Verde

•

Crème Caramel
Hogmanay Shortbreads

NEW YEAR'S EVE

Here's an attractive assortment of supper dishes for the traditional New Year's Eve party.

BEANSPROUT SALAD

This is a fresh and crunchy salad. You may wish to have extra dressing available on the side. Serves 20.

INGREDIENTS
100g (4 oz) button mushrooms, thinly sliced
2 tablespoons French dressing
450g (1 lb) fresh beansprouts
4 carrots scraped and cut into thin sticks
225g (8 oz) red cabbage, thinly shredded
3 cartons mustard and cress

METHOD
1 Put the mushrooms in a large salad bowl and pour over the French dressing. Leave to stand for 30 minutes.
2 Add all the remaining ingredients and toss well. Serve immediately, with extra French dressing if desired.

SMOKED MACKEREL AND OLIVE PÂTÉ

You may want to arrange this pâté on two serving dishes so you can replace the first with the second when it is almost gone and starting to look messy. Serves 20.

INGREDIENTS
1 onion, peeled and chopped
4 hard-boiled eggs, shelled and chopped
12 stuffed green olives, sliced
750g (1½ lb) smoked mackerel fillets, skinned and chopped
salt
freshly ground black pepper
1-2 garlic cloves, peeled and crushed
12 tablespoons plain yogurt

TO GARNISH
2 tablespoons chopped fresh parsley
16 stuffed green olives, sliced

METHOD
1 Put the onion and hard-boiled eggs into a food processor or blender and process until thoroughly chopped. Add the olives and smoked mackerel and process again until smooth.
2 Add salt and pepper, then the garlic and yogurt and process again until smooth.
3 Turn the mixture into a bowl, taste and adjust the seasoning, and stir well. (If too thick add more yogurt.)
4 Turn the pâté into 2 serving dishes and sprinkle with chopped parsley. Arrange sliced olives around the edge.

FROM THE FRONT Smoked Mackerel and Olive Pâté, Chinese Lettuce Salad, Beansprout Salad, Lasagne Verde.

CHINESE LETTUCE SALAD

A pretty green salad. Serves 20.

INGREDIENTS
2 green-skinned dessert apples, peeled,
cored and thinly sliced
2 tablespoons lemon juice
2 heads Chinese leaves, trimmed and finely
sliced
1 unpeeled cucumber, diced
2 green peppers, seeded, cored and sliced
1 bunch spring onions, trimmed and
chopped
1 head celery, trimmed and thinly sliced
2 bunches watercress, trimmed
300ml (1/2 pint) French dressing

METHOD
1　Put the apple slices in a large salad bowl
with the lemon juice, toss to coat thoroughly,
then drain.
2　Add all the remaining salad ingredients
and toss well. Cover and chill in the refrigerator until ready to serve. Pour over the French
dressing and toss again before serving.

LASAGNE VERDE

A delicious variation on the classic Italian
lasagne. Serves 20.

INGREDIENTS
450g (1 lb) lasagne verde
salt
3 tablespoons vegetable oil
750g (1 1/2 lb) lean minced beef
1kg (2 lb) minced pork
225g (8 oz) chicken livers, finely chopped
2 onions, peeled and finely chopped
2 garlic cloves, crushed
225g (8 oz) carrots, scraped and finely
chopped
4 tablespoons tomato purée
2 × 425g (15 oz) can tomatoes
450ml (3/4 pint) tomato juice
2 tablespoons Worcestershire sauce
1/2 teaspoon ground nutmeg
225g (8 oz) button mushrooms, chopped
(optional)
freshly ground black pepper

SAUCE
100g (4 oz) butter or margarine
100g (4 oz) plain flour
1.2 litres (2 pints) milk
2 teaspoons English mustard powder
225g (8 oz) mature Cheddar cheese, grated

METHOD
1　Cook the lasagne 3-4 sheets at a time in a
large saucepan of boiling salted water to
which 1 tablespoon of the oil has been
added, for about 6 minutes or until just
tender. Drain well and lay out on trays.
2　Put the minced beef and pork in a large,
heavy-based saucepan with the remaining oil
and cook until the fat runs, stirring frequently.
Add the chicken livers, onions, garlic and
carrots and cook gently for about 10 minutes,
stirring frequently.
3　Stir in the tomato purée, the tomatoes
with their juice and the Worcestershire sauce,
nutmeg and mushrooms. Season well with
salt and pepper. Bring to a boil, cover and
simmer gently for 30 minutes. Stir occasionally and taste, adjusting the seasoning
if necessary.
4　Make the sauce: melt the butter in a
saucepan, stir in the flour and cook for 1-2
minutes. Remove from the heat and gradually stir in the milk, then bring to a boil,
stirring frequently, and simmer for 2 minutes.
Season well with salt and pepper, then stir in
the mustard and 150g (5 oz) of the cheese
and stir until the cheese is melted.
5　Preheat oven 200°C, 400°F, Gas Mark 6.
6　Lightly oil 2 large baking dishes about
5cm (2 inches) deep. Beginning with a layer
of lasagne, make layers of lasagne, meat
sauce and cheese sauce, ending with cheese
sauce. Sprinkle with the remaining grated
cheese.
7　Bake toward the top of a preheated hot
oven for about 40-50 minutes or until well
browned on top. Reverse the dishes halfway
through the cooking time. Serve hot.

CRÈME CARAMEL

This vanilla-flavoured custard is rich and creamy. Topped with the burnt flavour of caramel it becomes the most delicious sweet ever, a favourite from nursery to adult dinner parties.

It is vital that the custards should not get too hot in the oven, or they will curdle, so a bain marie (water bath) is used to ensure an even, low temperature. Crème caramel is an ideal recipe for the busy hostess to prepare – it can be made well in advance and kept in a cool place. Serves 8.

INGREDIENTS
2 tablespoons cold water
150g (5 oz) caster sugar
3 tablespoons boiling water

CUSTARD
600ml (1 pint) milk
1 vanilla pod
4 large eggs
2 eggs yolks
40g (1½ oz) sugar

METHOD
1 Pour the cold water into a small, thick-based frying pan. Stir in the sugar, using a wooden spoon. Place over a low heat to dissolve the sugar, stirring occasionally.
2 When the sugar has dissolved, bring to a boil and boil without stirring until the sugar turns a dark, golden brown. Remove at once from the heat and slowly spoon in the boiling water, stirring to loosen the caramel.
3 Lightly oil 8 150ml (¼ pint) dariole moulds or ramekins. Spoon some of the caramel into each mould and cool until set.
4 Meanwhile, make the custard. Pour the milk into a saucepan, add the vanilla pod and bring slowly to a boil. Leave to infuse for about 10 minutes.
5 Crack the 4 eggs into a deep bowl and add the extra egg yolks. Add the sugar and mix with an electric beater until well blended and pale in colour.
6 Remove the vanilla pod from the milk, rinse and dry it and store in a jar of sugar for future use.
7 Preheat oven 160°C, 325°F, Gas Mark 3.

8 Pour the milk onto the eggs, stirring, and strain into a measuring jug. Skim off the froth from the top, or leave it to subside.
9 Divide the custard between the caramel-based moulds. Place in a large roasting tin, in 1cm (½ inch) of cold water. Cover with a double layer of foil, to prevent a skin forming on the surface of the custards.
10 Cook in a preheated oven for about 45 minutes until set. To test whether the custards are cooked, insert a fine skewer two-thirds of the way through each one; if it comes out clean the custard is cooked.
11 Remove the moulds from the water and, while still warm, ease the custard away from the side of the moulds with a small, sharp knife. Shake once and invert into individual glass dishes. Ease the moulds away and allow to cool completely before serving.

HOGMANAY SHORTBREAD

These shortbread biscuits may be frozen, well wrapped in cling film in a rigid container, for up to 3 months. Thaw for 1-2 hours at room temperature. Makes 12.

INGREDIENTS
100g (4 oz) unsalted butter
50g (2 oz) caster sugar
150g (5 oz) plain flour
25g (1 oz) rice flour
caster sugar, to decorate

METHOD
1 Heat oven 180°C, 350°F, Gas Mark 4.
2 Place the butter and sugar in a bowl and cream together until fluffy. Sift in the flours and work to form a soft dough. Knead lightly until smooth.
3 Roll the dough into a log shape, wrap in cling film and chill for 30 minutes. Cut the roll in slices and place on a greased baking sheet.
4 Bake in the oven for 15-20 minutes until golden around the edges.
5 Dredge with caster sugar and cool on a wire rack.

NEW YEAR'S DAY OPEN HOUSE

Have mineral water and plain wine and beer on hand as well as mulled wine. The canapés here are substantial enough to make a proper meal, especially if you add a few favourite desserts.

MULLED WINE

This warm wine is especially welcome on a cold day. Makes about 16 glasses.

INGREDIENTS
2 bottles of Burgundy or heavy red wine
¼ bottle gin
75g (3 oz) raisins
100g (4 oz) caster sugar
8 whole cloves
1 teaspoon cardamom seeds (optional)
5cm (2 inch) piece cinnamon stick
thinly pared rind of 2 lemons

METHOD
1 Put the wine, half the gin and all the remaining ingredients into a large saucepan.
2 Heat gently, stirring, until the sugar has dissolved, then bring to a boil. Turn the heat to the lowest setting and simmer very gently for at least 30 minutes. Stir in the remaining gin, reheat and serve at once.

STILTON DIP

Serve this with Cheese Bites (see right) and a plate of crudités such as sticks of celery and carrot, strips of green pepper and small florets of raw cauliflower.

INGREDIENTS
175g (6 oz) Stilton, rind removed
1 small onion, peeled and chopped
2 celery sticks, chopped
1 hard-boiled egg, chopped
salt
1 teapsoon paprika
1 teaspoon sugar
1 tablespoon lemon juice
1 tablespoon white wine vinegar
4-6 tablespoons vegetable oil

MENU
Mulled Wine

Stilton Dip with Cheese Bites,
Celery and Peanut Boats
Prune, Almond and Bacon Rolls
Smoked Cod's Roe Pinwheels
Cheese and Anchovy Twists
Cocktail Canapés
Curry Puffs with Watercress

METHOD
1 Put the Stilton, onion, celery and hard-boiled egg in a food processor or blender and process until smooth. Add all the remaining ingredients and process again until smooth. Taste and adjust the seasoning and turn into a small serving bowl.

CHEESE BITES

These can be frozen at stage 2. Allow to thaw until they are just able to be cut with a sharp knife and proceed as step 3 when ready to continue.

INGREDIENTS
150g (6 oz) plain flour
a pinch of salt
freshly ground black pepper
cayenne
100g (4 oz) butter, diced
65g (2½ oz) mature Cheddar cheese, grated
15g (½ oz) Parmesan cheese, grated
1 egg yolk
1 tablespoon water
milk, to glaze
2 tablespoons finely chopped walnuts

METHOD
1 Sift the flour with the salt, pepper and cayenne to taste into a mixing bowl. Add the butter and rub in until the mixture resembles fine breadcrumbs. Mix in the cheeses and stir in the egg yolk and water to bind.

2 Shape into a roll about 2.5cm (1 inch) in diameter and wrap in foil or cling film. Chill in the refrigerator until firm.

3 Preheat oven 190°C, 375°F, Gas Mark 5.

4 Cut into 5mm (¼ inch) slices and place on baking sheets lined with silicone paper. Brush with milk and sprinkle with walnuts.

5 Bake in a preheated moderately hot oven for 10-12 minutes. Transfer to a wire tray and leave to cool completely, then store in an airtight container.

CELERY AND PEANUT BOATS

A tasty snack dressed up with spices, onions and lemon juice.

INGREDIENTS
4 tablespoons crunchy peanut butter
25g (1 oz) butter
salt
freshly ground black pepper
1 tablespoon finely chopped spring onions or chives
a good pinch of dried thyme
pinch of garlic salt (optional)
15g (½ oz) fresh white breadcrumbs
a few drops of lemon juice
6 celery sticks, trimmed
paprika, to finish

METHOD
1 In a bowl, beat the peanut butter with the butter until smooth. Season well with salt and

CLOCKWISE FROM THE BACK Christmas Mull, Celery and Peanut Boats, Prune, Almond and Bacon Rolls, Stilton Dip with Cheese Bites, Crudités.

pepper and add the spring onions, herbs and garlic salt, if using. Stir in the breadcrumbs, adding enough lemon juice to give a spreading consistency.

2 Spoon the mixture into the cavity in the celery, then sprinkle lightly with paprika.

3 Cut the celery into 2.5cm (1 inch) lengths and arrange on a plate. Chill in the refrigerator until ready to serve.

PRUNE, ALMOND AND BACON ROLLS

Serve hot, speared with cocktail sticks. Makes 20.

INGREDIENTS
20 plump no-need-to-soak prunes, stoned
20 blanched whole almonds
20 rashers of streaky bacon

METHOD
1 Fill the cavity of each prune with an almond.

2 Lay the bacon rashers on a board and stretch them slightly with the back of a knife, then wrap one around each prune.

3 Arrange the prune, almond and bacon rolls in a foil-lined baking tin and cook under a moderate grill for 5-10 minutes, turning once, until the bacon is crispy.

SMOKED COD'S ROE PINWHEELS

As a variation you can spread the bread with 1 × 40g (1½ oz) can dressed crab mixed with 100g (4 oz) softened butter; or 100g (4 oz) smooth pâté mixed with 150g (5 oz) softened butter.

INGREDIENTS
100g (4 oz) smoked cod's roe
1-2 teaspoons lemon juice
100g (4 oz) softened butter
freshly ground black pepper
1 tablespoon chopped fresh parsley (optional)
1 small uncut brown loaf, crust removed
parsley sprigs, to garnish

METHOD
1 In a bowl, mash the cod's roe with the lemon juice with a fork, then beat in the butter until smooth. Season to taste with pepper and stir in the parsley, if using.
2 Cut the loaf lengthways into 4 thin slices.
3 Spread the bread slices with the smoked cod's roe mixture and roll up neatly beginning with a short end. Wrap the rolls tightly in cling film, screwing the ends together, and chill for at least 1 hour or overnight.
4 Cut the rolls crossways into thin slices and arrange on a plate. Garnish with parsley sprigs.

CHEESE AND ANCHOVY TWISTS

These can be served cold or warmed up in the oven before serving.

INGREDIENTS
100g (4 oz) puff pastry or shortcrust pastry
2 cans anchovy fillets, soaked in milk for 5 minutes, then drained
a little milk
2 tablespoons grated Parmesan cheese

METHOD
1 Preheat oven 220°C, 425°F, Gas Mark 7.
2 Roll out the pastry to a 30cm (12 inch) square about 3mm (⅛ inch) thick. Trim the edges neatly with a sharp knife. Cut the pastry into quarters then cut each quarter into strips 1-2cm (½-¾ inch) wide.
3 Cut the anchovy fillets in half lengthways. Brush the strips with milk, then lay a piece of anchovy on each pastry strip. Sprinkle with the Parmesan cheese.
4 Give each strip one or two twists and lay on a baking sheet lined with non-stick silicone paper. Bake in a preheated hot oven for about 15 minutes or until lightly browned. Transfer to a wire rack and leave to cool completely, then store in an airtight container.

COCKTAIL CANAPÉS

Do not make these too far in advance because the biscuits will lose their crispness.

INGREDIENTS
24 small biscuits
softened butter, for spreading
4 hard-boiled eggs
¼ cucumber, sliced
50g (2 oz) peeled prawns
50g (2 oz) cream cheese
50g (2 oz) smoked salmon pieces
1 × 100g (4 oz) asparagus spears, drained

METHOD
1 Spread 12 small biscuits with butter, then top with a slice of hard-boiled egg, half a slice of cucumber, a peeled prawn and sprig of parsley.
2 On 12 other biscuits, pipe 2 rows of cream cheese across the biscuits, place a small roll of smoked salmon in the centre of the cheese and top with an asparagus spear.

CURRY PUFFS WITH WATERCRESS

Makes about 25.

INGREDIENTS
75g (3 oz) butter
¼ pint water
65g (2½ oz) plain flour
pinch salt
1 onion, peeled and finely chopped

2 teaspoons curry powder
2 eggs, beaten
vegetable oil, for deep frying

SAUCE
4 tablespoons thick mayonnaise
2 tablespoons plain yogurt
*1 bunch watercress, trimmed and finely
chopped*
grated rind of ½ lemon

METHOD

1 Melt 50g (2 oz) of the butter with the water and bring to the boil. Sift the flour and salt together and add all at once to the pan. Stir quickly with a wooden spoon until the mixture is smooth and leaves the sides of the pan clean.

2 Meanwhile melt the remaining 25g (2oz) of the butter in a small saucepan, add the onion and fry over a gentle heat for about 7 minutes, until lightly browned. Stir in the curry powder, then cool slightly.

3 Add the curry and onion mixture to the choux paste. Gradually beat in the eggs a little at a time until the mixture is smooth and glossy.

4 Heat the oil to 180-190°C (350-375°F) or until a cube of bread browns in 30 seconds.

5 Drop small teaspoons of the choux mixture into the oil, about 6 at a time. Fry for about 3-4 minutes, turning if necessary, until well puffed up and golden brown. Drain on kitchen paper and keep warm while frying the remainder in the same way.

6 Combine the sauce ingredients in a small bowl and stir well to mix. Garnish with a sprig of watercress, if desired. Stand the bowl containing the watercress dip on a large plate surrounded by the puffs speared with toothpicks if desired.

*CLOCKWISE FROM FRONT Cheese and
Anchovy Twists, Curry Puffs with Watercress Dip,
Smoked Cod's Roe Pinwheels, Cocktail Canapés.*

AROUND THE WORLD AT CHRISTMAS

Everyone has traditional Christmas favourites – dishes that you grew up with, and that you now make for your own family. They taste especially good because they are spiced with childhood memories. Families all over the world have just such traditional foods. And because some foods, like German Stollen and the French Bûche de Noel (Yule Log) are so popular, they have almost become synonymous with their home country and how Christmas is celebrated there.

Here are recipes for five holiday specialities from other countries that you might like to bring to your table this season.

BÛCHE DE NOEL

This Bûche de Noel makes a splendid centrepiece for any buffet table.

INGREDIENTS
4 eggs
100g (4 oz) caster sugar
65g (3½ oz) plain flour
15g (½ oz) cocoa
25g (1 oz) butter, melted and cooled

FILLING
4 tablespoons double cream
1 tablespoon milk
1 × 250g (8¾ oz) can sweetened chestnut spread

CRÈME AU BEURRE AU CHOCOLAT
75g (3 oz) sugar
4 tablespoons water
2 egg yolks
100-175g (4-6 oz) unsalted butter
50g (2 oz) plain chocolate, broken into pieces
sifted icing sugar
marzipan holly leaves and berries, to decorate (see pages 84-5 for basic marzipan recipe)

METHOD
1 Preheat oven 190°C, 375°F, Gas Mark 5.
2 Line a Swiss roll tin, 30 × 25 cm (12 × 10 in), with greased greaseproof paper. Put the eggs and sugar into a bowl and whisk until the mixture is very thick and pale and the whisk leaves a heavy trail when lifted.
3 Sift the flour and cocoa together twice and fold into the mixture, followed by the melted and cooled butter.
4 Turn into the prepared tin, making sure there is plenty of mixture in the corners. Bake in the preheated oven for about 15-20 minutes, or until just firm and springy to the touch.
5 Turn out onto a sheet of greaseproof or non-stick silicone paper dredged with caster sugar. Peel off the lining paper, trim off the edges of the cake with a sharp knife, then roll up the cake with the sugared paper inside. Cool on a wire tray.
6 Whip the cream and milk together until stiff, then fold into the chestnut spread.
7 Unroll the cake carefully, remove the paper and spread evenly with the chestnut mixture. Reroll carefully.
8 For the crème au beurre: place the sugar in a heavy-based pan with the water and heat gently until dissolved. Bring to a boil and boil for 3-4 minutes to 110°C, 225°F, Gas Mark ¼, or until the syrup forms a thin thread.
9 Pour the syrup in a thin stream onto the egg yolks, whisking all the time. Continue to whisk until the mixture is thick and cold. Beat the butter until soft and gradually beat in the egg mixture.
10 Place the chocolate with 1 tablespoon water in a bowl over a pan of hot water and stir continuously until smooth and melted. Cool, then beat into the syrup mixture.
11 Coat the cake with the chocolate mixture; then mark attractively with the tines of a fork. Chill until set. Before serving, dredge lightly with icing sugar and decorate with holly berries and leaves, fashioned out of marzipan.

STOLLEN

This is the famous German Christmas cake bread, quite delicious to eat. It is a slow riser because of the large amount of fruit, but well worth the time it takes to make.

INGREDIENTS

25g (1 oz) fresh yeast or 15g (½ oz) dried yeast
2 tablespoons warm water
75g (3 oz) caster sugar
pinch of salt
6 tablespoons warm milk
2 tablespoons rum
few drops almond essence
400g (14 oz) plain flour
1 egg, beaten
150g (5 oz) unsalted butter, softened
50g (2 oz) raisins
50g (2 oz) glacé cherries, chopped, washed and dried
50g (2 oz) currants
25 g (1 oz) angelica, chopped
50g (2 oz) cut mixed peel
40g (1½ oz) flaked almonds
sifted icing sugar

METHOD

1 Blend the yeast in the water. If using dried yeast, add 1 teaspoon of the sugar and leave in a warm place until frothy. Dissolve 50g (2 oz) sugar and the salt in the milk. Add the rum, almond essence and yeast liquid to the milk mixture.

2 Sift the flour into a bowl, making a well in the centre. Add the yeast mixture, egg, 75g (3 oz) softened butter cut into small pieces, and the fruits and nuts. Mix to a soft dough and knead for 10 minutes by hand, or 4-5 minutes in a large electric mixer fitted with a dough hook.

3 Replace the dough in a bowl, cover with cling film or a damp cloth and put to rise in a warm place until doubled in size – about 2 hours.

4 Knock back the dough and knead until smooth, then roll out to a rectangle about 30 × 20 cm (12 × 18 inches).

Stollen, a German speciality.

5 Melt the remaining butter and brush liberally over the dough; then sprinkle with the remaining sugar. Fold one long side over just beyond the centre and then the other long side to overlap the first piece well. Press lightly together and slightly taper the ends.

6 Place on a greased baking sheet, brush with melted butter and leave in a warm place until almost doubled in size.

7 Preheat oven 190°C, 375°F, Gas Mark 5.

8 Bake for about 45 minutes, until well risen and browned. Cool on a wire rack. Before serving dredge heavily with sifted icing sugar and serve cut into fairly thin slices.

VASILOPITTA

This is a New Year's Cake served at the stroke of midnight on New Year's Eve in Greece. St Basil is the patron saint of Greece so the cake is also named after him. It is usually much larger than this version and always has a lucky coin baked into it, although the ingredients do vary from family to family. When it is cut, a piece is offered to the Holy Mother and St. Basil and the rest cut up for the assembled gathering. Any left over is supposed to be given to the poor on the following day. If the lucky coin is in the piece left for St. Basil, then everyone should have a happy year.

INGREDIENTS
350g (12 oz) plain flour
1 tablespoon baking powder
1 teaspoon ground nutmeg
225g (8 oz) unsalted butter
450g (1 lb) caster sugar
4 large eggs
250ml (8 fl oz) orange juice
grated rind of 1 large orange
flaked or blanched almonds

METHOD
1 Line a tin approximately 30×25×5cm (12×10×2 in) with greaseproof paper. Preheat oven 180°C, 350°F, Gas Mark 4.
2 Sift the flour, baking powder and nutmeg together.
3 Cream the butter and sugar until very light and fluffy then beat in the eggs, one at a time, following each with a spoonful of flour; then beat in about one-third of the flour.
4 Gradually beat in the orange juice, alternating with the remaining flour and orange rind, until smooth and evenly blended. Drop in the coin wrapped in foil.
5 Turn into the prepared tin and either sprinkle with flaked almonds or write the new year's date on top of the cake with blanched almonds.
6 Bake in a preheated oven for 50-60 minutes until golden brown and just firm to the touch. Turn out carefully onto a wire tray and leave to cool.
7 Serve cut into squares or diamonds.

FILHOS DE NATAL

These Christmas fritters from Spain are traditionally served dipped in honey. Here they are sprinkled with nuts for extra interest. They are best eaten fresh. Makes about 60.

INGREDIENTS
2 teaspoons dried yeast
1 teaspoon caster sugar
3 tablespoons warm milk
500g (1 lb 2 oz) strong white flour
1 teaspoon salt
4 eggs
3 tablespoons brandy
oil for deep frying
clear honey
approx 50g (2 oz) chopped toasted almonds
or hazelnuts

METHOD
1 Dissolve the yeast and sugar in the milk and leave to stand in a warm place until frothy – about 20 minutes.
2 Sift the flour and salt into a bowl and make a well in the centre. Pour in the yeast liquid, beaten eggs and brandy and mix to a smooth, elastic dough.
3 Knead on a floured surface for 5 minutes by hand or for 2-3 minutes in a large electric mixer fitted with a dough hook. Replace the dough in the bowl, cover with cling film or a damp cloth and leave to rise in a warm place (an airing cupboard is ideal) for about 2 hours, or until doubled in size.
4 Knock back the dough and knead until smooth. Roll out on a floured surface to about 5mm (¼ inch) thick. Cut some of the dough into strips about 5cm (2 inches) long and 1cm (½ inch) wide. Cut others into strips 7.5-10cm (3-4 inches) long and knot.
5 Heat the oil to about 190°C, 375°F or until a cube of bread browns in 30 seconds, and fry the fritters a few at a time until golden brown, turning over when necessary. Remove with a slotted spoon and drain.
6 Dip a wet brush in the honey and brush over the fritters, then sprinkle with the nuts. Serve hot, warm or cold.

AO "A" TEA ROA

The Maori name for this Christmas pudding, Ao "A" Tea Roa, describes the long white cloud that is always visible over the islands of New Zealand as you fly in. Roast turkey is traditionally served on Christmas Day followed by this pudding, which is very suitable for their warm Christmas weather. Serves 6-8.

INGREDIENTS

THE PUDDING
225g (8 oz) plain flour
225g (8 oz) soft brown sugar
175g (6 oz) sultanas
350g (12 oz) raisins
50g (2 oz) cut mixed peel
grated rind of 1 lemon
½ teaspoon mixed spice
100g (4 oz) softened butter
2 teaspoons bicarbonate of soda
350ml (12 fl oz) boiling water
2 eggs, beaten

LONG WHITE CLOUD
1 × 425g (15 oz) can apricot halves
¼ teaspoon ground cinnamon
1 litre (2 pint) carton or large block vanilla ice cream
2-3 tablespoons brandy

METHOD

1 Sift the flour into a bowl, add the sugar,

LEFT TO RIGHT Ao "A" Tea Roa, Filhos de Natal, Vasilopitta.

dried fruits, peel, lemon rind and spice and mix well. Cut the butter into small pieces and dot over the mixture.

2 Dissolve the bicarbonate of soda in the water and pour over the mixture. Mix lightly, cover with a cloth and leave overnight.

3 Next day add the beaten eggs and mix thoroughly. Turn into a greased 1.7 litre (3 pint) or 2 × 900 ml (1½ pint) pudding basin. Cover with greased greaseproof paper (giving room for expansion) and then foil or a pudding cloth, and tie securely with string. Place in a large pan (or pans) of boiling water, so that the water comes halfway up the basins, and simmer for 3 hours.

4 Line a freezer tray or other container approximately 30 × 10cm (10 × 4 inches) with double foil and grease well. Remove the warm Christmas pudding from the bowl and pack it into the container, making it about 4cm (1½ inches) thick. Chill until required.

5 Purée the apricots with some of the juice and flavour with the cinnamon.

6 To serve: unmould the pudding on a warmed long serving dish. Put slices or scoops of ice cream along the top of the pudding and coat with the apricot sauce. At the table, pour warmed brandy around the pudding on the warmed dish and set alight.

CARDS AND WRAPS

GREETINGS FOR CHRISTMAS

It was during the late 19th century that Christmas cards came into their own. Previously, people had exchanged Christmas greetings by letter, and schoolchildren often prepared Christmas Pieces for their parents or grandparents, a kind of sampler for their best handwriting on special paper with a printed border.

The Valentine card had been around for some time, so it is quite surprising that it took the Christmas card so long to get off the ground. It is generally thought that the person responsible for the first Christmas card was Henry Cole, director of the newly founded Victoria and Albert Museum. In 1843 he commissioned H.C. Horsley, R. A. to produce a suitable design. It depicted, in its central panel, a jolly family sitting down to their Christmas dinner, and raising their glasses in a toast, while two smaller side panels portrayed acts of seasonal charity, feeding the hungry and clothing the naked. In 1846 1,000 copies of this design were printed and sold for a shilling a copy.

The idea didn't really catch on, however, and it was not until the 1860s that English printers recognized a potential business opportunity and started manufacturing cards in bulk. The American market for cards was quite small at this time, and since there were no US Christmas card makers, English printers exported theirs across the Atlantic to sell.

A decade later, a young German immigrant by the name of Louis Prang printed the first American-made Christmas cards from his shop in Boston. But that first year – 1874 – he didn't sell to the US market, but rather to the larger and more established British card market. It wasn't until a year later that his cards were sold in America.

In the late decades of the century the practice of sending cards both in England and the United States became so widespread that the post office had difficulty coping with the seasonal mail. A correspondent to *The Times* after the Christmas rush of 1877 described the sending of Christmas cards as a "social evil", and complained at "the delay of legitimate correspondence by cartloads of children's cards". But in 1883 that same paper concluded:

A snow-filled landscape provides the subject for this atmospheric Christmas card.

This wholesome custom has been . . . frequently the happy means of ending strifes, cementing broken friendships and strengthening family and neighbourhood ties in all conditions of life. In this respect the Christmas card undoubtedly fulfils a high end, for cheap postage has constituted it almost exclusively the modern method of conveying Christmas wishes, and the increasing popularity of the custom is for this reason, if no other, a matter for congratulation.

Early mass-produced cards were often more like Valentine cards than Christmas cards, for the simple reason that the manufacturers already produced Valentines and it was easy to use the same card and just change the greeting. So Christmas greetings were conveyed with cupids, bows, lace edging, and as with most things Victorian, flowers everywhere. Even Prang, who had not sold Valentine cards earlier, kept his first cards to non-Christmas themes: flowers, shells and other images from nature.

Pretty soon, however, Christmassy themes began to predominate, with the traditional scenes of snow-laden landscapes, holly and mistletoe, Christmas trees and bells, Santa Claus, plum puddings and robins. There is a legend that robins got their red breasts by fanning with their wings the fire that was warming the baby Jesus, and scorched themselves, hence their association with Christmas.

It is surprising how few Christmas cards had religious themes, because piety was an important element in the Victorian Christmas. An astonishing number had nothing to do with Christmas whatever; there were flowers,

A nineteenth century Christmas card showing Santa Claus and reindeer delivering presents.

dogs and cats, horses and cows, even a famous series of nudes at the seaside! In 1894 a lengthy study was published on the subject of Christmas cards. It commented on the incongruous nature of much of the subject matter and deplored:

tragic sunsets, haunted churchyards, consumptive choirboys, monsters of might-make land, pictures of accidents dear to the farce writer, and, in short, the subjects which are in vulgar parlance "weird" and alarming on the one hand, and distinctly uncomfortable on the other.

The humour in comic cards was often pretty crude, and likely to offend if sent to the wrong person. "I am a poor man," writes Mr Pooter in *The Diary Of A Nobody*, "but I would gladly give ten shillings to find out who sent me the insulting Christmas card I received this morning". Poor old Pooter never could take a joke.

THOUGHTFUL GREETINGS
If you are one of those stalwart souls who had the strength to go back to the stores the day after last Christmas and scoop up cards and gift wraps and tags at half price, then you're

all set for this year. If you didn't, then you will have to pay for it – literally – this year. For many, the extra money is well spent; it is worth not having to think about heavy-duty consumerism right in the middle of post-Christmas peace and quiet.

But perhaps little money need be spent after all on wrapping paper, tags and cards this year. A bit of imagination and some time and effort can make a small outlay go a long way. Old cards can be recycled into gift tags. Creative gift wrap can be fashioned from almost anything that will fit around the package: scraps of craft paper, the painted backs of shopping bags, colourful comics and even fabric. Greeting cards, invitations and Christmas stationery can be cut and pasted, printed, and stencilled at home with simple things, many of which you probably already have.

Children, especially, find designing cards and colouring their own wrapping papers for friends, grandparents and teachers a real treat. Working with simple shades in the nonrestricted forms of cards and large sheets of paper allow them to draw and colour, cut and paste and even print simply and easily and, if they are old enough, with little adult help. And making, rather than buying, cards and paper helps children – and adults – to appreciate the meaning of recycling and shows them ways to transform old, seemingly obsolete things into new, useful items.

Even if you don't want to make all your own gift wraps and cards, personalizing some with your own handiwork can make your gifts and greetings to special people unique. Adding a handmade ribbon rose to a package, creating your own Christmas newsletter on letter paper you have decorated, or wrapping a present in something that makes a second present, like a basket or even a pair of humorous Christmas socks, can be a satisfying way for you to show someone that your Christmas wishes are warm and genuine.

A CHRISTMAS NEWSLETTER

Christmas newsletters are not for everyone, certainly, but more people this year than last will replace cards containing short messages with long letters filled with news of the year and wishes for the season.

Perhaps a good reason for their popularity is the word processors and copying machines that make the onerous task of writing to masses of friends and family easy. Then there is the very real need of keeping many people up-to-date with the changes and events that certainly happen in any given year, especially in as mobile a society as ours. And some people find commercial Christmas cards too impersonal for their tastes; they would rather compose their own greetings.

Newsletters can be tucked in cards, bought or homemade, or they can be written on stationery decorated for Christmas so that you have an all-in-one card-newsletter.

For the card-newsletter decorate a plain sheet of letter paper by drawing a Christmassy border around the perimeter or designing a letterhead at the top that incorporates your name and address with a holiday image. Use this original as your master, making as many copies as you need on a copying machine. Don't go through the trouble of doing it in colour unless you will be running off copies on a colour copier.

AVOIDING CHRISTMAS CARD PROCRASTINATION

Some people love to get Christmas cards ready for posting. Others see it as little more than another chore to get out of the way before Christmas Day. If you need a bit of motivation, you might like to give one of these ideas a try:
● About the middle of November, make a list of all the people you want to send cards to. Total up the number and divide that number by the weeks left between now and the middle of December. That is how many cards you will plan to sign and address each week. For instance, if you want to send cards to 60 people, you should plan to write out and address 15 cards each week for the next four weeks.
● Plan a night (or two nights if you have a lot of cards to send) in early December and reserve it as your card-writing night(s). Light a fire in the fireplace, put on some Christmas carols, pour yourself a glass of sherry or a cup of mulled wine or hot chocolate to get yourself into the Christmas mood. Maybe gather around you some photos of dear friends and family, then write away!

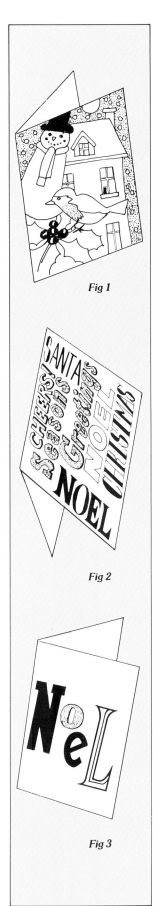

Fig 1

Fig 2

Fig 3

HOMEMADE CHRISTMAS CARDS

Think of Christmas cards as little gifts of warm wishes and good cheer for now and the New Year, as tokens of friendship and affection. Don't dash off a card with only your name at the bottom to long-distance friends or cousins that may hear from you only this one time a year; take a few moments to write a personal note, or slip in a Christmas newsletter (see below). Or use one of these handmade card ideas to really personalize your holiday greeting.

1 Make picture collages of Christmas images by pasting cut-outs from old Christmas cards onto the front of folded card paper. Keep themes and colour schemes in mind as you make the collages, and select images that work well together. For instance, you could work within old-fashioned scenes, white winter scenes, cheerful red and green themes. Avoid cutting around images so that you end up with regular shapes; rather cut close around the outline of the images themselves.

2 Make word collages by cutting and pasting at different angles Christmas greetings in different sizes and colors (Fig 2). Alternatively, cut out single letters of different colours and sizes to make up your own words of greeting (Fig 3).

3 Make photo collages by cutting out small photos of members of your family and pasting several either by themselves or along with other Christmas images. As with picture images, the most effective results come from cutting close around people to create odd shapes rather than squares or circles.

4 Draw an outline of a familiar figure like a Santa Claus (or the head of a reindeer) and paste little buttons on for eyes, maybe a nose, and perhaps for Santa's pompom on the tip of his cap. Draw in the other features with ink or paint. The result is very simple, but the three-dimensional additions are very effective (Fig 4).

5 Paper chains, left flat so that the receiver has the pleasure of unfolding them, make lovely cards. They can simply be left unadorned, just as a series of identical shapes, or they can be decorated. Take a long card that is thin and light.

Fold it into accordion folds. Draw on the top fold an outline of a simple image: a gingerbread man or woman, Santa Claus, a Christmas tree, a snowman, a bell. Then cut around the outline, being sure to cut through all the layers. Decorate it if you wish by drawing in details.

6 Send cards that can be hung on the tree. Roughly cut out an image from a used Christmas card or decoration and paste it on card paper that has been folded in half, being sure to place the top of the image right at the fold. Then cut carefully around the outline of the image, right through the two layers of card paper. Pierce a small hole through the card a little below the fold and insert a piece of ribbon or string for a hanger (Fig 5).

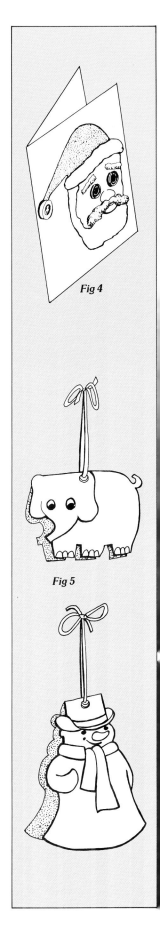

Fig 4

Fig 5

SPONGE PRINTS

Fig 1

Fig 2

STENCILLING CARDS AND WRAPPING PAPER

Decorating cards and paper with stencils is easy for all but very young children to do. Make your own stencils by drawing or tracing simple, obvious Christmas shapes. Use a waterproof paper such as a plastic card or waxed cardboard. You can make negative or positive stencils. Positive stencils have the shapes cut out of their centres and negative stencils have all but the actual shapes cut away.

1 Cut positive stencils with a craft knife and negative stencils with either a craft knife or a pair of sharp scissors so that images are crisp and neat.

2 If possible, it is best to tape the stencil down on your card or wrapping paper so that it doesn't move around. Masking tape can usually be removed from smooth-finished paper without ripping or leaving marks. Negative stencils can be taped onto the card by putting little rolls of masking tape or pieces of double-sided masking tape between the stencil and the card.

3 Positive stencils, if larger than the card, can be taped to newspaper placed under the card so that there won't be any risk of tape marks nor any risk of stray paint getting where you don't want it – an almost foolproof stencilling method for children. (Many children will find colouring-in positive stencils with felt-tip pens easier than using paints.)

4 Use water-based acrylic paints and brush, spray or roll them over the stencil. With negative stencils be careful not to get paint beyond the outer edges of the stencil.

5 Let the paint dry before removing the stencil and using it again.

6 For stencilling gift wrap paper, stencil on several images in a fixed or random pattern. And for more elaborate designs on large cards or paper, create a still-life or scene with several stencilled images.

SIMPLE PRINTING TECHNIQUES

Sponge printing and potato printing are very easy ways for you to mass-produce your own greeting cards.

Sponge prints

1 With a felt-tip pen draw shapes on ordinary kitchen sponges (Fig 1). The thicker the sponges, the easier they will be to handle, especially for children. Then cut the shapes out (Fig 2).

2 Pour a little acrylic paint in a dish and carefully dip a sponge shape into the paint so that the sponge takes up some paint but not so much that it drips. Do not squeeze the sponge.

3 Then gently lift the sponge away from the dish and press it down carefully onto your card paper (Fig 3). Practice printing on scrap paper before you print on cards.

Fig 3

POTATO PRINTS

Fig 1

Fig 2

Potato prints

1   Begin by cutting a potato in half (Fig 1), being sure to cut straight and not on a slant. Then with a felt-tip pen or a small paintbrush dipped in acrylic paint, draw an image on the potato (Fig 2). Alternatively, you can carve in the outline with a pocket knife or paring knife.

2   Then carve away everything but your image so that your image stands about 5mm (¼ inch) or more above the rest of the potato (Fig 3). Be careful not to slant your cuts under the the remaining image; rather, slant them away so that the image has a wide base that will not break off as you print.

3   When you are ready to print, place the card on several layers of newspaper to cushion the surface. Then paint over the raised image with a paintbrush filled with acrylic paint or dip it into a dish of paint just so that the raised image picks up paint (Fig 4). Try out your potato print several times first on scrap paper before you begin serious printing so that you can determine how best to hold the potato and how often to apply more paint (Fig 5).

4   You can print a single image on each card, the same image in different colours, or a few images (from different potatoes) in the same or different colours. This printing technique can also be used for gift wrap paper.

THE WORD'S THE THING

Practise writing out the message you'll be putting in your card so that you are sure it will fit nicely right where you want it. Don't type or cut and paste out a message, hand write it.

Fig 3

Fig 4

Fig 5

PRETTY PRESENTATIONS

Everyone loves to get a Christmas gift, no matter how small or simple it may be. If time has been spent wrapping it attractively, then the gift is all the more special.

Gift wrapping takes time and should not involve a last-minute panic and a final dash around the stores looking for Christmas papers and red and green ribbons. Choose your wrappings earlier in December and make an occasion for all the family to enjoy, providing them with boxes collected in advance, a good adhesive, double-sided tape – and a pair of scissors for everyone involved. Here are many ideas for exciting gift wraps.

1   Choose a theme for all the gifts – perhaps gold foil throughout – and use sections from white paper doilies instead of ribbons.

2   Buy plain papers as well as those with Christmas designs – they will help to create different effects and transform boxes into interesting shapes (see the little train and the shirt box in the picture).

3   Tissue paper makes good gift wrap; wrap the box in a bright colour, fold and snip pieces from a second, paler colour and overwrap the box for a lacy effect.

4   Children may not appreciate good gift papers – consider wrapping their gifts in pages from colored comics, taped together, or in bright wallpaper.

5   Newspaper makes an unusual – and smart – gift wrap, especially for a man. Tie the gift in bright red ribbon for contrast.

6   Pages from magazines or Sunday supplements can be used to make a collage gift wrap. Choose advertisement or feature story pages with a large area of colour for the basic wrap. Cut and glue on from other pages, to make themes or motifs.

7 Personalize gifts with names and messages. Wrap the gift in a plain paper; cut letters from patterned paper, or use rub-on letters available from stationery stores.

8 Let children make their own gift paper; a pad of artist's layout paper will provide large-sized sheets. Half-potatoes or apples can be cut into designs for block-printing with poster colours (see earlier), or try the effects of corks, pencil ends, pieces of sponge or cotton balls, string dipped in paint, bottle tops, etc. Or, stencil patterns through paper doilies with painting pens.

9 Cotton fabric makes a good wrap for gifts and is especially useful for oddly shaped presents. Use it over white tissue paper for the best effect.

10 For striking, modern gift tags, tear a random shape from a sheet of plain bright-coloured gift wrap. Write your message in a contrasting pen.

11 Craft foil is a little expensive but is ideal for small, awkwardly-shaped gifts, such as bottles, tins, or pencils. It is usually double-sided, and leftover scraps can be used for a wide variety of decorative ornaments, such as holly leaves, bells and stars.

12 Gold or silver doilies used over white or black tissue paper, can be used to wrap small, round gifts.

13 Sections cut from silver and gold doilies add glitter to a package. Cut out the circular center for snowflakes, cut motifs for gift tags, and use the lacy edges for a garland around the edges of a box.

14 Write glittering messages with glue and glitter. Spread a line of glue thinly, sprinkle the glitter and leave it to dry. A dry paintbrush is useful for applying glitter in small quantities.

15 Use dressmaker's pinking shears for the edges of crêpe paper or tissue paper. Crêpe

Beautifully wrapped Christmas presents make an enticing addition to the Christmas tree.

paper also pulls into a decorative edge – stretch it between the fingers.

16   Use bits of last year's Christmas cards for making gift tags – but choose the areas carefully. Motifs can be cut out and glued to white, or coloured, card tags; cut out greetings and write personal messages on the other side. The secret is to measure and cut the tags very carefully for a professional look (see the tags in the picture). Punch holes in the tags and tie them on with narrow ribbon, or thread a large-eyed needle with gold crochet thread and "sew" the tags on.

17   Use real woven satin ribbons to tie gifts when you know the recipient will appreciate the ribbon as a "second" gift.

18   Look for special cut-edge gift ribbons, made from cotton and acetate fabrics; they come in festive prints and plain colours and tie beautiful bows. Some have glittering threads that pull the ribbons up into "instant" bows.

19   For economical gift ties, consider glitter knitting wool, gold or silver crochet thread, red package twine.

20   Special gifts need little wrapping, other than cellophane, if the container is part of the gift. For instance:

A flowerpot containing a pair of gardening gloves, a packet or two of seeds for a gardener.

A china jelly mould with special packs of herbs or spices, and a pretty cook's apron, for a cook.

An inexpensive round basket, filled with small, perfumed soaps.

A growing plant, with small bows of gold ribbon tied to its branches.

21   Make your own gift bows and rosettes from ribbons or strips cut from gift wrap papers.

22   Awkwardly-shaped gifts need special treatment. Wrap bottles in tissue paper first, then a thin paper or gift wrap foil over the top, gathering the ends up around the neck. Snip the top edge into petal shapes, or fringe it; tie ornaments around the bottle neck, strings of glass beads, multi-bows of narrow ribbons, etc. Aluminium foil makes a good gift wrap for bottles.

23   Soft items, such as clothing, are best wrapped in a Christmas cracker shape. Roll the gift in tissue paper and tape it. Cut thin card to fit around the shape and half as long again. Tape it around the gift. Wrap in a large piece of gift paper, tie at the ends of the card to make a Christmas cracker shape. Fringe or pink the gift paper ends. Cut a decorative shape from another paper to decorate the Christmas cracker.

24   Christmas cracker shapes are also good for long gifts of different kinds but pad the gift with tissue paper first.

25   Round gifts can either be tied in fabric or a soft paper, or tied into a "second gift", such as a scarf or a handkerchief. Alternatively, change the shape with corrugated card taped

RIBBON FINISHES

RIBBON TIPS

Curling or crimping ribbon has a ribbed surface and is about 3mm (⅛ inch) wide. Drawn over a knife blade it forms "springs". Ribbon that sticks to itself when moistened makes rosettes.

Cut 4 23cm (9 inch) lengths and form them into figure-of-eights, sticking the ends together.

Stick "eights" together in twos, to make rosettes, then stick two rosettes together. Make a small loop for the middle.

FLAT LOOP

Cut ribbon into 30, 25, 20 and 15cm (12, 10, 8 and 6 inch) lengths. Dampen the ends and form the pieces into rings. Flatten the rings and dampen inside to form double loops. Stick loops one to another, the longest at the bottom, the smallest on top. Make a loop on top to finish.

A MULTIBOW

Tie ribbon around the gift, making a double knot. Lay 3 or 4 10cm (4 inch) pieces across the knot. Bring up the ribbon ends and knot over the pieces, pulling them into a multi-bow.

STARBURST

Cut pieces of ribbon, 10 cm (4 inches) long. Fishtail the ends or cut diagonally (round them off for a flower shape). Dampen the middle of each piece and twist it. Lay twists on top of each other, dampening them to secure. Use longer and smaller pieces for a different effect, and mix colours also. Ends can also be fringed.

CHRYSANTHEMUM

Lay ribbon in a zigzag pattern. Pick it up and twist wire around the middle. Pull out the petals.

around the gift, then top-wrap.

26 Big items, such as a doll's house, can be wrapped in newspaper first, then decorated with brightly coloured, self-adhesive tape.

27 Put large gifts into a large plastic bag; black bin liners look good tied with red, white and green ribbons, or smaller white bin liners can be decorated with shapes cut from coloured or foil papers. Wrap the gift in masses of brightly coloured tissue paper first to mask its shape as much as possible.

28 Look at haberdashery counters for decorative trims – thick coloured cords, inexpensive nylon lace, braids, silver buttons.

29 Stationers and art shops may have decorative items also – packs of fancy paper shapes, or coloured spots, for making patterns on plain paper wrappings.

30 Tubes are useful "boxes" for all kinds of gifts and simple to make. Roll the gift in thin cartridge paper or card and tape the joint. Stand the tube on the card or paper and draw around the end. Cut out 2 circles, cutting out 12mm (½ inch) from the drawn line. Using scissors, cut into the edge, up to the line. Spread a little glue on the cut tabs and fit them carefully into the ends of the tube.

31 Collect boxes all through the year. To cover a box with gift paper, open up the box, separating the glued joints, and trace around the flat box, adding 12mm (½ inch) all around. Spread glue on the extra 12mm (½ inch) and fold it onto the flat box. Leave to dry, then glue the box back together again.

32 Christmas stockings are fun for everyone. Make stockings from felt and use them from year to year, each member of the family having a special, personalized design, or make them disposable from inexpensive fabric. Machine stitch the edges together over a strip of tissue paper, tearing it away afterward.

33 If gifts are to be posted, take time to pack them correctly. Stationers can provide stiff cardboard and corrugated card for strengthening boxes collected from supermarkets. Tape all the joints of the box first, then cut pieces of card to fit 2 opposite sides and the bottom in 1 piece, and then a second piece to cover the remaining opposite sides and bottom in 1 piece. Cut a piece of the stiffening card to fit on top of the gift.

34 Another way of using supermarket boxes it to cut off the flaps from 2 boxes of similar size. Put the gift in 1 box, place the second box over the top to make a lid. Tape the edges and tie with string before wrapping in strong brown paper.

FINISHING TOUCHES

A gift, however simple, is appreciated all the more when it is lovingly wrapped in pretty paper. But it's the finishing touches that make gifts extra inviting.

Scented paper

For a truly luxurious finishing touch, wrap your flower-decorated gift with scented paper. If possible, match the fragrance to the flower decoration or to the colour of the wrapping paper.

To give fragrance to ordinary wrapping paper, spread a handful of pot pourri over the bottom of a large cardboard box and place a sheet of wrapping paper on top. Instead of pot pourri you could use one or two sprays of scented dried flowers or scented sachets. Add a second layer of pot pourri (or other scented material) and place another sheet of paper on top. Make as many layers as you like, then cover the box tightly. Leave it for 2 or 3 weeks, opening it to turn the paper occasionally so that it fully absorbs the scent.

Dried flower decorations

Dried flowers offer even more scope for decorations than fresh – particularly if a present has to be taken a long way.

One method is to stick dried flowerheads all over the wrapping paper: simply dab transparent glue wherever you want to place the flowers and press them on gently. Rather than dotting the flowerheads on at random, you could make the floral initials of the person for whom the gift is intended. Decorate the ribbon as well as (or instead of) the wrapping paper, if you wish. Again, dab on glue and press on the dried flowerheads. Decorate the ribbon bow, too, by gluing a flowerhead in the centre, or attach tiny flowers to the trailing ribbon ends.

Add a fresh flower

Wrapping and giving a gift on the same day provides the perfect opportunity to use seasonal fresh flowers as decorations, and this simple, but thoughtful touch will transform even the plainest-looking package.

When you have finished wrapping and ribboning, tuck a single flower or a tiny posy behind the ribbon-tie – matching colours look best. An unwrapped gift, such as a bottle of wine, looks that bit more special decorated this way. Just tie a ribbon bow around the neck of the bottle and tuck in a tiny posy. (Fresh flowers need special care when used as decorations.)

Satin ribbon roses

If you are running short of fresh or dried flowers, the answer is to make your own using paper or ribbon – they can look just as attractive as the real thing, and they will keep for a long time.

MAKING A SATIN RIBBON ROSE IN 6 EASY STEPS

MATERIALS

1 87cm (35 inch) length of red satin ribbon (for large roses)
2 70cm (28 inch) length of narrow red satin ribbon (for smaller roses)
3 stub wire
4 fine wire for binding
5 florist's binding tape
6 needle and red thread
7 tape measure
8 scissors

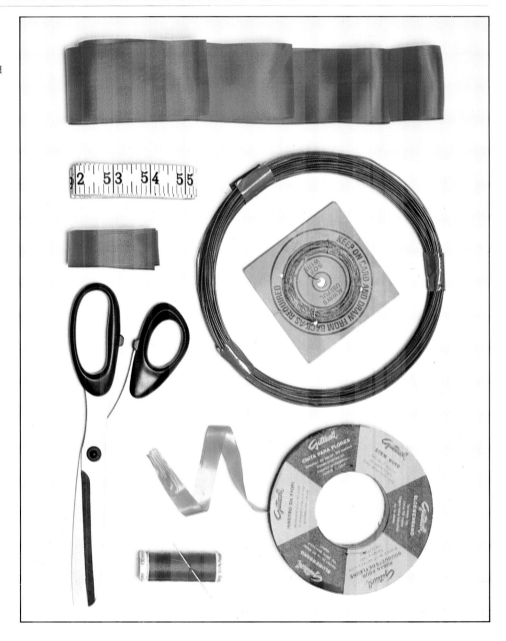

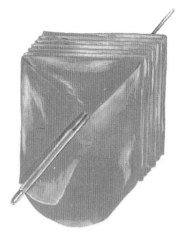

1 Measure and cut a length of ribbon. Take 1 end of the ribbon and fold it to make a right angle; make another right-angled fold in the opposite direction.

2 Continue making right-angled folds so that the ribbon is square in shape and there is a tiny hole in the centre. Leave a ribbon "tail" about 5cm (2 inches) in length that will form part of the stem.

3 Cut a 15cm (6 inch) length of stub wire and bend back 1 end so that it resembles a hair grip. Then, holding the ribbon square firmly in 1 hand, push the looped wire through the hole in the centre of the ribbon square. Thread the remaining 5cm (2 inches) of ribbon through the bent back loop of stub wire.

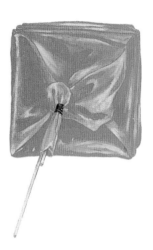

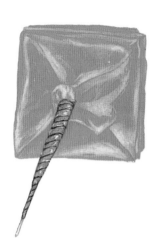

4 Twist the ribbon clockwise so that it coils around and around to form the centre of the rose. Turn the ribbon square over to check the rose centre and gently pull the wire back through the flower so that the wire cannot be seen from the front.

5 Bind the first fold with the leftover ribbon securely to the stem with fine wire. (Hold the square firmly while working or it will slip out of shape.) If necessary, use a needle and thread to stitch through the centre of the rose to hold it together.

6 Neatly bind the base of the stem with florist's binding tape to make a natural-looking "stalk". For a long-stemmed flower, push a longer stub wire up into the centre of the flower and wrap florist's binding tape along the length of stem. Mounted on long stems, a spray of ribbon roses can be used like silk flowers as a decorative feature in the bedroom.

THROW A PARTY

COME ONE, COME ALL

Entertaining is far less formal than it used to be; gone are the days of lengthy menus with everything done to etiquette-book standards. Today the host or hostess simply sticks to the one cardinal rule of entertaining: the comfort and enjoyment of the guests. If you like people and want to please them, you are well on your way to being a good host or hostess.

The secret of successful entertaining is individuality – in other words, your own style. Only you can entertain with the special feeling for colour, design, food, drink and atmosphere that is your personal style. Good food and good conversation are virtually inseparable, and if you provide the former in convivial surroundings, the latter will surely follow.

Mr. Fezziwig's Ball.

• Invite guests in numbers that you can cope with, bearing in mind the space that you have, the number of plates, knives, forks, and so forth.
• Do as much preparation in advance as possible (see Planning Ahead in Chapter 6, Festive Fare), leaving yourself free to enjoy your guests, and allowing guests time to enjoy your company.
• Deal with as much cleaning up as you can before guests arrive so that you have a neat kitchen in which to finish off and serve food.
• Plan it so that you have at least half an hour to relax before your guests arrive.

• Have drinks and canapés, if you're serving them, all ready. Turn on music that will not interfere with conversation. Light candles to soften the setting, to create a warm and friendly mood.
• Greet each guest at the door yourself and make them feel at home right away.
• Keep the "cocktail hour" to under an hour; 45 minutes is about right. If longer, people may drink and nibble enough to dull their appetites for what follows, or worse, they might get restless and very hungry. You may wish to put the times for drinks and for the meal on the invitation, such as "Drinks at 8:00, dinner at 8:45."
• Remember that one disappointing dish will not spoil the party. Ignore it or make light of it. Guests will hardly remember it, but they might remember if it makes you flustered or dampens your spirits.

PLANS AND INVITATIONS
The mix and number of people you plan to invite will dictate the type of party you will have. Few people have a table that will seat more than about eight for a sit-down dinner, but most homes can accommodate 20 people for a buffet party.

Once you have decided on the type of party you wish to give, start planning whom you are going to invite. When you have worked this out, organize the invitations and keep a good record of the replies, or you may lose track of those who have accepted and those who won't be able to come and for whom replacements may be needed. For something larger than a dinner party, it is easy to get carried away by over-enthusiasm, and that is when you find that the party you had originally intended for 20 has suddenly mushroomed into a gathering of 40.

There are no hard-and-fast rules when it comes to sending invitations. Generally speaking, invitations by telephone suffice for most adult occasions, especially for those that are fairly casual. A telephone call will give you, if you wish, the chance to mention who else is coming, what time the dinner will actually be served, and other news that might make your guests feel comfortable. But sending out written invitations, although often considered more formal, might actually be easier than calling guests, especially if you or they are working or otherwise usually busy during the day or evening. Written invitations are more polite for formal occasions and make it easier for you to keep a check on who has sent back their RSVPs. Because Christmas is the busiest social time for most people, give as much advance warning of the party as possible.

Blind Man's Buff, the children's party game, illustrated by W. St. Clair Simmons.

A SIT-DOWN DINNER

This will most likely be a three- or four-course dinner for six to twelve people. Because the food will clearly be the focus of the evening, choose the menu with care. Complement colours, textures, ingredients and spices and balance light courses with richer ones. Keep canapés, if you're serving them with before-dinner drinks, light so that dinner is clearly the main event. If you feel that place cards are too formal, ask guests to alternate woman-man and not to sit near partners. After a leisurely meal encourage your guests to move to the livingroom for coffee and chocolates or petits fours. It is a gracious way of giving people the opportunity to move about a little and perhaps sit next to someone else for a while. It also moves everyone away from an untidy table.

BUFFET PARTIES

A long table on which food is presented for guests to serve themselves is the best way for

The Queen of Sheba, a variation of Blind Man's Buff for adults.

Bishop, a warming punch (recipe page 152).

give them, in addition to regular napkins, large napkins for spreading over laps. And use china plates or sturdy plastic or paper dishes rather than the flimsy ones that can bend easily if not supported by a table.

COCKTAIL PARTIES

A cocktail party is usually a gathering of a relatively large mix of people for drinks — alcoholic and non-alcoholic — and snacks. It usually lasts for two or three hours in the early evening. Sometimes it takes the place of dinner and sometimes it doesn't. Most people appreciate knowing if they should plan dinner after the party or can expect there to be enough canapés to satisfy them, and as host or hostess you can enlighten them beforehand or make mention of the food on the invitations.

Rather than putting drinks and foods all in one place, spread them out so that people have reason to circulate about the room. Wine is always popular and so, generally, is beer. But these days mineral water with a slice of lemon or lime or mineral water mixed with orange juice is sometimes even more popular; serve it very cold in white wine glasses. For the holidays there are many hot drinks like grog and mulled wine and cold punches and champagne drinks that help to get people into the Christmas spirit. You'll find recipes for several special drinks later in this chapter; there are also a couple of them in Chapter 6.

having more than 12 or so for dinner. Since buffets usually involve a greater variety of dishes than do sit-down dinners, plan to have both hot and cold foods. That way you can have some dishes ready and waiting a little ahead of time, and you're not overloading your oven at the last minute. If quantities will be large, it is nice to prepare two serving dishes of each food rather than one large one so that you can remove the almost-empty one and replace it with a fresh one; a large one tends to look less appetizing after half the guests have helped themselves to it. Place drinks on another table to avoid congestion, and don't bring out the desserts until the main course has been cleared away.

While guests will not expect to sit at a table to eat, they will appreciate a tray table or a low table to share with others. At the least

CANAPÉS AND SNACKS

Since most people will probably be standing and (hopefully) talking, plan finger foods; have some hot and some cold. It's always nice to have some warm ones, full of flavour and straight from the oven, like the marinated Liver and Bacon Kebabs and the Crispy Ricotta Parcels featured here. But unless you have help, keep such canapés to a minimum; otherwise you'll spend more time in the kitchen taking foods in and out of the oven than with your guests.

MARINATED CHICKEN LIVER AND BACON KEBABS

Small wooden skewers for these little kebabs can be found in kitchen shops. Serves 8.

INGREDIENTS
350g (12 oz) chicken livers
350g (12 oz) streaky bacon, rinded
4 teaspoons Worcestershire sauce
4 teaspoons mushroom ketchup
2 tablespoons dried mustard
2 tablespoons dried mustard
1 teaspoon lemon juice
1 tablespoon tomato purée
50g (2 oz) butter, melted
watercress, to garnish

METHOD
1 Cut the chicken livers into 2.5cm (1 inch) pieces. Stretch the bacon rashers on a board with the back of a knife. Cut each rasher across in two and roll it up.
2 Thread the liver pieces and bacon rolls alternately onto small skewers.
3 Blend together the Worcestershire sauce, ketchup, mustard, lemon juice, tomato purée and butter.
4 Place the kebabs close together in a deep dish and pour the sauce over them. Cover, chill and marinate them for up to 6 hours.
5 Place the kebabs on a rack and grill under a high heat for 5-10 minutes, basting with the remaining sauce as they cook. Serve hot, garnished with watercress.

Variation Kebabs can be served as a main dish or a first course. For a main dish, accompany them with a green salad and French bread or on a bed of rice. Try using cubes of pork or lamb interspersed with onion and green pepper.
Simple marinade Combine 4 tablespoons oil, 4 tablespoons lemon juice, 2 tablespoons chopped parsley, 1 crushed garlic clove, salt and pepper.
Moroccan marinade Combine 1 small chopped onion, $1/2$ teaspoon salt, 1 teaspoon ground cumin, $1/2$ teaspoon black pepper, 4 tablespoons oil, and 1 teaspoon paprika for an extra-spicy flavour.

CRISPY RICOTTA PARCELS

Filo pastry wraps neatly around a flavoured cheese filling for a delicious finger food. Serves 8.

INGREDIENTS
225g (8 oz) ricotta cheese, softened
100g (4 oz) frozen spinach, chopped and thawed
100g (4 oz) smoked ham, finely chopped
$1/4$ teaspoon ground nutmeg
freshly ground black pepper
8 sheets filo pastry (strudel leaves)
75g (3 oz) butter, melted

METHOD
1 Preheat oven 220°C, 425°F, Gas Mark 7.
2 Place the cheese in a bowl. Squeeze the spinach dry in a sieve and add to the cheese with the ham, nutmeg and pepper to taste. Mix them together well.
3 Lay out the sheets of pastry on a work surface and keep them moist under a damp tea towel. Taking out 1 sheet of pastry at a time, cut lengthwise into 3 equal strips and brush well with butter.
4 Place a teaspoon of cheese at 1 end of each strip. Fold the pastry diagonally over the filling to enclose it in a triangle of pastry and continue to fold it over, working along the strip to finish with a neat triangular-shaped parcel of several layers of buttered pastry.
5 Brush with more butter and place on a baking sheet. Repeat the process with the remaining filling, pastry and butter. This will yield 24 small parcels.
6 Bake in the preheated oven for 8-10 minutes until golden brown. Serve hot.

Marinated chicken liver and bacon kebabs; Crispy ricotta parcels.

THE FESTIVE BOWL

Drinks for your Christmas celebrations need to be planned as carefully as the festive foods. It adds to the festive feeling if guests are offered a traditional hot punch or grog on arrival and when leaving.

Some people prefer not to drink alcohol, particularly if they are driving home afterward, but this need not mean their drinks are limited to straight fruit drinks or mineral water. Interesting non-alcoholic drinks are included here so that everyone can have a special celebration drink.

Punches

Punch is traditionally served from a large bowl with a ladle. Antique wash bowls make charming punch bowls, or alternatively a large mixing bowl can be used; arrange greenery around the sides to mask the utilitarian appearance. If you do not have a bowl of suitable size, serve from a large cooking pot. Punch should be served freshly made and hot.

Do not be tempted to serve guests with more than one – or two – punch drinks. Most punches are very palatable and easy to drink, but as some recipes have a mixture of alcoholic drinks in them it is easy to give your guests more than is good for them!

HEARTWARMER

This one packs a punch! Serves 12.

INGREDIENTS
200ml (7 fl oz) red grape juice
225g (8 oz) brown sugar
350ml (12 fl oz) dark rum
1.5 litres (2½ pints) dry white wine
450ml (¾ pint) red wine

METHOD
1 Warm the grape juice with the brown sugar until the sugar has completely dissolved. Stir in the rum and put aside.
2 Put the white wine and red wine together in a saucepan and heat until they are hot but not boiling. Add the rum and grape juice mixture and stir together. Serve hot.

CHRISTMAS PUNCH

A punch that smells just like Christmas. Serves 8.

INGREDIENTS
10 sugar cubes
2 large oranges
8 cloves
1 teaspoon cinnamon
1 teaspoon ground nutmeg
150ml (¼ pint) water
thinly peeled rind and juice of 2 lemons
1.2 litres (2 pints) dry cider
150ml (¼ pint) rum or brandy

METHOD
1 Rub the sugar cubes over the oranges to absorb the zest.
2 Squeeze the juice from 1 orange and put into a saucepan with the sugar.
3 Cut the second orange into eighths. Push a clove into the peel of each segment. Add to the juice and sugar, sprinkle on the spices and stir. Leave to marinate for 15 minutes.
4 Add the water, lemon rind and juice. Heat gently without stirring until the sugar dissolves, then add the cider. Continue heating until hot.
5 Add the rum or brandy and serve hot.

BISHOP

Do the final preparation of this punch at the serving table so all can enjoy the flaming orange. Serves 12.

INGREDIENTS
3 oranges
24 cloves
½ bottle of inexpensive port
1 tablespoon clear honey
2 tablespoons brandy, warmed

METHOD
1 Heat oven 180°C, 350°F, Gas Mark 4.
2 Stud 2 of the oranges with cloves and bake in a dish in the oven until the oranges begin to go soft and slightly brown (about 15 minutes).

3 Heat the port and honey together in a pan and add one of the cooked oranges. Simmer for about 15 minutes.

4 Put the second baked orange into a ladle or a large spoon and pour the brandy over it. Set the orange alight and, while it is still burning, lower it into the port.

5 Slice the third orange thinly and add to the punch. Serve hot in glasses, making sure there is a slice of orange in each glass.

MULLED DRINKS

Mulls were traditionally mixed at the fireside and heated with a red-hot poker.

MULLED ALE

Don't substitute beer or light ale; it won't taste the same. Serves 10.

INGREDIENTS
1.2 litres (2 pints) brown ale
150ml (1/4 pint) rum or brandy
3 tablespoons well-packed brown sugar
6 cloves
1 teaspoon ground ginger
pinch of ground nutmeg and cinnamon
thinly peeled rind and juice of 1 lemon
thinly peeled rind and juice of 1 orange
600ml (1 pint) water
orange slice, to decorate

LEFT TO RIGHT *Mulled Ale; Mulled Claret; Egg Nog.*

METHOD
1 Put all ingredients except the orange slice into a large pan. Bring slowly to a boil, stirring all the time to dissolve the sugar.

2 Turn off the heat and leave to stand for a few minutes. Strain into a warmed jug and serve, with a slice of orange on top.

MULLED CLARET

Heat but do not boil the wine and port. Serves 9

INGREDIENTS
1 bottle claret or other wine
1/4 bottle inexpensive port
600ml (1 pint) boiling water
brown or white sugar to taste
pinch of ground nutmeg
cinnamon stick

METHOD
1 Heat the wine and port together in a saucepan, pour in the water and stir.

2 Add the sugar and nutmeg and serve hot, with a stick of cinnamon.

Grogs

A hot grog, served on a cold night, warms the heart and builds up Christmas spirit.

GOODNIGHT GROG

This grog also uses tea. Serves 8.

INGREDIENTS
900ml (1 1/2 pints) Indian tea, strained
300ml (1/2 pint) dark rum or whisky
2 tablespoons brown sugar or 1 1/2
tablespoons clear honey
5cm (2 inch) cinnamon stick
pinch of mixed spice

METHOD
1 Put the tea into a saucepan with the rum or whisky, sugar or honey, the cinnamon stick and the spice. Heat gently, stirring constantly. Leave to stand for a few minutes, remove cinnamon and serve warm.

GINGER SNAP

The ginger wine and nutmeg gives this drink its snap. Serves 4.

INGREDIENTS
300ml (½ pint) water
275ml (9 fl oz) ginger wine
2 tablespoons lime juice
1 tablespoon brown sugar
1 pinch of ground nutmeg

METHOD
1 Heat the water to boiling and pour over the other ingredients in a bowl or jug.
2 Stir until the sugar dissolves. Serve hot.

WINE CUP

A sparkling wine punch with a hint of citrus. Serves 8.

INGREDIENTS
thinly peeled rind of 1 lemon
90ml (3 fl oz) white rum
1 miniature bottle of orange-flavoured liqueur
2 bottles red wine
3 bottles ginger ale

METHOD
1 Marinate the lemon peel in the rum and liqueur for about 2 hours.
2 To serve, pour over the Bordeaux and ginger ale and stir. Chill with ice cubes.

CIDER CUP

The cider here is the alcoholic one. Serves 8.

INGREDIENTS
1 litre (1¾ pints) bottle dry cider
1 litre (1¾ pints) bottle soda water
1 wineglass of brandy
1 tablespoon lemon juice
2 tablespoons sugar (optional)

TO DECORATE
thin strips of cucumber peel
thin strips of lemon rind

METHOD
1 Chill the cider and soda. Pour into a

chilled bowl with the brandy and lemon juice and stir well. If desired, add sugar to sweeten.
2 Decorate with cucumber and lemon peel strips and serve in chilled glasses.

LOVING CUP

Serve this in small glasses as it's a strong punch. Serves 12.

INGREDIENTS
8 sugar cubes
2 lemons
½ bottle medium sweet or sweet sherry
¼ bottle brandy
1 bottle dry sparkling white wine

METHOD
1 Rub the sugar cubes over the lemons to absorb the zest.
2 Peel the lemons thinly and remove as much of the pith as possible. Slice the lemons thinly and put aside.
3 Put the lemon peel, sherry and brandy and sugar cubes in a jug and stir until the sugar is dissolved. Chill for about 30 minutes.
4 Pour in the wine just before serving and float the lemon slices on top.

SPICY FRUIT PUNCH

Fruit juice can be mixed together and diluted with a variety of soft drinks – almost any combination works.

INGREDIENTS
600ml (1 pint) orange juice
600ml (1 pint) apple juice
150ml (¼ pint) water
½ teaspoon ground ginger
½ teaspoon mixed spice
brown or white sugar to taste (optional)
1 apple, thinly sliced, to decorate

METHOD
1 Place the juices, water and spices in a pan and bring gently to the boil, stirring in sugar to taste. Simmer for 5 minutes.
2 Pour into a warmed punch bowl and serve with slices of apple on top.

Syrups

Flavoured syrup makes a delicious base for cups and for soft drinks. Try experimenting with different flavours so you have a wide selection of drinks to offer friends.

ORANGE SYRUP

Make this before Christmas and bottle it ready for use. Citric acid can be found in some supermarkets and chemists.

INGREDIENTS
thinly peeled rind and juice of 3 large oranges
900ml (1½ pints) water
1kg (2 lb) granulated sugar
1 tablespoon citric acid

METHOD
1 Place the orange peel in a pan with the water and sugar. Heat gently, stirring until all the sugar is dissolved. Bring to the boil and boil for 10 minutes. Remove from the heat and leave to stand overnight.
2 The next day, stir in the orange juice and citric acid. Strain and pour the syrup into bottles. Seal tightly with a cork and store for up to 3 months.

Variations

Lemon syrup is made in the same way, or a mixture of oranges and lemons makes an interesting flavour.
Ginger lemon Slice 25g (1 oz) of the ginger root into the syrup before boiling.
Lemon syrup drinks For a pleasantly soothing nightcap, dilute lemon syrup with hot water and add a pinch each of ground cloves, cinnamon and allspice.

CHAMPAGNE DRINKS

Good champagne is a drink all on its own and needs no dressing up. Less expensive champagnes and sparkling wines form the basis of delicious light drinks, suitable for morning parties.

A Buck's Fizz, made of equal quantities of champagne and fresh orange juice, is a classic of its kind.

EGG NOG

Dutch in origin, egg nog is a delicious rich drink for a holiday brunch. Serves 8-10.

INGREDIENTS
10 egg yolks
100g (4 oz) caster sugar
475ml (16 fl oz) brandy

METHOD
1 Beat the egg yolks with the sugar until thick and light coloured and all the sugar is dissolved.
2 Fold in the brandy. Serve immediately in small glasses.

SPARKLING COCKTAIL

A delicious and surprisingly inexpensive party drink just right for a special toast. Serves 1.

INGREDIENTS
1 small sugar cane
2 drops of bitters
1 tablespoon brandy
dry sparkling white wine

METHOD
Place the sugar cube, bitters and brandy in a large wineglass. Leave until the sugar has dissolved. When ready to serve, fill up with the sparkling wine.

CALVADOS TODDY

A warming drink which serves 1.

INGREDIENTS
calvados
1 teaspoon sugar
hot water
ground nutmeg

METHOD
1 Put about 2.5cm (1 inch) of calvados in a thick glass.
2 Add the sugar, fill the glass with hot water and sprinkle the toddy with a little nutmeg.

SUPPER FOR TEN

This light supper, followed by 2 luscious desserts, is ideal for a post-Christmas supper party. For a change, it is the first course that is hot, so you need not worry about setting out the main course a bit ahead of time. The main dish, Curried Turkey Salad, uses left-over turkey, but the delicate spices and fruit will not remind anyone of a leftover Christmas dinner.

MENU

Carrot and Coriander Soup

Herb Bread
Curried Turkey Salad
Tomato, Bean and Artichoke Salad

Rum Syllabubs with Brandy Snaps
Spiced Sponge Roll

CARROT AND CORIANDER SOUP

A colourful, lightly spiced start to the meal. Serves 10.

INGREDIENTS
75g (3 oz) butter or margarine
225g (8 oz) onions, peeled and chopped
750g (1½ lb) carrots, scraped and sliced
3 tablespoons plain flour
1.2 litres (2 pints) chicken stock
salt
freshly ground black pepper
1 tablespoon ground coriander seeds
1 bay leaf
1 tablespoon lemon juice
600ml (1 pint) milk
150ml (¼ pint) single cream
2 tablespoons chopped
fresh parsley, to garnish

METHOD
1 Melt the butter in a large saucepan. Add the onions and sauté over a gentle heat for about 5 minutes or until soft and lightly coloured. Add the carrots, stir to coat in butter, and sauté for another 2-3 minutes.
2 Stir in the flour and cook for 1-2 minutes, then gradually stir in the stock and bring to the boil.
3 Season well with salt and pepper and add the coriander, bay leaf and lemon juice. Cover the pan and simmer gently for about 30 minutes or until the carrots are very tender.
4 Discard the bay leaf and purée the soup in a food processor or blender, or pass through a sieve.

5 Return to a clean pan with the milk and return to the boil. Taste and adjust the seasoning, stir in the cream and reheat gently. Serve at once in warmed soup bowls, garnished with chopped parsley. Serve with herb bread (see below).

HERB BREAD

Garlic and herbs spice up plain French bread.

INGREDIENTS
1 long French loaf
175g (6 oz) butter
1 clove garlic, peeled and crushed
2 tablespoons dried mixed herbs
salt
freshly ground black pepper

METHOD
1 Preheat oven 200°C, 400°F, Gas Mark 6.
2 Cut the loaf diagonally into slices about 2.5cm (1 inch) thick, without cutting through the bottom crust.
3 Beat the butter in a bowl until soft and creamy, then beat in the garlic, herbs, salt and pepper. Spread the herb butter on both sides of each slice of bread.
4 Wrap the loaf in foil and bake in a preheated oven for 10-15 minutes. Serve hot, cut into slices.

CURRIED TURKEY SALAD

A lovely mixture of cold turkey, garlic sausage, fruit and spices. Serves 10.

CLOCKWISE FROM LEFT Curried Turkey Salad, Herb Bread, Carrot and Coriander Soup, Tomato, Bean and Artichoke Salad

INGREDIENTS

450g (1 lb) long-grain rice
salt
3 tablespoons chopped parsley
grated rind of 1 lemon
200ml (7 fl oz) mayonnaise
6 tablepsoons French dressing
1½-2 teaspoons curry powder
freshly ground black pepper
900g-1.25kg (2-2½ lb) cooked turkey meat, diced
225g (8 oz) garlic sausage, sliced
1 × 425g (15 oz) can pineapple pieces, drained
1 × 425g (15 oz) can sliced mangoes, drained and roughly chopped
1 bunch spring onions, chopped
225g (8 oz) cooked peas
8-10 celery sticks, sliced
mustard and cress, to garnish

METHOD

1 Cook the rice in a large saucepan of boiling salted water for 15-20 minutes or until just tender. Drain and rinse under cold running water, then drain again. Turn into a bowl and mix in the parsley and lemon rind.

2 In a large bowl combine the mayonnaise and French dressing with curry powder and salt and pepper to taste.

3 Add the turkey meat and turn in the dressing to coat thoroughly. Chop half the garlic sausage and add to the bowl with all the remaining ingredients. Mix lightly to coat evenly. Cover and chill for at least 1 hour.

4 Arrange the rice around the edge of a large serving dish and spoon the turkey into the centre.

5 Roll the remaining slices of garlic sausage into cones and arrange around the edge of the salad. Garnish with mustard and cress.

TOMATO, BEAN AND ARTICHOKE SALAD

Whole cherry tomatoes can be substituted for the tomato quarters here. Serves 10.

INGREDIENTS
750g (1½ lb) French beans, trimmed
2 × 425g (15 oz) can artichoke hearts, drained
150ml (¼ pint) French dressing
salt, freshly ground black pepper
750g (1½ lb) tomatoes, quartered

METHOD
1 Cook the beans in a large pan of boiling salted water for 3-5 minutes. Drain and cool. Cut the beans into 5cm (2-inch) lengths and place in a bowl.
2 Cut the artichoke hearts into quarters and add to the beans with the dressing and salt and pepper. Toss lightly but thoroughly and transfer to a large dish. Arrange the tomato wedges around the edge of the dish.

RUM SYLLABUBS

A frothy, sweet but very light dessert. Serves 6-8.

INGREDIENTS
150ml (¼ pint) medium white wine
finely grated rind of 1 orange
4 tablespoons caster sugar
4-5 tablespoons rum or Cointreau
600ml (1 pint) double cream

METHOD
1 Put the wine, orange rind and sugar in a large bowl, stir to mix and leave to stand for about 1 hour.
2 Add the rum or Cointreau and then gradually pour in the cream. Whisk until the mixture stands in soft peaks.
3 Pour into 6-8 glasses and chill in the refrigerator for up to 30 minutes. Serve with brandy snaps.

BRANDY SNAPS

These light and very delicate biscuits are well worth the effort. Makes 12-16.

INGREDIENTS
50g (2 oz) butter
50g (2 oz) golden syrup
50g (2 oz) caster sugar
50g (2 oz) plain flour
¼ teaspoon ground ginger

METHOD
1 Line baking sheets with silicone paper and grease several wooden spoon handles. Preheat oven to 160°C, 325°F, Gas Mark 3.
2 Melt the butter with the golden syrup and sugar, then remove from heat.
3 Sift the flour and ginger together and beat into the melted mixture.
4 Place teaspoons of the mixture well apart on the baking sheets and spread out a little. Bake for 8-10 minutes or until golden brown.
5 Cool until just firm enough to remove with a spatula, then immediately wind around the spoon handles. If the brandy snaps become too brittle before winding, return to the oven for a minute or so and try again. Leave to cool on a wire rack until firm, then slide off the handles.

SPICED SPONGE ROLL

Whipped cream inside and out make this a luscious holiday indulgence. Serves 8.

INGREDIENTS
4 eggs
100g (4 oz) caster sugar
100g (4 oz) plain flour
¼ teaspoon ground ginger
¼ teaspoon mixed spice
25g (1 oz) butter, melted and cooled
icing sugar, sifted

FILLING
450ml (¾ pint) double cream
4-6 tablespoons ginger marmalade
1 × 300g (11 oz) can mandarin orange segments, drained
a few pieces of stem ginger, (optional)

METHOD

1 Grease 30×25cm (12×10in) Swiss roll tin, line with greaseproof paper. Lightly flour. Preheat oven 190°C, 375°F, GM5.

2 Put the eggs and sugar into the top of a double boiler. Place it over gently simmering water and whisk until the mixture is thick and the whisk leaves a thick trail when lifted. Remove from the heat.

3 Sift the flour, ginger and spice together twice and fold lightly and evenly into the egg mixture. Finally fold in the cooled butter using a large metal spoon.

4 Pour the mixture into the prepared pan and spread out lightly, making sure the corners are well filled. Bake for 15-20 minutes or until pale brown and just firm and springy to the touch.

5 Turn the sponge onto a sheet of grease-proof paper lightly sprinkled with icing sugar. Peel off the lining paper immediately and trim the edges of the sponge neatly with a sharp knife. While still warm roll up from a short edge, with the paper inside. Leave to cool completely on a wire rack.

6 Whip the cream until stiff. Reserve 2 tablespoons and fold the ginger marmalade into the remainder.

7 Unroll the sponge carefully and remove the paper. Spread the ginger cream over the sponge. Reserve 8 of the best mandarin orange segments for decoration and arrange the remainder over the ginger cream. Reroll the sponge carefully, dredge with icing sugar and place on a serving dish.

8 Put the reserved cream in a piping bag fitted with a star nozzle. Pipe a line of cream down the centre of the roll. Decorate with the remaining mandarins and pieces of stem ginger, if using. Chill in the refrigerator until ready to serve.

FRONT Spiced Sponge Roll BACK Rum Syllabubs with Brandy Snaps

A JOINT CHRISTMAS PARTY

The Christmas season is the busiest time of the year for most people. At the very least there are presents to be bought, a tree to be decorated, cakes to be baked, and cards to send. Having friends over to share the holiday spirit is usually an important part of Christmas, too, but on top of everything else, it can seem just too much.

A party organized as a joint effort may be the answer. If each person or family brings a dish, the work – and expense – of a dinner party is shared among several people. As host or hostess, you can concentrate your efforts on decorating the house, arranging the table and the drinks and perhaps preparing one or two dishes. There is also less work for you to do during the party, and less work cleaning up afterward.

Joint parties are particularly good for informal family get-togethers where the guestlist can quickly grow into a small crowd. Children, often fussier eaters than grownups, will have several dishes to choose from and will be particularly happy if their parents had the good sense to bring a dish that they know their children will enjoy.

It's quite usual on these occasions for the host or hostess to divide the meal into courses – for instance, appetizer, main dish, salad or side dish, and dessert – and ask each guest or family to bring a dish for one of those courses. This way you can be certain that you don't end up with five desserts and only one main dish!

Or you may decide to plan the menu yourself, complete with recipes, or use the one here, and then ask each guest or family to make one of the dishes. This way you can be certain that all the dishes will work well together. It will also allow you to accommodate someone who likes to cook but isn't very sure of their skills in the kitchen. You could ask this person to bring one of the easier dishes, such as Spinach and Walnut Salad, in the menu here.

As the host or hostess you may decide to make the centrepiece dish – a substantial food around which all the other dishes can sit, such as Honey-Glazed Ham.

MENU

Honey-Glazed Ham

Creamy Noodles
Green Beans with Almonds
Spinach and Walnut Salad
Courgette Salad

Red Fruit Salad
Thumbprint Biscuits

The party menu below is designed to appeal to most palates. The dishes, except for the ham, are all relatively easy and fairly quick to prepare, which is important when you are deciding what other people should make. There should be enough food here to feed a hungry group of 16 adults. Add, subtract or substitute to suit your guestlist.

TIPS FOR JOINT PARTIES

● If arranging the menu yourself, choose dishes that are not difficult or expensive to make, unless you are planning a gourmet dinner.
● Even though you might have a menu prepared, with a dish in mind for each guest, it would be nice to let your friends know that you're receptive to their suggesting an alternative dish – one of their choosing – for that particular course.
● Ask guests to write their names on a piece of freezer tape and stick it on the bottom of their serving dish, this way you'll know what belongs to whom at going-home time.
● Joint parties are best arranged as buffet dinners, with all the dishes except the desserts placed on the serving table at the same time. Desserts, tea and coffee can be brought out when the main part of the meal is over and the table is cleared. Because everyone helps themselves, no one need wonder if the person who made a particular dish is supposed to serve it, or if that is left to the host or hostess.
● If wine is appropriate at your party, you could ask each guest to bring along a bottle, as well as their dish.

HONEY-GLAZED HAM

This is great for a party because it's large enough to feed a crowd, and leftovers can be put to good use. Carve the first few slices but keep the rest whole and let guests slice and serve themselves.

INGREDIENTS
3.5kg (8 lb) shank end of gammon
2 bay leaves
4 whole cloves
6 black peppercorns
1 large onion, peeled and sliced
600ml (1 pint) sweet cider
50g (2 oz) soft dark brown sugar

GLAZE
100g (4 oz) clear honey
about 2 tablespoons whole cloves
3 tablespoons demerara sugar

METHOD
1 Soak the ham in cold water overnight, or bring it to a boil in a large pan of water, then drain. Pat the ham dry on kitchen paper.
2 Place the ham in a pan large enough for the ham and cooking liquid. Put in the bay leaves, 4 cloves, peppercorns, onion, cider and dark brown sugar. Pour on enough cold water to cover. Bring the water to the boil, skimming if necessary. Cover the pan, lower the heat and simmer for 2 hours 35 minutes, or 20 minutes to the pound.
3 Remove the ham from the stock and allow to cool (reserve the stock for soup). When it is cool enough to handle, carefully cut away the skin. Trim off some of the fat, taking care to leave a smooth, even surface.
4 Preheat oven 220°C, 425°F, Gas Mark 7.
5 Brush all over the surface of the ham with the honey. Stick the 2 tablespoons cloves into the fat to make a lattice pattern. Sprinkle the sugar over the fat.
6 Place the ham in a roasting tin and bake for 30 minutes, turning the meat once.
7 Transfer the ham to a dish to cool. Wrap it in foil and chill in the refrigerator. Remove it from the refrigerator and leave at room temperature for 4-5 hours before serving.

Honey-glazed ham provides a festive touch to any buffet table.

CREAMY NOODLES

This is an easy dish to make and one that almost everyone likes. For children you may wish to leave out the olives. Serves 16.

INGREDIENTS
1 kg (2 lbs) green ribbon noodles
550g (1 lb 4 oz) cream cheese
225g (8 oz) chopped black olives
100g (4 oz) butter
5 tablespoons chopped fresh parsley
1½ tablespoons dried basil
salt, freshly ground black pepper

METHOD
1 Preheat the oven to 180°C, 350°F, Gas Mark 4. Lightly butter two large casserole dishes.
2 Cook the noodles in boiling salted water until tender but not soft – about 10 minutes; keep them hot. Melt the butter and set it aside. Cut the cream cheese into small cubes and toss it with the noodles and olives until the cheese melts. Stir in the melted butter, basil, parsley and salt and pepper to taste.
3 Place half the noodle mixture in each casserole dish. Cover with lid or foil and bake for 20 minutes.

FRENCH BEANS WITH ALMONDS

The addition of the almonds elevates french beans to something quite special. Serves 16.

INGREDIENTS
1.75kg (4 lbs) french beans, trimmed
50g (2 oz) butter
2 crushed garlic cloves
2 cups slivered almonds
¼ cup lemon juice
salt
freshly ground black pepper

METHOD

1 Place the beans in a large pot of about 1 cup boiling water and simmer for about 12 minutes. Drain.

2 Meanwhile, melt the butter in another pan and fry the garlic and slivered almonds until lightly browned stirring all the time. Stir in the lemon juice and season to taste with salt and pepper.

Spinach and walnut salad.

3 Add the beans to the pan and cook, tossing gently, until they are heated through.

SPINACH AND WALNUT SALAD

Raw spinach will quickly become a family favourite. Serve as a starter or accompaniment to a hot dish. Serves 16.

INGREDIENTS
450g (1 lb) young spinach leaves, washed and stems removed
100g (4 oz) shelled walnuts, slightly chopped
10 shallots or 3 small onions, very finely chopped

DRESSING
2 tablespoons white wine vinegar
6 tablespoons walnut or olive oil
salt
freshly ground black pepper

METHOD

1 Tear the spinach leaves into pieces and place in a wooden salad bowl. Stir in the walnuts and shallots or onions. Cover and chill for 10 minutes.

2 Place the vinegar, oil and seasoning in a screw top jar and shake until blended. Pour the dressing over the salad and toss well to coat the leaves.

COURGETTE SALAD

A raw vegetable salad that marinates in its dressing. Serves 16.

INGREDIENTS
1.35 kg (3 lb) courgettes, thinly sliced
12 spring onions, peeled and finely chopped
3 tablespoons chopped fresh chives
300ml (½ pint) olive oil
50ml (2 fl oz) white wine vinegar
3 garlic cloves, crushed
salt
freshly ground black pepper
3 tablespoons capers

METHOD

1 Mix the courgettes with the spring onions and chopped chives in a salad bowl.
2 Mix the olive oil with the wine vinegar, garlic, salt and pepper to taste, then add the capers.
3 Stir the dressing into the salad ingredients, so that the courgettes are evenly coated. Allow the salad to stand in a cool place for 1 hour to allow the flavours to mingle.

RED FRUIT SALAD

A Christmas-coloured fruit salad that is easy to make. Fluffy yoghurt ensures the perfect light accompaniment. Serves 16.

INGREDIENTS
2 × 425g (15 oz) cans black cherries, pitted and drained with juice reserved
450ml (¾ pint) apple juice
1.75kg (4 lb) firm pears
1kg (2 lb) frozen raspberries
750g (1½ lb) black grapes, halved and seeded

TO SERVE
Fluffy yogurt (see below)

METHOD

1 Place the cherries in a large serving bowl. Put the cherry juice into a saucepan with the apple juice.
2 Peel, core and slice the pears and add to the pan. Bring to the boil and simmer for about 6 minutes. Add the contents of the pan to the cherries.
3 Sprinkle the still frozen raspberries over the warm fruit and leave at room temperature until thawed.
4 Finally add the grapes, mix well, and chill until required. Serve alone or with Fluffy yogurt.

Fluffy yogurt
1 Turn 600ml (1 pint) yogurt into a bowl and stir with a fork until smooth.
2 Whisk 4 egg whites until very stiff and fold evenly through the yogurt.

3 Sprinkle lightly with grated nutmeg and serve with the Red Fruit Salad.

THUMBPRINT BISCUITS

Call in the children to help you press their thumbs into the dough before you bake it. Makes about 6 dozen biscuits.

INGREDIENTS
225g (8 oz) butter or solid (not tub) margarine
450g (1 lb) caster sugar
4 eggs
2 teaspoons vanilla essence
450g (1 lb) plain flour
2 teaspoons baking powder
½ teaspoon bicarbonate of soda
apricot and raspberry jams

METHOD

1 Preheat the oven to 180°C, 350°F, Gas Mark 4 and grease baking sheets.
2 Beat the butter or margarine and then add the sugar and beat again until light and fluffy. Add the eggs, one at a time, then add the vanilla essence and beat well.
3 Sift together the flour, baking powder and bicarbonate of soda. Then add this mixture gradually to the butter mixture, beating until a soft dough forms.
4 Cover the bowl and chill the dough for about 1 hour or until cold and easy to handle.
5 Roll the dough between the palms of your hands into small balls (about 2.5cm, 1 inch in diameter) and place on the baking sheets about 5cm (2 inches) apart. Then push your thumb into the centre of each ball to slightly flatten it and create a little well in the middle. (You may want to dip your thumb in ice water as you go along to keep the dough from sticking.) Then fill each well with one of the jams.
6 Bake for 15-20 minutes, taking care not to brown the biscuits.

A CHILDREN'S CHRISTMAS

If you are planning to have your Christmas dinner in the evening it may be more practical to give the children a special Christmas feast of their own at lunchtime. The menu is planned for six children but could easily be doubled up for a bigger party. Older children and young teenagers will enjoy Crunchy Chicken and Peppermint Ice Cream Mice just as much as the smaller children!

To create a festive atmosphere it's fun to have individual place settings for each child. Start with brightly coloured paper plates and napkins, then add a jolly paper hat or maybe a balloon with the child's name drawn in felt-tip pen so that when it's blown up the name expands! There are endless ways to make the meal full of gaiety.

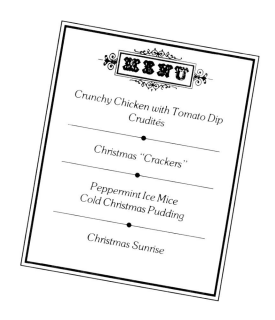

MENU

Crunchy Chicken with Tomato Dip
Crudités

Christmas "Crackers"

Peppermint Ice Mice
Cold Christmas Pudding

Christmas Sunrise

CRUNCHY CHICKEN WITH TOMATO DIP

Easy-to-eat finger food for hungry children. Serves 6.

INGREDIENTS
4 chicken breasts, skinned and boned
1 egg, beaten
4 packets unsalted crisps
¼ teaspoon dry mustard
¼ teaspoon paprika
salt
freshly ground black pepper
margarine or butter, for greasing

FOR THE TOMATO DIP
50g (2 oz) cream cheese, softened
150ml (¼ pint) natural yogurt
2 tablespoons tomato relish
2 tablespoons finely diced green pepper
salt, freshly ground black pepper
raw vegetable sticks

METHOD
1 Heat the oven to 220°C, 350°F, Gas Mark 7. Cut the chicken pieces into chunks and dip them in beaten egg to coat.
2 Pierce the crisp bags and crush the crisps in them, using a rolling pin. Pour the crushed crisps into a bowl and mix in the mustard, paprika and seasoning. Toss the coated chicken chunks in the mixture.
3 Grease baking sheets with margarine or butter and place the chicken chunks on the sheets. Bake in the oven for 15-20 minutes or until the chicken is tender.
4 For the tomato dip, blend the cream cheese gradually into the yogurt until the mixture is smooth. Stir in the relish and the green pepper and season to taste.
5 Serve the hot chicken chunks on cocktail sticks ready to dip, accompanied by sticks of raw carrot, red pepper, green pepper and celery.

Variation Instead of using chicken pieces, you can also use drumsticks for the children to eat with their fingers. Increase the baking time to 30-40 minutes and serve the dip on the individual plates.

CHRISTMAS CRACKERS

When they're done these look like traditional Christmas crackers. The surprise is the frankfurter! Serves 6.

INGREDIENTS

9 sheets filo pastry (strudel leaves) or 450g (1 lb) puff pastry
75g (3 oz) margarine or butter, melted
18 cocktail-sized frankfurters (or cooked sausages)
6 tablespoons smooth chutney
mint leaves, to garnish

METHOD

1 Heat oven 220°C, 425°F, Gas Mark 7.
2 Lay out the sheets of pastry on a work surface and keep them moist under a damp tea towel.
3 Take 1 sheet of filo pastry at a time. Cut in half widthwise to give 2 small rectangles. Brush with melted margarine or butter. Place a frankfurter at 1 short side and spread a teaspoon of chutney on it. Roll up the sausage inside the pastry, working from the short side. If you are using puff pastry, roll it out thinly, cut into rectangles and wrap once around the frankfurters.
4 Pinch the pastry at either side of the frankfurter to resemble a Christmas cracker and brush again with margarine. Repeat to use the remaining ingredients to make 18 crackers.
5 Place the crackers on a baking sheet and bake in the oven for 10 minutes until golden brown. Serve hot, with extra chutney if desired, and garnished with mint leaves.

CLOACKWISE FROM TOP Christmas Crackers; Crunchy Chicken with Tomato Dip; Cold Christmas Pudding; Christmas Sunrise; Peppermint Ice Mice

PEPPERMINT ICE MICE
Fun to look at, fun to eat. Serves 6.

INGREDIENTS
300ml (½ pint) milk
2 egg yolks
50g (2 oz) caster sugar
2 teaspoons cornflour
300ml (½ pint) double cream, whipped
½ teaspoon peppermint essence, or to taste
few drops green food colouring

TO DECORATE
liquorice strips
flaked almonds
silver dragees

METHOD
1 Whisk the egg yolks and sugar together until very light and thick. Blend the cornflour with a little of the milk to a smooth cream. Strain the remaining milk onto the egg yolk mixture and whisk until blended. Stir in the cornflour.

2 Set the mixture in a bowl over a pan of simmering water. Cook until the mixture coats the back of a wooden spoon.

3 Cool the custard, pour into a shallow container and freeze until of a mushy consistency. Turn out and whisk until smooth. Fold in the cream, peppermint essence and a few drops of colouring. Pour into a container, cover, and freeze until solid.

4 Allow to soften in the refrigerator for 1 hour before serving. To serve, scoop out small and large rounds of ice cream for heads and bodies. Push in strips of liquorice for tails, slivered almonds for ears and silver dragees for eyes, to represent mice.

COLD CHRISTMAS PUDDING
Simple strawberry or raspberry jelly dressed up for Christmas. Serves 6.

INGREDIENTS
75g (3 oz) white fondant icing or white marzipan
few drops of green food colouring
icing sugar
2 packets strawberry or raspberry jelly
75g (3 oz) sultanas
50g (2 oz) glacé cherries, halved
25g (1 oz) blanched almonds, chopped
15g (½ oz) angelica, chopped
a little whipped cream, to decorate

METHOD
1 Make holly leaves by kneading the rolled icing or marzipan with green food colouring. Roll out to 5mm (¼ inch) thickness between sheets of greaseproof paper, dusting with icing sugar to prevent the mixture from sticking. Cut out the leaves with a cutter or cardboard template. Lay the leaves over the rolling pin to give them a slight curve and leave to dry overnight.

2 Make up the jelly according to package directions, using 50ml (2 fl oz) less water than directed. Leave the jelly to cool. When it is on the point of setting, stir in the sultanas, cherries, almonds and angelica. Pour the jelly into 6 small moulds and allow to set completely.

3 Turn out by dipping the moulds in hot water for a few seconds. Decorate each pudding with a little whipped cream and the holly leaves.

Variation A firmer jelly, which can be sliced with a knife and served with cream, is made by increasing the amount of dried fruit and nuts.

CHRISTMAS SUNRISE

Be sure to serve these in clear plastic glasses so children can see the "sunrise". Serves 6.

INGREDIENTS
300ml (½ pint) fresh orange juice
2 tablespoons lemon juice
600ml (1 pint) lemonade, chilled
3 tablespoons grenadine syrup

METHOD
1 Mix together the orange juice, lemon juice and lemonade and pour into tall glasses.
2 Carefully pour the grenadine into each glass to that it sinks to the bottom, giving a sunrise effect. Serve with decorative straws.

COLA FLOAT

A special party drink that is always popular. Serves 6.

INGREDIENTS
900 ml (1½ pints)
6 scoops vanilla easy scoop ice cream

METHOD
1 Fill 6 glasses three-quarters full with cola then place a scoop of ice cream on top. Serve with straws.

APPLE AND GINGER FIZZ

A cooling fizzy drink that children adore. Serves 6.

INGREDIENTS
600ml (1 pint) apple juice
300ml (½ pint) ginger ale
ice cubes
1 red-skinned apple

METHOD
1 Place the apple juice and ginger ale in a jug. Add ice cubes. Thinly slice the apple, discarding the core. Float the apple slices on the drink and serve.

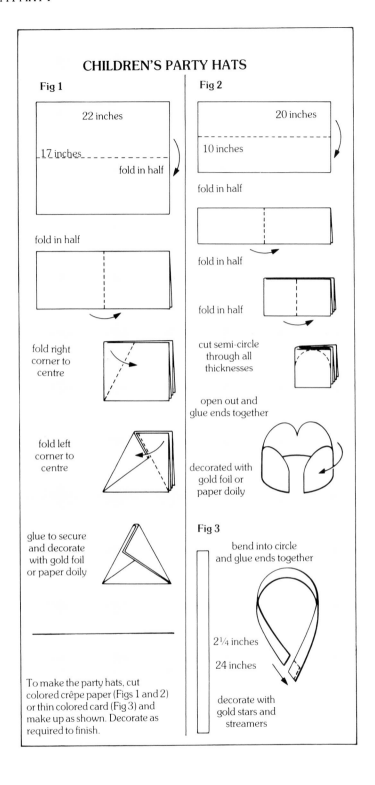

CHILDREN'S PARTY HATS

Fig 1

22 inches
17 inches
fold in half

fold in half

fold right corner to centre

fold left corner to centre

glue to secure and decorate with gold foil or paper doily

Fig 2

20 inches
10 inches
fold in half

fold in half

fold in half

cut semi-circle through all thicknesses

open out and glue ends together

decorated with gold foil or paper doily

Fig 3

bend into circle and glue ends together

2¼ inches
24 inches

decorate with gold stars and streamers

To make the party hats, cut colored crêpe paper (Figs 1 and 2) or thin colored card (Fig 3) and make up as shown. Decorate as required to finish.

CAROLS FOR CHRISTMAS

SONGS FOR ONE AND ALL

Singing carols is a part of Christmas that can be enjoyed in gatherings both large and small. For some, the mention of carols will bring to mind an outing to church to share in the traditional Christmas Eve service, perhaps by candlelight; for others it will conjure up a picture of a family gathering around the piano, or perhaps the electronic keyboard or synthesizer (possibly newly acquired from Santa Claus). Whatever form such music making takes, it continues a tradition that is centuries old, although many of the "traditional" carols are the result of much more recent revival and rearrangement.

The word *carol* originally comes from the French *caroler* meaning to dance in a ring. The earliest carols told the biblical stories surrounding the birth of Christ (from the appearance of the Angel Gabriel to the Virgin Mary, through the visits of shepherds and kings to the crib, to Herod's massacre of the Holy Innocents), and they were sung to simple, popular tunes, often with a refrain or chorus repeated after each verse. They were performed when revellers gathered together outside the church after the festive service to sing and dance in the churchyard. However, such behaviour was generally viewed with considerable disapproval by medieval church authorities: it was not until the fifteenth century that the popular carol was able to flourish in peaceful coexistence with traditional plainsong chants and other kinds of church music. By this time, carols were admitted inside the church, where they served to provide music for the various Christmas processions.

Once established, the popular folk tradition thrived until it came up against puritanical restraints once more, this time in the form of Oliver Cromwell and the Long Parliament, who, apart from throwing up their hands in horror at the mention of dancing, in 1647 abolished the festival of Christmas altogether! Although the Restoration of King Charles II to the throne swiftly brought about the reinstatement of music, dance and drama as courtly entertainment, the folk tradition of carol singing was not so fortunate. It was not until the early years of this century that this rich tradition was rediscovered and performed either in authentic style, or with carols skilfully arranged in keeping with more modern choral style. Meanwhile, in the 1850s one Rev. J. M. Neale discovered a sixteenth century Swedish carol collection *Piae Cantiones*, and published many items from it in translation (including *Good King Wenceslas*). Thus

A church spire dominates this wintry scene which beautifully evokes the spirit of Christmas.

many of our most popular carols come not from the original folk tradition but from more recent developments – and many more are not originally English. Apart from those found in *Piae Cantiones*, the tune of *Hark the Herald Angels Sing* was written by Mendelssohn, and *Silent Night*, as *Stille Nacht*, is still one of Germany's most popular Christmas melodies. Of those that do date back to earlier times, several mix Latin and English words – a time-honored device for popularizing and explaining the traditional Latin texts of the Medieval Church.

A word about performing the carols in this chapter: the accompaniments are very simple, providing the melody line for anyone who is able to read music. Suit your singing style to the mood of the carol, for while many carols encourage us to make merry and to make a merry noise, others are lullabies, originally designed to send an infant to sleep.

For an especially celebratory start to the festive season, why not try the age-old English custom of carol singing. On Christmas Eve, or earlier if you prefer, gather together family, friends and neighbours, wrap up warm, and carrying torches and percussion instruments go out and entertain the neighbourhood – it could soon become a local tradition! End the evening round an open log fire with warm drinks and festive snacks in a friend's home.

Merry Christmas!

WHILE SHEPHERDS WATCHED

1
While shepherds watched their flocks by night,
All seated on the ground,
The angel of the Lord came down,
And glory shone around.

2
'Fear not,' said he (for mighty dread
Had seized their troubled mind);
'Glad tidings of great joy I bring
To you and all mankind.

3
'To you in David's town this day
Is born of David's line
A Saviour, who is Christ the Lord;
And this shall be the sign:

4
'The heavenly Babe you there shall find
To human view displayed,
All meanly wrapped in swathing bands,
And in a manger laid.'

5
Thus spake the seraph; and forthwith
Appeared a shining throng
Of angels praising God, who thus
Addressed their joyful song:

6
'All glory be to God on high,
And to the earth be peace;
Good-will henceforth from heaven to men
Begin and never cease.'

Nahum Tate

THE FIRST NOWELL THE ANGEL DID SAY

1
The first Nowell the angel did say
Was to certain poor shepherds in fields as they lay;
In fields where they lay, keeping their sheep,
On a cold winter's night that was so deep:

Nowell, Nowell, Nowell, Nowell,
Born is the King of Israel!

2
They looked up and saw a star,
Shining in the east, beyond them far;
And to the earth it gave great light,
And so it continued both day and night:

3
And by the light of that same star,
Three Wise Men came from country far;
To seek for a king was their intent,
And to follow the star wherever it went:

4
This star drew nigh to the north-west;
O'er Bethlehem it took its rest,
And there it did both stop and stay
Right over the place where Jesus lay:

5
Then entered in those Wise Men three,
Full reverently upon their knee,
And offered there in his presence
Their gold and myrrh and frankincense:

6
Then let us all with one accord
Sing praises to our heav'nly Lord,
That hath made heav'n and earth of naught,
And with his blood mankind hath bought:

Traditional

IN THE BLEAK MID-WINTER

1
In the bleak mid-winter
Frosty wind made moan,
Earth stood hard as iron,
Water like a stone;
Snow had fallen, snow on snow,
Snow on snow,
In the bleak mid-winter
Long ago.

2
Our God, heaven cannot hold him
Nor earth sustain;
Heaven and earth shall flee away
When he comes to reign:
In the bleak mid-winter
A stable-place sufficed
The Lord God Almighty
Jesus Christ.

3
Enough for him, whom cherubim
Worship night and day,
A breastful of milk,
And a mangerful of hay;
Enough for him, whom angels
Fall down before,
The ox and ass and camel
Which adore.

4
What can I give him
Poor as I am?
If I were a shepherd
I would bring a lamb;
If I were a wise man
I would do my part;
Yet what can I give him—
Give my heart.

Christina Rossetti

SILENT NIGHT

1
Silent night, holy night,
All is calm, all is bright;
Round yon virgin mother and child
Holy infant so tender and mild,
Sleep in heavenly peace,
Sleep in heavenly peace.

2
Silent night, holy night,
Shepherds first saw the sight,
Glories stream from heaven afar
Heavenly hosts sing Alleluia:
Christ the saviour is born,
Christ the saviour is born!

3
Silent night, holy night,
Son of God, love's pure light;
Radiance beams from thy holy face,
With the dawn of redeeming grace,
Jesus, Lord, at thy birth,
Jesus, Lord, at thy birth.

Joseph Mohr,
Tr. Anon.

HARK! THE HERALD-ANGELS SING

1
Hark! the herald angels sing
Glory to the new-born King;
Peace on earth and mercy mild,
God and sinners reconciled:
Joyful all ye nations rise,
Join the triumph of the skies,
With th'angelic host proclaim,
Christ is born in Bethlehem.

Hark! the herald angels sing
Glory to the new-born King.

2
Christ, by highest heaven adored,
Christ, the everlasting Lord,
Late in time behold him come
Offspring of a virgin's womb:
Veiled in flesh the Godhead see,
Hail the incarnate Deity!
Pleased as man with man to dwell,
Jesus, our Emmanuel.

3
Hail the heaven-born Prince of peace!
Hail the Sun of Righteousness!
Light and life to all he brings,
Risen with healing in his wings;
Mild he lays his glory by,
Born that man no more may die,
Born to raise the sons of earth,
Born to give them second birth.

C. Wesley and others

WE THREE KINGS

1
We three kings of Orient are;
Bearing gifts we traverse afar
Field and fountain, moor and mountain,
Following yonder star:

O star of wonder, star of night,
Star with royal beauty bright,
Westward leading, still proceeding,
Guide us to thy perfect light.

2
Born a king on Bethlehem plain,
Gold I bring, to crown him again—
King for ever, ceasing never,
Over us all to reign:

3
Frankincense to offer have I;
Incense owns a Deity nigh;
Prayer and praising, all men raising,
Worship him, God most high:

4
Myrrh is mine; its bitter perfume
Breathes a life of gathering gloom:
Sorrowing, sighing, bleeding, dying,
Sealed in the stone-cold tomb:

5
Glorious now, behold him arise,
King, and God, and sacrifice!
Alleluia, alleluia;
Earth to the heavens replies:

J. H. Hopkins

GOOD KING WENCESLAS

1
Good King Wenceslas looked out,
On the Feast of Stephen,
When the snow lay round about,
Deep and crisp, and even:
Brightly shone the moon that night,
Though the frost was cruel,
When a poor man came in sight,
Gath'ring winter fuel.

2
'Hither, page, and stand by me,
If thou know'st it, telling,
Yonder peasant, who is he?
Where and what his dwelling?'
'Sire, he lives a good league hence,
Underneath the mountain,
Right against the forest fence,
By St. Agnes' fountain.'

3
'Bring me flesh, and bring me wine,
Bring me pine-logs hither:
Thou and I will *see* him dine,
When we bear them thither.'
Page and monarch, forth they went,
Forth they went together;
Through the rude wind's wild lament
And the bitter weather.

4
'Sire, the night is darker now,
And the wind blows stronger;
Fails my heart, I know not how;
I can go no longer.'
'Mark my footsteps, good my page;
Tread thou in them boldly;
Thou shalt find the winter's rage
Freeze thy blood less coldly.'

5
In his master's steps he trod,
Where the snow lay dinted;
Heat was in the very sod
Which the Saint had printed.
Therefore, Christian men, be sure,
Wealth or rank possessing,
Ye who now will bless the poor,
Shall yourselves find blessing.

J. M. Neale

O COME, ALL YE FAITHFUL

1
O come, all ye faithful,
Joyful and triumphant
O come ye, O come ye to Bethlehem;
Come and behold him
Born the King of Angels:

O come, let us adore him,
O come, let us adore him,
O come, let us adore him, Christ the Lord!

2
God of God,
Light of light,
Lo! he abhors not the Virgin's womb;
Very God,
Begotten not created:

3
Sing, choirs of angels,
Sing in exultation,
Sing, all ye citizens of heaven above;
Glory to God
In the highest:

4
Yea, Lord, we greet thee,
Born this happy morning,
Jesus, to thee be glory given;
Word of the Father,
Now in flesh appearing:

Tr. F. Oakeley,
W. T. Brooke and others

AWAY IN A MANGER

1
Away in a manger, no crib for a bed,
The little Lord Jesus laid down his sweet head.
The stars in the bright sky looked down where he lay.
The little Lord Jesus asleep in the hay.

2
The cattle are lowing, the baby awakes,
But little Lord Jesus no crying he makes.
I love thee, Lord Jesus! Look down from the sky,
And stay by my side until morning is nigh.

3
Be near me, Lord Jesus; I ask thee to stay
Close by me for ever, and love me, I pray.
Bless all the dear children in thy tender care.
And fit us for heaven, to live with thee there.

Anon.

I SAW THREE SHIPS

1

I saw three ships come sailing in,
On Christmas Day, on Christmas Day,
I saw three ships come sailing in,
On Christmas Day in the morning.

2

And what was in those ships all three?
On Christmas Day, on Christmas Day,
And what was in those ships all three?
On Christmas Day in the morning.

3

Our Saviour Christ and his lady.
On Christmas Day, on Christmas Day,
Our Saviour Christmas and his lady.
On Christmas Day in the morning.

4

Pray, whither sailed those ships all three?
On Christmas Day, on Christmas Day,
Pray, whither sailed those ships all three?
On Christmas Day in the morning.

5

O, they sailed into Bethlehem,
On Christmas Day, on Christmas Day,
O, they sailed into Bethlehem,
On Christmas Day in the morning.

6

And all the bells on earth shall ring,
On Christmas Day, on Christmas Day,
And all the bells on earth shall ring,
On Christmas Day in the morning.

7

And all the angels in heaven shall sing.
On Christmas Day, on Christmas Day,
And all the angels in heaven shall sing.
On Christmas Day in the morning.

8

And all the souls on earth shall sing,
On Christmas Day, on Christmas Day,
And all the souls on earth shall sing,
On Christmas Day in the morning.

9

Then let us all rejoice amain!
On Christmas Day, on Christmas Day,
Then let us all rejoice amain!
On Christmas Day in the morning.

Traditional

INDEX

PICTURE ACKNOWLEDGEMENTS

The publishers would like to thank the following organizations and individuals for their kind permission to reproduce the photographs in this book:

The Bridgeman Art Library: 41; 75; 175; 186; 187; 188; 189
Camera Press Ltd: 23
Christmas Archives: 89b; 136; 137
The Dickens Museum: 148
Mary Evans Picture Library: 88; 149t
Fine Art Photographs: 55; 89t; 138; 168; 169; 171; 176; 177; 183
Hulton/Bettman Archive: 6; 7; 40; 54
The Illustrated London News: 149b
Peter Newark's American Pictures: 9
Octopus Publishing Group Ltd: (Sue Atkinson) 37; 39; 59; 61; 64; (Michael Boys) 91; (Christine Hansombe) 85; 86; (Jerry Harpar) 92; (James Jackson) 119; 121; 123; 124; 125; 129; 131; 133; 135; 157; 159; 161; 162; (Duncan McNicol) 10; 31; 33; 47; 52; 53; 78; 80; 113; 150; 151; 153; 165; (Constance Spry Foundation/Spike Powell) 11; (Constance Spry Foundation/Martin Brigdale) 21
Orbis Publishing Ltd: (Anthony Blake) 96; (J. Bouchier) 26; 27; 28; 50; (Camera Press) 22; 32; (Chris Crofton) 12; 13; 15; 16t; 17; 99; 100; 101; (David Garcia) 69; (Garden Picture Library) 93; (N. Hargreaves) 19t; 30; 75; 97; (Peter Higgins) 107; (Anne Hodgeson) 76; 77; (R. McMahon) 20; 65; 66; 67; 68tl; 68tr; 70; 72t; 146; (NHPA) 90; (M. Smallcombe) 103; 104; 105; (Syndication International) 19b; (Shona Wood) 72b; 73
The Telegraph Colour Library: 14; 185
Elizabeth Whiting and Associates: 2; 108; 109
World Press Network Ltd 1991: (Country Homes and Interiors) 18; 25; (Maison Marie Claire) 4; 95